For Linda Jennings,
  Strangers is an American
saga of migration, family, and
community and hence, it is each
of ours. Enjoy the exploration!
    In Sisterhood,
      Lillian Serece Williams

Strangers in the Land of Paradise

BLACKS IN THE DIASPORA
Darlene Clark Hine,
John McCluskey, Jr., and
David Barry Gaspar
General Editors

$\mathscr{S}$TRANGERS
IN THE
LAND OF $\mathscr{P}$ARADISE

The Creation of an African American
Community, Buffalo, New York
1900–1940

BY
Lillian Serece Williams

INDIANA UNIVERSITY PRESS   BLOOMINGTON & INDIANAPOLIS

This book is a publication of

Indiana University Press
601 North Morton Street
Bloomington, IN 47404-3797 USA

http://www.indiana.edu/~iupress

Telephone orders   800-842-6796
Fax orders   812-855-7931
Orders by e-mail   iuporder@indiana.edu

The paper used in this publication meets the minimum requirements of American National
Standard for Information Sciences—Permanence of Paper for Printed Library Materials,
ANSI Z39.48-1984.

Manufactured in the United States of America

Library of Congress Cataloging-in-Publication Data

Williams, Lillian Serece.
Strangers in the land of paradise : the creation of an African American community,
Buffalo, New York, 1900–1940 / Lillian Serece Williams.
p.   cm. — (Blacks in the diaspora)
Includes bibliographical references and index.
ISBN 0-253-33552-3 (cloth : alk. paper)
1. Afro-Americans—New York (State)—Buffalo—Social conditions—20th century.
2. Afro-Americans—New York (State)—Buffalo—Social life and customs—20th
century. 3. Buffalo (N.Y.)—History—20th century. 4. City and town life—New York
(State)—Buffalo—History—20th century. 5. Migration, Internal—United States—
History—20th century. I. Title. II. Series.
F129.B89N48   1999
974.7'9700496073—dc21   98-54228

ISBN 0-253-21408-4 (pbk : alk. paper)

2   3   4   5   6   05   04   03   02   01   00

For my mother,

ADA LUCILLE WILLIAMS,

and

to the memory of my father

JAMES LOUIS WILLIAMS, SR.

(1915–1985)

Contents

TABLES

LIST OF ILLUSTRATIONS

PREFACE

*What was taken by outsiders to be slackness, slovenli-
ness or even generosity was in fact a full recognition of
the legitimacy of forces other than good ones. . . . The
purpose of evil was to survive it and they determined
(without ever knowing they had made up their minds
to do it) to survive floods, white people, tuberculosis,
famine and ignorance. They knew anger well but not
despair. . . .*[1]

Bessie Williams, Joseph Brown, and the other southern blacks who made
their way to Buffalo at the turn of the twentieth century arrived with the
full intent of enhancing their economic, social, and political circumstances.
They knew well the stifling effects of the Jim Crow laws that governed
their native southern communities. They became a part of the masses of
blacks who left the South and thus registered their outrage over limited
job opportunities, political repression, and social ostracism under the
southern system of apartheid. Buffalo was the terminus for many of those
who had earlier sought refuge in other northern, urban communities.
Consequently, these migrants had experienced northern-type segregation
and its impact upon black lives. Still, these newcomers arrived with their
southern culture and with optimism that it would support them as they
sought to exploit the opportunities that Buffalo offered.

Their approaches to these perceived opportunities would vary, as
did their experiences. The migration was an economic success story
for the Williamses. Bessie Williams found work as a domestic, like so
many other black women, while her husband, Daniel, secured a position
at the Bethlehem Steel mill in Lackawanna. Joseph Brown, on the other
hand, found employment in the more volatile building trades industry
and subsequently experienced economic hardships.

The post–World War I years were difficult ones for many Buffalo blacks. The paternalistic relationship between blacks and wealthy whites which had characterized many interactions at the turn of the century had been rendered virtually obsolete. Therefore, new solutions were necessary to address new challenges. Williams became a follower of Marcus Garvey and a member of the Republican party, while Brown joined the Prince Hall Order of Masons and at the same time also sought to become a civil servant. Occasionally these migrants brought their collective forces to bear in an attempt to alleviate the harsh realities of some of their lives and to redress the grievances of African Americans throughout the nation. But the stories of Brown and Williams mirrored those of other African Americans who resided in Buffalo at the time, whether they were newcomers or long-time residents.

During the 1960s and 1970s the studies that emerged in black urban history emphasized the racial segregation and the "tangle of pathology" that resulted when African Americans migrated to urban communities. In this conceptual framework their families and communities were impacted negatively. Scholars contended that the migrants suffered such ills as anomie, disease, poverty, and weakened family ties, and that solving the immediate problems of food, shelter, and a livelihood sapped most of their energies.[2] These studies focused upon the formation of the "ghetto" in northern cities, i.e., the physical and institutional development of black residential communities. Invariably blacks' experiences were perceived as deleterious to the maintenance of their cultural forms and to their goals of self-determination. Racism was the key to understanding African American communities and blacks were passive in the process.[3] Yet this paradigm limits our understanding of the intricacies of the migration of African Americans, as the experiences of Williams and Brown suggest.

Their communities were alive, vibrant, and considerably complex. George Edmund Hayes, writing in 1913, observed that there was a distinct black world growing up in the cities of America—neighborhoods "isolated from many of the impulses of the common life and little understood by the white world."[4] Essayist, novelist, and lecturer Frank Hercules described Harlem as a "many faceted community that is the complete world on its own terms."[5] So, too, were the other emerging African American communities across the country. In 1973 historian John Blassingame contended that this description was apt for nineteenth-century communities, too. He noted that Savannah, Georgia provided blacks with a "large arena to develop a variety of social, intellectual, and creative talents, and to build [a] community infrastructure. . . ."[6]

In the 1980s and 1990s a new genre of cultural studies on African Americans in the cities at the turn of the century emerged that recognized such perceptions, and their authors used new approaches and methodologies to elucidate black migration and settlement. These authors contend that black communities were fertile fields in which to study not only race relations and ghetto formation, but also proletarianization. They further noted that black urban communities were arenas in which to scrutinize the ways African American southern culture was transplanted and facilitated the migration and settlement processes.[7] These observers concluded that such black communities showed tremendous strength, despite the harsh realities of many of their residents' lives. These studies have enhanced our knowledge of the kin and friendship networks that brought them to the urban environment and sustained them after their arrival. We now have a better sense of what the move meant for them. Historian Richard Thomas wrote that the process of community-building for African Americans was fueled by a "commitment to struggle for freedom and equality."[8] In other words, the migrants were active agents in the process.

The trend in the field of black urban history has been for earlier theoretical approaches or methodologies to be relegated to the archives as the field continued to evolve. Despite all of their limitations, race-relations and ghetto-formation models, as well as the cultural studies approach, all offer new insights and perspectives on black urban history. It seems to me that a blending of the earlier perspectives with evolving methodologies and theoretical approaches could only further enhance our understanding of the migration and settlement of blacks in cities. A case in point is the "new social history" that is now nearly a generation old.[9] Yet this "new social history" that was so important in shedding light on black family life has virtually been ignored when addressing blacks' migration to and settlement in cities. It can permit scholars to better understand the meaning of the migration experience for both the elite and the working classes, especially for those groups that may not have left large bodies of manuscript data. Furthermore, this methodology can elucidate how gender and age affected the experiences of black migrants.

My Buffalo study clearly falls within the genre of cultural studies that have emerged since the 1980s and blends its research methodology with that of the new social history. It also offers to the "cultural school" much of the corroborative evidence to substantiate contentions predicated upon certain demographic and economic factors, such as age, occupation, or gender. The time is now ripe for historians to integrate the best insights of the new social history and the emerging field of cultural studies.

Strangers in the Land of Paradise: The Creation of an African American Community, Buffalo, New York, 1900–1940 is a social and economic study that examines the black community as a cultural entity with distinct institutions, values, and lifestyles. It delineates values and institutions that the black migrant population brought with it from the South to the northern, urban environment, as well as those that evolved as a result of their interaction with native blacks and the city itself. It also explores the process by which they adapted to their new setting. Central to my thesis is the contention that the black community developed both as the result of the external forces of discrimination and segregation and, equally significantly, as a result of a self-conscious effort on the part of African Americans in their quest for self-determination.

The Buffalo, New York African American community was selected for this study because Buffalo's location on the Great Lakes resulted in its becoming a significant manufacturing town which created employment opportunities for large numbers of unskilled and semi-skilled black workers after the outbreak of World War I. As Joe William Trotter has documented, this creation of a class of black factory workers was a key ingredient in shaping turn-of-the-century black communities. Secondly, until the eve of the Great Depression, Buffalo's black community was quite small, which permits one to conduct a composite study of the effects of migration, industrialization, and urbanization on the black community at the micro level. Furthermore, Buffalo was more typical of the communities in which turn-of-the-century blacks resided. In contrast to the great cities in the North, like Chicago and New York with their teeming populations, blacks typically resided in cities, like Buffalo, with small African American populations. Their experiences provide genuine insight into the lives of black migrants and allow scholars an opportunity to ascertain why these individuals brought their memories, hopes, and dreams, along with their families, as they relocated to the "Queen City of the Great Lakes" and other urban centers. Their ways enabled them to create enduring communities.

The book examines the growth and development of Buffalo, the movement of European immigrants and African American migrants into the city, and their ability to secure an economic foothold. It tests the extent to which family and friendship networks for blacks were a significant force in their migration and acculturation. It also describes the establishment of institutions that African Americans created to shape their modern, urban community.

ACKNOWLEDGMENTS

Strangers in the Land of Paradise: The Creation of an African American Community, Buffalo, New York, 1900–1940 is the result of the support of many individuals and institutions. I would like to take this opportunity to express to them my sincere appreciation.

This book began as a doctoral dissertation under the direction of Michael H. Frisch at the University at Buffalo, State University of New York. I wish to thank Professor Frisch and my other committee members, William C. Fischer and David Gerber, for their encouragement and guidance.

A Rockefeller Foundation Minority Scholars Fellowship and the Nuala McGann Drescher Award of the United University Professionals afforded me the luxury of researching and writing full-time. I also have benefited from faculty research grants from the University at Buffalo and the University at Albany. I especially wish to thank Arthur Butler, former Provost of the College of Arts and Sciences at the University of Buffalo, whose generous support provided for the encoding of the New York State manuscript census data. Daniel Wulff, Interim Vice President for Research at the University at Albany, and the Women's Studies Department provided funding for the reproduction of many of the photographs. Assistance from Francine Frank, former Dean of the Humanities College, and H. Patrick Swygert, former President of the University at Albany, permitted me access to the resources of the Hollis Burke Frissell Library at Tuskegee University and the Moorland-Spingarn Research Center at Howard University.

Throughout my professional career, it has been my privilege to count among my staunchest supporters the foremost historians in the field of United States history. The late Herbert G. Gutman first kindled my interest in United States social history when I was still an undergraduate student; he inspired me to join his other students in conducting studies of Buffalo's ethnic communities. Mary Frances Berry, V. P. Franklin, and Laurence A. Glasco read several versions of my manuscript and were key members of my intellectual debating team. Allen Ballard, Graham Barker-Benfield,

John Bracey, Bettye Collier-Thomas, Monroe Fordham, Kenneth Hamilton, William M. King, Adrienne Lash Jones, John Blassingame, Ralph Watkins, the late Nancy L. Grant, and the late Gertrude W. Marlowe were extremely generous with their time. They either read and critiqued several chapters of my manuscript, shared their research with me, or spent countless hours discussing this project with me. Consequently, I received from them spiritual and intellectual sustenance over the long haul. In the early stages, my conversations with Thomas J. Davis, Spencer Crew, and James Horton were invaluable as we pursued the study of black urban life. I owe a special debt to Joe William Trotter, who read the final version of my manuscript with care and staunchly supported its publication. My editors Darlene Clark Hine and Joan Catapano encouraged me to write this book and provided crucial guidance throughout the process.

Friends and colleagues at the University at Buffalo, the University at Albany, and Howard University formed an important part of my community. I benefited from their intelligence, creativity, and nurturance. I want especially to acknowledge Barbara Seals Nevergold, Peggy A. Rabkin, Iris Berger, Florence B. Bonner, Shirley J. Jones, Mary Nell Morgan, A'Lelia Perry Bundles, Patricia Guthrie, June O. Patton, Linda Nicholson, Judy Scales-Trent, Joan Schulz, and Naomi Zack, scholars in their own right, and Marijo Dougherty and June Baranco Gumbel.

Over the years, the professional organizations in my field have given me a forum to disseminate my research findings and, most importantly, have provided comments and critics. I am especially grateful to the Association for the Study of Afro-American Life and History, which consistently included me on its programs.

All historians owe a debt of gratitude to the archivists and librarians who facilitate their work. I am particularly grateful to Debra Newman Ham, formerly of the National Archives and the Library of Congress; Joseph Howerton of the National Archives; Janet Sims-Wood at the Moorland-Spingarn Research Center at Howard University; Mary Wolfskill, Director of the Manuscript Division of the Library of Congress; and Adrienne Cannon, Director of the African American Division of the Library of Congress. Deborah Curry and Dean Meredith Butler of the University at Albany libraries facilitated my efforts to collect manuscript data. James Corsaro, Associate Librarian, Manuscripts and Special Collections, helped me to navigate the vast resources of the New York State Library, and Craig Williams duplicated maps from its collections. The administration and staff of the Buffalo and Erie County Historical Society were extremely supportive. I especially wish to thank Dr. William Siener, Mary Bell, Yvonne Foote, and Patricia Virgil. Christopher Densmore, University at Buffalo Archivist, and former archivist Shonnie Finnegan have always been staunch and enthusiastic supporters of my research efforts. Mary Levey, Director of the National Historic Preservation Center and Archives at Girl Scouts of the USA, and her staff, especially Ameeta Kumar, were always available to fulfill my requests for additional data, despite their demanding schedules. I wish to thank each of these repositories, the Hamburg Historical Society, and the individuals for granting me permission to quote sources and to reproduce photographs and maps from their collections. Mark Schmidt prepared many of the photographs for publication.

Buffalo city clerk Charles Michaux spearheaded my efforts to secure permission to publish municipal documents. I wish to thank Council-woman Rose Marie LoTempio for introducing into the Council a res-olution authorizing me to publish these documents and the Common Council for enacting it.

I would like to thank those Buffalo residents who so graciously opened their homes to me and who provided detailed accounts and insights into their family life and the institutions in Buffalo's African American community. I am especially grateful to the late Joseph Brown, Ora Curry, Theresa Evans, Frank Garrison, Arthur Griffa, Raymond Jackson, and Bessie Williams.

Barbara J. Williams-Jenkins and University at Albany secretaries Eileen Pellegrino and Ronaline M. Saunders typed several versions of this manu-script. My graduate students Reginald Hicks, Robin Hicks, and Weihua Zheng provided research assistance, and I also benefited from our in-tellectual exchanges. Felix Wu, Donald Voss, Brian Heaton, and Mari-anne Simon provided technological skills at a critical time and assisted me in producing many of the graphs.

My deepest gratitude goes to my family for their love and encour-agement throughout this process. Ada Lucille Williams, my mother, is my inspiration and my staunchest supporter; she also shared her un-published essays with me. My siblings provided sustenance and sound advice. Thanks, James, Jr., Rafi Taha, Barbara J. Williams-Jenkins, Patricia A. Williams, Joyce M. Williams, Stephanie L. Williams Cowart, Isaac L. Williams, and T. Christopher Williams. My nieces and nephews are con-stant reminders of what is really important in life, and they helped me to keep this project in perspective. I also am grateful to my Washington, D.C., "family" of Annette Dunzo, James Kennedy, and Francoise Pfaff, for making the task easier.

I dedicate *Strangers in the Land of Paradise: The Creation of an African American Community, Buffalo, New York, 1900–1940* to my mother, Ada L. Williams, and to the memory of my father, James L. Williams, whose guidance, unconditional love, and support still sustain me on this journey.

Lillian Serece Williams
Washington, D.C.
September 25, 1998

Strangers in the Land of Paradise

Introduction

With its well-appointed harbor and railway lines, nineteenth-century Buffalo offered ample transportation systems. Consequently, the steel industry, the grain milling business, and the livestock business flourished in the city and attracted large numbers of workers for readily available unskilled and semi-skilled jobs. As the United States increasingly entered the First World War, African Americans came to Buffalo to fill these positions. Buffalo also was just south of the resort and tourist center Niagara Falls, whose power plants facilitated the development of industry on the Niagara Frontier. Its Statler Hotel, with 1,000 rooms, attracted many visitors to the city, and meeting their needs meant that Buffalo also could offer a variety of domestic and other service jobs for newcomers.

Moreover, on the eve of the twentieth century Buffalo was picturesque, with its circles and wide, tree-lined boulevards that connected its vast park system, the creation of landscape architect Frank Law Olmsted. The sprawling mansions of the chief beneficiaries of the city's boom lined Delaware Avenue, Elmwood Avenue, Richmond Avenue, and Jewett Parkway. They heralded its preeminence and pundits dubbed Buffalo the "City of Lights." Buffalo was, indeed, a city of beauty and glitter. For some it seemed like Paradise.

In 1901 Buffalo hosted the Pan American Exposition, which highlighted it as one of the most modern and technologically advanced cities in the hemisphere. Its macadam-paved streets and electric street lights set it apart from other American cities. The exhibit area was flanked by Olmsted's Delaware Park and the lake and drew thousands from near and far. Visitors were justifiably impressed. Buffalo continued to prosper. What these advances would mean for black residents or for those who wended their way to Buffalo on the eve of the twentieth century is the other side of the story.

In 1905, the African American population of Buffalo was small, just

Midway Parade, Pan-American Exposition, Buffalo, 1901. This
Frances Benjamin Johnston photo depicts the city's opulence,
as well as the stereotype of people of African descent that had
become ingrained in scholarly and popular circles by the eve
of the twentieth century. Courtesy of Library of Congress.

slightly over 1,200.[1] It was to remain a fairly small community until
after World War I. A decade later, in 1915, this community had grown
to just a little over 1,600. Yet by 1925, Buffalo's black community experienced a tremendous growth; it numbered about 9,000 then.[2] Despite
the tremendous increase, blacks in Buffalo comprised a small percentage
of the city's total population, about .02 percent in 1905, and slightly
less than 1 percent (.9 percent) in 1925.

By the 1920s these individuals, mainly old residents of Buffalo, had
their hegemony within the community challenged by the most recent
arrivals, some of whom were college-educated. But most of them were
"workers," in pursuit of the prospect of higher wages and relative job
security that conditions in Buffalo promised. At this juncture, it was
quite evident that southerners were providing the leadership in the

Buffalo African American community, and as we shall see, they swelled the membership rolls of organizations like the NAACP. Many of these spokesmen were of working-class backgrounds and several of them had established businesses that catered to their community's needs.

African Americans experienced grave housing situations in Buffalo. By 1900, there had emerged a distinct "Negro" district located east of the downtown business district. The core of this area included William Street, South Division, Michigan Avenue, and Broadway. However, blacks had not encountered strict residential segregation. The nineteenth-century pattern whereby black families were found residing in the same house or in adjacent buildings on a block where the dominant population was white was still prevalent. A few blacks also continued to live in the same house with whites and apparently experienced little discord. Buffalo whites, unlike those in other northern cities, did not organize "neighborhood improvement associations" to challenge the rights of blacks to reside in those areas where they could afford to live.[3] However, the informal sanctions and traditions against race-mixing often were equally effective. Buffalo also offered few large apartment buildings or tenement dwellings. So blacks and the immigrant groups that preceded them to the city dwelled in one- or two-family structures, usually with small front and back yards. This architectural style often made invisible the deplorable conditions under which newcomers lived. Housing conditions reached critical stages by the 1930s, when the African American population peaked.[4]

In 1905, African Americans in Buffalo lived in all but five of the city's wards (1, 2, 4, 9, and 10). Two-thirds, however, resided in wards 6 and 7, near the downtown commercial districts (see map 1). By 1915, blacks were found in all but six of Buffalo's 27 wards. Although this represents a slightly constricted community, we must look at the changes which occur within the wards themselves to understand how the community was developing physically. Wards 6 and 7 were still the most populous, with nearly three-fourths of all African Americans in the city residing within their boundaries. After 1915, the Buffalo black community experienced rapid expansion (see map 2). By 1925, blacks who found homes in wards 6 and 7 declined to 60 percent; simultaneously, the black population of contiguous wards increased substantially (see map 3). In 1915, no blacks were found in ward 8; a decade later, 9 percent of the black population dwelled there. The black population of wards 2 and 3 had also increased from zero in 1915 to 6.2 percent and 4.5 percent, respectively, in 1925. Blacks in ward 14 had more than doubled in number between 1915 and 1925, from 2.6 percent to 6.9 percent.

By 1937, the African American population reached its highest density levels. They increasingly located in the Cold Spring section near downtown, where 12,000 of the estimated 13,000 black population resided.[5]

But to understand the physical development of the black community and the impact of the growing numbers upon that population and the city, an examination at the micro level is warranted because the black community was still small in comparison to the white population. In the fourth ward blacks comprised 1,417 of the total 21,981; the most populous location for African Americans was ward 5, with 8,817 of the 25,774 residents. In 1937 only 95 of the 25,625 residents of ward 6 were black. In ward 8 the blacks comprised 1,552 of the 23,307 people there and 875 of the 17,044 who lived in ward 12.[6]

As a result of these changes, African Americans increasingly were restricted to two areas of settlement within the city, the Ellicott and Masten Park districts, both of which had been recently abandoned by various immigrant groups (see map 4). A few more economically successful and socially connected blacks were able to purchase homes on Lyth and Laurel streets in the Jefferson-Delavan neighborhood, a contiguous region just to the north. The older black sections of Buffalo were already in a state of rapid decline and the huge influx of new arrivals severely taxed the community's resources.

As the number of African Americans in Buffalo increased, white citizens began to devise new tactics of discrimination and segregation. Previously, the sections of the city open to black residents had been restricted somewhat, but it was usually possible for an individual black to secure a "letter of recommendation" from an influential white person which would allow him access to better housing. After 1915, it was not only more difficult to secure housing in "restricted" sections, but blacks were also being segregated in theaters and restaurants. Moreover, the popularity of the film *Birth of a Nation* and the inroads which the Ku Klux Klan made into Buffalo's white community were indicative of the rapid deterioration in race relations.[7]

The newcomers who began to swell the black community after 1900 did not have the interracial contacts of the older residents. As a result, they were affected more directly by external social factors—the shortage of adequate housing facilities, the adverse health conditions, the lack of recreational facilities, and the increased segregation imposed upon Buffalo blacks. At the same time, their own set of demographic and social characteristics rendered them more vulnerable to these external conditions, but also provided them with the means necessary to cope with them. It is to these internal characteristics of the black community that we now turn.

At the turn of the century, the most striking feature among Buffalo blacks was their abnormal age distribution. Like most northern black communities at the time, the Buffalo black population contained a disproportionate number of young people.[8] (See figure 1A.) Throughout the period from 1905 to 1925, over three-fourths of black males and females were under the age of forty. Sociologist Charles Johnson had noted this disparity among blacks, also. In 1923, Johnson wrote, "[The Buffalo black community] is overweighted in the adult age groups and there are too few children."[9] He found that over half of the black population fell between the ages of twenty and forty years, while only 37 percent of Buffalo whites could be categorized as young adults.[10] (See figure 1B.)

As a result of the unnatural growth of the African American population, males comprised over half of the population. But this ratio varied according to age. The ratio of male youths to female youths hovered around 100 for the census years 1905, 1915, and 1925. Yet for the young-adult group, ages nineteen to twenty-nine, there was an excess of males.[11] For men ten to twenty years older, this excess reached critical proportions, with 28 to 40 percent more males than females. These unfavorable sex ratios, the result of increased migration, portended serious problems for black families, as well as for the black community in general. The 1930 census revealed that the abnormal sex ratios continued, with the largest numbers falling in the age group between 30 and 34 years, where there were 1,028 males and 844 women, or a ratio of 122.[12]

These findings—the unusually small number of children and the expanding adult categories, especially around the marriageable ages—suggest that the increase in population could be attributed to the migration of blacks from the South. Johnson noted that at the same time that northern centers such as Buffalo were experiencing an increase in their young adult population, the South experienced a decline; southern states simultaneously witnessed an increase in the proportion of blacks who were over the age of sixty-five. These social characteristics had far-reaching implications for the developing black community of Buffalo.

PART I

Blacks in Twentieth-Century Buffalo: Structural Development

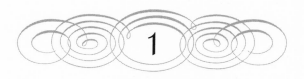

The Early Years

*Ships at a Distance Have
Every Man's Wish on board.*[1]

Buffalo's location at the source of the Niagara River and on the eastern shore of Lake Erie made it suitable for development as a commercial center. From the early days of Indian settlement in western New York, Buffalo had been the seat of the fur trading industry. Under the French and later the British, it maintained this status. Following the American Revolution, new possibilities for growth and development in western New York led to the dredging of Buffalo harbor, making Buffalo an ideal location for the terminus of the Erie Canal.[2] The investment in the canal paid handsome dividends to the village. In 1820, only 120 vessels had entered and departed from Buffalo harbor; by 1826, just one year after the construction of the canal, 418 vessels came through the Buffalo harbor.[3] In 1827, the number of ships that sailed through the Buffalo port had more than doubled since the previous year; now nearly 1,000 ships came through the western New York port. Throughout the nineteenth century, Buffalo continued its phenomenal growth as a center of commerce.

In 1816, the village population was a mere 400. After the completion of the Erie Canal in 1825, Buffalo experienced a massive increase in population. Many of those who worked on the canal remained in the area. By 1830, the population had soared to 8,653. The following year 10,000 people resided in the township of Buffalo and in the fall of 1832 it became incorporated as a city. Buffalo had become the gateway to the west. Many of the pioneers who were headed west in search of fame and fortune stopped off at Buffalo. Many remained. The population continued to increase by leaps and bounds, such that by 1850 it had reached 42,000 and just thirty years later it approached 118,000.[4]

As Buffalo's population increased, it experienced even more ethnic diversity. By 1870, two of every five Buffalonians were foreign-born. There were small groups of British, Scottish, Welsh, French, and Dutch settlers prior to the construction of the Erie Canal. Fleeing famine, persecution, and widespread unemployment, a large wave of Germans immigrated to the United States and many of them settled in Buffalo.[5] The Germans were followed by other European ethnic groups. Poles began to settle in large numbers after 1874; by 1884, they had established a well-defined community with their own churches, schools, fraternal organizations, and their first newspaper, *Polak w Americe.* The Polish community was one of the fastest growing in the city.[6] The Italians formed another large colony of immigrants in Buffalo. By 1890, they had established businesses that catered to their own needs, and simultaneously had introduced to Buffalo aspects of their unique culture that included foods (like peanuts and popcorn fritters) and leisure activities such as billiards; they also published their own newspaper, *Il Corriere Italiano.*[7] Immigrants from other countries settled in Buffalo in smaller numbers, including Hungarians, Ukrainians, and Greeks.

All of the ethnic groups that came to Buffalo arrived with the intention of improving their economic status. Although their ability to exploit the new environment was dependent upon a number of factors, Buffalo offered them ample opportunity to find unskilled and semi-skilled jobs. Supportive industries, designed to produce items for those who were westward bound, sprang up in Buffalo. Furniture, tools, stores, hardware, farm implements, and leather goods were manufactured, some as early as 1812.[8]

After the construction of the Erie Canal, lumber and metal products became important components of the Buffalo economy. The shipyard industry, based upon passenger service at first, boomed by the 1840s and 1850s as a result of the transport of coal and grain. Buffalo factories handled about 8,000 barrels of flour in 1829. The invention of the grain elevator increased productivity tremendously. In 1830, over 180,000 barrels of flour were milled in Buffalo and the "Queen City of the Great Lakes" was well on its way to becoming the grain center not only of the United States, but of the world.[9] The livestock business flourished in mid-nineteenth-century Buffalo, too. In 1860, the Dold Packing Company was founded. It became one of the major packing houses in Buffalo, and by 1920 it employed some 2,000 workers, who earned cumulatively three million dollars in annual wages. Buffalo ranked first in sheep handling and had the second largest horse market in the country.

The Great Lakes traffic was soon preempted by the railroads. By the turn of the century, Buffalo was second only to Chicago as a rail center. Many newcomers found employment working for the railroad companies. Moreover, the railroads, because of their connection to the Pennsylvania coal fields, facilitated the establishment of the iron industries in Buffalo. Iron smelting had begun in 1860; the Pratt and Letchworth Company and the Buffalo Forge Company were pioneering in this field, and later they were joined by the Bethlehem Steel Company and the Republic Steel Corporation.

The availability of inexpensive transportation was instrumental in changing Buffalo from a commercial to a manufacturing city.[10] Buffalo's developing industries needed large supplies of unskilled and semi-skilled workers for production. Thus, huge waves of migrants flocked to the city—first European immigrants, and then southern African Americans.

Black people had lived in Buffalo long before its incorporation as a city in 1832. As early as 1792, Joseph Hodges, a black fur trapper, interpreter, and grog shopkeeper, was in western New York and was instrumental in attracting other settlers to the area. (Hodges left Buffalo in 1807 to live on the Cattaraugus Seneca Indian Reservation in upstate New York.)[11] By 1816, the year that the town was incorporated, sixteen blacks lived in Buffalo, nine of them slaves. The black population increased gradually: by 1828, it had reached only 60. In stark contrast to the foreign immigrant populations, the African American group remained small throughout the nineteenth century. Blacks were attracted to Buffalo because of its proximity to Canada and the freedom from slavery that it promised and because Buffalo offered plenty of job opportunities. Buffalo was also a site on the Underground Railroad. Despite its attractions, on the eve of the Civil War, the black populace numbered only about 500, many of whom were fugitive slaves or their descendants.

In the nineteenth century, most African Americans resided just east of the downtown business district and near the posh residences on Elm and Oak streets where many of them worked. Systematic residential segregation was absent from nineteenth-century Buffalo.[12] Although it was not unusual for African Americans to live in clusters on a block, many others obtained quarters in the same dwelling on a street in which the dominant population was white. While their homes were modest in every sense of the word, blacks maintained well-kept properties and seldom had encounters with either their neighbors or law enforcement officials.[13]

Even though their numbers were small, black Buffalonians had developed a keen sense of the meaning of community that resulted from the legacy of bondage that affected all African Americans and the social ostracism that they experienced. Further, these shared feelings were buttressed by the early establishment of their own independent institutions that gave them a sense of control over their destiny.[14] The church was one of the first such organizations. It also was one of the first community organizations that blacks in Buffalo established. In 1831, when the black population numbered only about sixty, the community organized two churches. The Vine Street African Methodist Episcopal Church (on Vine and Washington streets in the downtown area) and the Michigan Avenue Baptist Church (on Michigan near Broadway Street) were important pillars of the community. The latter church was a station on the Underground Railroad that led to Canada. The Colored Presbyterian Church and St. Philip's Episcopal Church were founded within the next three decades.[15] These churches served as the social center of the fledgling black community, as well as the site of political activity for blacks.[16] These were roles that the black church had played historically. Its independent status allowed it to provide the community with a sanctuary to devise and deliberate appropriate strategies for creating a free African American community.

Buffalo African Americans and those across the country began to organize lyceums and literary societies during the first half of the nineteenth century as another dimension of their program to build a free community. Many of these efforts were black responses to inadequate educational systems. But they went beyond this. Such projects also provided alternative educational institutions to the poorly equipped and staffed African schools that the Buffalo Board of Education had established for them and allowed blacks to design a curriculum that reflected their self-determinationist goals. African Americans utilized them not only to improve their reading and writing skills, but also to encourage literary expression by providing critics and avenues for publication. Buffalo blacks had founded the Debating Society and the Young Ladies Literary Society before 1837.[17] James Whitfield, a local poet, was prominent in black literary circles.[18] These societies also offered recreational forums and sometimes dispensed social services. They continued to flourish during the nineteenth century and enriched the life of the black community.

Its size did not preclude Buffalo's African American community from voicing sentiments on the issues of the day, especially those that directly affected their status. Buffalo African Americans were at the center and on the cutting edge of black political thought during this period. Abolitionism stirred their collective conscience and galvanized support from some sectors of the white community. Buffalo had been a stop on the Underground Railroad since the War of 1812, and blacks and their white allies aided escaped slaves in their attempts to find freedom in Canada. Two of the city's blacks were leaders in the anti-slavery movement. George Weir, Jr., clothier, grocer, and the son of the pastor of the Vine Street AME Church, became a member of the Buffalo City Anti-Slavery Society in 1838.[19] Abner H. Francis, a wealthy merchant, was elected treasurer in 1848.[20]

Many of the rural areas of western New York were known for their involvement with the Underground Railroad and were important stops on the lecture circuit for abolitionists. William Wells Brown—runaway, steamboat operator, and lecturer—settled with his family in Buffalo in 1836 and became a lecturer for the Western New York Anti-Slavery Society. He found the Buffalo environment favorable for his abolitionist agenda, and for offering a greater variety of occupational choices. His involvement with abolition in Buffalo provides a glimpse into the activities of African Americans in the movement in Buffalo and the surrounding region, while it also illustrates the schizophrenia that often characterized race relations in the area at the time.[21]

Brown's occupation as a sailor provided a convenient means of aiding runaways to freedom. Using the lake steamer that he operated out of Buffalo harbor, Brown transported many a runaway from "injustice" to a "sanctuary" in Canada. He also joined other African Americans in their attempts to protect escaped slaves from their captors.[22] Shortly after Brown arrived in Buffalo, a slave catcher from Nashville, Tennessee came to Western New York to recapture the Stanfords, a couple and their infant child who had sought refuge in nearby St. Catharines, Ontario. The patrol was successful and after a brief layover in Buffalo, it proceeded south to Hamburg, where a group of blacks from Buffalo, including Brown, apprehended the party and brought the runaways back to the city. The slave catcher appealed to the Erie County sheriff for redress. Later that same day, a heavily armed group of fifty predominantly black men escorted the family to Black Rock Ferry to board a boat to St. Catharines. When the rescuers were overtaken by the sheriff and a posse of seventy, a melee ensued; amidst the confusion, the Stanfords escaped. The rescuers were arrested for breaking the peace on the Sabbath and twenty-five of them were found guilty and ordered to pay steep fines of five to fifty dollars.[23] In some instances these fees amounted to one-tenth of the annual wages of some blacks in the city. So abolitionism cost many of them dearly financially, while it also brought them tremendous psychological gratification, for they actively were engaged in their own "emancipation," as well as that of the slaves. It was evident to them that no African American was free as long as slavery existed.

The Niagara Frontier provided ample opportunities to repeat such efforts, for some slaves, travelling with their owners, came to Buffalo en route to Niagara Falls, the resort town just to the north. Others came on their own, bent upon fleeing to Canada. In another incident, Buffalo abolitionists retained Millard Fillmore to represent an alleged fugitive. Better known for signing into law the Fugitive Slave Act of 1850, Fillmore provided pro bono service and noted that it was "his duty to help the poor fugitive."[24]

Buffalo abolitionists enjoyed a number of such victories. Nevertheless, this liberal stance regarding slavery did not translate necessarily into similar views regarding the status of free blacks. Nor were the rural areas of Western New York and Buffalo itself uniformly of abolitionist sentiment. When Dr. John H. Hopkins, the bishop of the Diocese of Vermont, addressed the Young Men's Association of Buffalo in 1851, he proposed a two-prong approach to deal with slavery and the free black population. For the slave he advocated compensated manumission, followed by emigration. Hopkins also believed that this proposal should accompany a gradual emancipation policy that included freeing slaves at the age of twenty-five. Under this plan the children of the slaves would become the wards of the state. In turn the state would establish and operate industrial training schools and apprentice the children out at age fourteen to finance the program. Hopkins suggested that his plan should be palatable because it would control free blacks and at the same time limit the increase in their numbers. While Hopkins' address so impressed the Young Men's Association that it requested a copy for publication, it is just such sentiment that led blacks to conclude that they, increasingly, would have to act independently.[25]

Race prejudice prevailed even in those outlying areas that also had produced many staunch supporters of abolitionism. William Wells Brown's lecture tour in the region illustrated the disdain that many whites felt for the African American population. Anti-Slavery Society lecturers like Brown sometimes found themselves in the position of simultaneously advocating racial equality and abolitionism. In late 1843 Brown travelled to Attica, a small town just east of Buffalo, to lecture. At the conclusion of his session, he discovered that he could not secure lodging at any of the town's inns because of their exclusionary racial policies. Consequently, Brown returned to the church where he had lectured to spend the night under the most spartan of conditions. A few months later, in the winter of 1844, Brown faced a hostile audience in East Aurora, just to the south of Buffalo, where he was pelted with eggs and other foodstuffs.[26]

As a consequence of such incidents and the articulation of proposals by proponents of gradual and compensated manumission like Hopkins, blacks were united more closely in their quest for political, economic, and social emancipation. Both Abner Francis and George Weir played prominent roles in the National Negro Convention Movement, chairing key committees and serving as delegates from Buffalo. This organization not only sought the abolition of slavery, but also lobbied for increased job opportunities for blacks, free public schools so that black youngsters would have a level playing field, and, finally, political rights guaranteed by the ballot so that other achievements that blacks hoped to gain would be safeguarded.[27]

The Vine Street AME Church of Buffalo hosted the National Negro Convention of 1843. The six representatives from Buffalo were Francis,

Weir, William Wells Brown, William Hall, Samuel H. Davis, and Henry Thomas.[28] The highlight of this convention was a spirited debate between Frederick Douglass, former slave and Rochester publisher, and college-educated Henry Highland Garnet, a Troy minister, over whether blacks should use force to overthrow the institution of slavery. The stage for this debate had been set by the chairman, a Buffalo cooper named Samuel Davis, who had moved to the city from Connecticut some time before and who would become pastor of the Michigan Avenue Baptist Church.[29] In his address to the Convention, Davis delineated the major issues of debate and contended:

> . . . we wish to secure for ourselves, in common with other citizens, the privilege of seeking our own happiness in any part of the country we may choose, which right is now unjustly, and we believe, unconstitutionally denied us in a part of this Union. We wish also to secure the elective franchise in those states where it is denied us—where our rights are legislated away, and our voice neither heard nor regarded. We also wish to secure, for our children, especially the benefits of education, which in several States are entirely denied us and in others are enjoyed only in name. These, and many other things, of which we justly complain, bear most heavily upon us as a people; and it is our right and our duty to seek for redress, in that way which will be most likely to secure the desired end.[30]

This conference indicated the growing despair that large numbers of African Americans felt about the failure of federal, state, and local governments to address their concerns. The convention also heightened the growing dissatisfaction with Garrisonian abolitionism and represented an abandonment of its tenets by some prominent blacks. Moreover, the debates indicated that the new generation of African Americans would insist on speaking for themselves.

Indeed, Buffalo was a magnet for many nineteenth-century activists. James Whitfield articulated the concerns of many early nineteenth-century black reformers. Born in 1822 in New Hampshire and educated in the New York school district, Whitfield settled in Buffalo and was a lifelong barber. But his passion was poetry and this became the vehicle through which he articulated his views on race, democracy, and the American Dream.[31] Like many of his contemporary black writers, Whitfield highlighted the inconsistencies in the United States credo, as his poem "America" illustrates:

> America, it is to thee,
> Thou boasted land of liberty,
> It is to thee I raise my song,
> Thou land of blood, and crime, and wrong,
> It is to thee my native land,

> From which has issued many a band
> To tear the black man from his soil,
> And force him here to delve and toil,
> . . . Was it for this that wealth and life
> Were staked upon that desperate strife,
> Which drenched this land for seven long years
> With blood of men and women's tears?
> When black and white fought side by side,
> Upon the well-contested field, . . .
> And made the proud invader yield.[32]

Whitfield's poetry was highly acclaimed by colleagues like William Wells Brown, the outspoken abolitionist who had resided in Buffalo for a time, Frederick Douglass, and the noted physician and emigrationist Martin Delaney. During a visit to Whitfield's shop Douglass lamented that "the malignant arrangements of society had chained him in the barber shop."[33] By 1850 Whitfield had become prominent in black literary circles not only in Buffalo, but also across the nation.

Unlike Abner Francis and George Weir, Whitfield—by 1838 and at sixteen years of age—had become an avowed emigrationist and remained committed to that ideology throughout his life. In a letter written as part of a call to the 1854 Cleveland National Convention on Emigration, Whitfield stated:

> The American government, the American churches and the American people, are all engaged in one great conspiracy to crush us. A scattered and oppressed minority, chained from birth to a sense of inferiority will never be integrated equals in American society, for all avenues to education, higher employment, and political power will remain closed to them.[34]

He further observed that "while the negro servant is viewed with a certain degree of complacency, the negro gentleman is regarded with unmitigated hatred." He concluded that he had "no faith left in the justice of this country," for whites would never relinquish their power. Yet by 1862, with the outbreak of the Civil War, Whitfield apparently became less pessimistic about African Americans' prospects for integration into the American system. At that time he noted that "the United States Government must form an alliance with her own people, i.e., the people of color."[35]

Reformers perceived that the city of Buffalo provided an environment that was conducive to open debate. Several other national conventions that held some importance for African Americans met in Buffalo before the Civil War. The National Liberty Party, organized in Warsaw, New York in 1839, held its 1847 convention in Buffalo. Garnet addressed

THE EARLY YEARS 17

the 148 conference delegates and Brown attended his session. The Free Soil Party convened in the "Queen City" the following year.[36]

Many of the blacks who settled in Buffalo were employed in service occupations as porters, servants, domestics, and waiters. But African Americans also worked in a number of skilled and professional positions in the nineteenth century. In 1855, for example, 16 percent of black males were barbers, 8 percent were sailors, 6 percent were employed in the building trades, and the crafts and professions employed 4.5 percent each. By the 1870s Peyton Harris's and Robert Talbert's investments in real estate in Erie County had paid handsome dividends.[37] This was the best economic situation that African Americans would experience until long after the post–World War I migration.[38]

The black community of Buffalo was composed of a small group of enterprising individuals bent upon preserving the freedom which was so dear to them and succeeding economically as other ethnic groups had before them. Indeed, they did make some modest gains. Nearly one in four black family heads owned real property in 1855, less than native-born whites and Germans (43–44 percent), but more than the Irish (18 percent).[39] A report of the Overseer of the Poor in November 1867 indicated that only two indigent blacks had sought public aid.[40] Black churches, lodges, families, and other community institutions provided for their own.[41] Given the transient nature of nineteenth-century America, the black community was fairly stable and experienced persistence rates comparable to other ethnic groups in the city.[42]

After the Civil War, African Americans in Buffalo continued the struggle for their constitutional rights which they had begun to wage during the antebellum era. Community celebrations reinforced blacks' commitments to each other, while they also served as instruments to present their political opinions to city officials and other residents. The ratification of the Fifteenth Amendment to the Constitution was an important milestone in their quest for freedom and self-determination. This was especially important to the black community because the New York State property ownership qualification of $250 virtually had disfranchised the entire black male population.[43] This was a huge sum, for in 1855 the average homeowner in Buffalo had $150 in real estate.[44] Only thirty-one African Americans met the property qualifications needed to exercise the franchise in 1855. They celebrated the passage of the Fifteenth Amendment in 1870 with a thirty-eight-gun salute near the Michigan Avenue Baptist Church. This was followed by a special worship service at the church, in which Reverend A. S. Brokenburgh delivered a sermon based upon scripture appropriately taken from the Book of Exodus. Each year thereafter local blacks arranged a massive celebration at the St. James Hall and parades to commemorate the passage of the Fifteenth Amendment.[45]

Nineteenth-century black Buffalonians were cognizant of the power of the news media, and the manner in which the local press depicted African Americans was another issue that caught their attention. A group of "colored" men noted their dissatisfaction with one of the local newspapers after publication of a news feature about a camp for blacks at Fort Erie, Ontario:

> The colored people of Buffalo desire it to be very distinctly understood that they do not, in any form, way, manner, or shape, agree with the directors of the colored camp at Fort Erie, that the *Buffalo Courier* is their friend, or that they intend to "hurl to the winds of destruction" the *Buffalo Express*. The young man that penned that article is a stranger to Buffalo, and knows nothing of the relative position of the two papers toward the colored people, he is very ignorant about the *Courier*. If he professes to such "progressive" republicanism, to such, "true Republican spirit of elevation." How in the name of common sense can we address the *Courier* as "dear *Courier*," the known traducer of our race—a paper that we have always classed among our bitter and most unrelenting opponents, and the "embodiment" of all infamous sheets opposed to our "true Republican spirit of elevation. . . .[46]

Black Buffalonians, like those nationwide, valued education and fought valiantly to secure the best possible education for their children. Peyton Harris, the real estate investor, was an ardent proponent of quality education for African American children. In 1847 he observed that the African school was a sham. "In very deed," he contended, "it has not reached the dignity and elevation of education. It has been rudimental. . . . To comprehensiveness it has never yet made any pretension; to profundity not the most distant approach." Despite such pronouncements, the Buffalo Common Council's Committee on schools refused to take action, arguing that the very existence of the African School placed black children on an equal plane. Leading black critics continued to question the committee's actions and policies. But Henry Moxley was instrumental in initiating the movement that resulted in the integration of the Buffalo Public School System. In 1832, at age twenty-four, Moxley, a barber, had come to Buffalo as a runaway slave. He immediately established a lucrative barber shop. Influenced by the passage of the Civil Rights Act of 1866, which provided for equal enjoyment by blacks of all the laws regarding person and property which benefitted whites, Moxley, in June of 1867, petitioned "to have his children admitted to the school in District 32," where they resided. This struggle was a protracted one and ultimately involved Robert Talbert and a number of members of the Colored Presbyterian Church, including John Simpson and George Weir, Jr. These skilled workers and businessmen also had been active in the abolitionist and the National Negro Convention movements. Finally, in 1881, the District Council of Buffalo agreed to permit the students to be enrolled in their neighborhood schools. Previously, African American youngsters had been transported outside of their neighborhoods to the poorly equipped Vine Street African School, which had been established for them; earlier attempts at integrating Buffalo's schools had been thwarted.[47]

Other issues affecting blacks were foremost on this community's mind, and it continued to express its views throughout the nineteenth century. The Buffalo Amateur Debating society met on October 24, 1879, at the Sparsfield Hall, to ratify the nominations made by the Republican state, county, and city conventions. For this occasion, blacks arranged to have Professor Solomon Day, principal of the "colored" school in Dayton, Ohio, address the society. Day reminded the audience of the terrible conditions which blacks suffered in the Democratic South. But his lecture was mainly a refutation of the allegations made about the black migration and the African Americans' marriage to the Republican party by the southern press.[48] Day commented that

> [Migration] toward the West [was] the wisest and best thing it was possible for [the black man] to do—the only thing that promises him and his posterity a future worth living for. When his crying of agony and his dying wail during the years intervening between his freedom and his resolve to leave the South was bourne upon nearly every breeze that wafted from the South; when his terrible condition of poverty, political ostracism, and of countless cruelties and wrongs were proclaimed in the North, the press and all the leaders of a certain political party said it is a Radical lie and the Negro of the South, said they, is in perfect enjoyment of all his political rights, happy and contented and regularly voting the Democratic ticket from choice; just as soon as the exodus to Kansas begins this same press and these same leaders say he has been persuaded to leave by Northern Radicals to swell the vote of the Radicals and to increase the northern representation in Congress by the census 1880.[49]

Publishing their own newspapers was one means to address the bias that blacks discerned in the local media coverage about them and their issues. Francis Peregrino, a South African nationalist who had settled in Buffalo, used the *Spectator*, the newspaper that he previously had edited in South Africa and Brazil, as a forum to express some of the black community's opinions. In 1897, he wrote a letter to the prominent theologian Dr. T. Dewitt Talmidge of Washington, D. C., inquiring why he constantly delivered sermons deploring "the mistreatment of Armenians and yet failed to speak about the lynching of blacks."[50] Black Buffalonians, in April 1897, joined forces with African Americans in

Albany, Syracuse, and Rochester to endorse the nomination of a local black attorney, Albert M. Thomas, for the position of consul general to Haiti.[51]

The sporadic actions of these blacks indicate a persistent dedication to improving their status in Buffalo. They seized upon opportunities to highlight the inconsistencies in the actions of America's staunchest proponents of democratic principles and human rights. Moreover, these Buffalonians saw their struggle as a nationwide one and joined other organizations that pledged to redress the grievances of blacks across the country.

Just as antebellum blacks in Buffalo had spoken out against their oppression and had fostered literary endeavors, those who were present in the Gilded Age continued this practice. At the 1880 commencement exercises of the University of Buffalo Medical School, Reverend Joseph Robert Love, class representative and rector of the St. Philip's Episcopal Church, was called upon to give a toast. Love, believed to be the first black graduate of the University of Buffalo, observed that for the first time in the history of the school a black man had been asked to address the alumni banquet. Love further noted that "the time was fast coming when the colored American citizen would emerge from his social ostracism of the past and meet his white brothers on the equal plane of education and merit in pursuit of the various avocations."[52] In January 1897, the local black community honored Dr. W. E. B. DuBois for the publication of his doctoral dissertation, *The African Slave Trade*, the first volume in a prestigious Harvard University historical series.[53]

At the turn of the century African Americans organized a number of social and economic institutions. Women played key roles in this trend. Imbued with the concept of self-help and mutuality, African American women across the nation were concerned about uplifting their communities by devising programs and strategies to carry them into the twentieth century. They also were concerned about the increasing stridency of the physical and verbal sexual assaults by whites on all black women, regardless of their "class, age, or reputations." In response to these considerations black women joined forces and established the National Association of Colored Women (NACW) in Washington in 1896.[54]

In 1899 social worker Susan Evans helped to establish an NACW affiliate in Buffalo, the Phyllis Wheatley Club, named in honor of the eighteenth-century black poet. She was joined by twenty other women, including Mrs. Charles Davis, a graduate of Hampton Institute, and Oberlin College graduate Mary Burnett Talbert, who would become renowned in national and international reform movements.[55] The Phyllis Wheatley Club would be in the forefront when creating programs and strategies for the development of Buffalo's modern black community. It founded

Believed to be Robert
Talbert, Sr. Taken from
the Talbert Family Col-
lection. Courtesy of
Lillian S. Williams.

Harris/Qualls/Talbert
women. Taken from the
Talbert Family Collection.
Courtesy of Lillian S.
Williams.

The Reverend Dr. Joseph Robert Love, rector of St. Philip's Episcopal Church and first African American graduate of the University of Buffalo School of Medicine. Courtesy of the National Library, Jamaica.

William H. Talbert. Courtesy of the Buffalo and Erie County Historical Society.

Mary Burnett Talbert. Courtesy of the Buffalo and Erie County Historical Society.

Sarah May Talbert, daughter of William and Mary Talbert and later a graduate of the New England Conservatory of Music. Courtesy of the Buffalo and Erie County Historical Society.

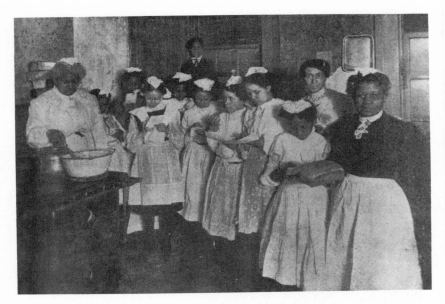

Mrs. John Bell and her cooking class at St. Luke's AME Zion
Church, 1906. Courtesy of *The Buffalo Illustrated*, New York
State Archives.

A Sunday school class at Saint Luke's AME Zion Church,
1906. Courtesy of *The Buffalo Illustrated*, New York State
Archives.

Mary Burnett Talbert, standing fourth from left, with members of the Phyllis Wheatley Club outside the Michigan Avenue Baptist Church. Courtesy of Nannie Helen Burroughs Collection, Library of Congress.

Portrait of Mary Burnett Talbert as Worthy Matron of the Naomi Chapter #10 Order of the Eastern Stars, affiliate of Prince Hall Masons. Courtesy of the Buffalo and Erie County Historical Society.

Twentieth Century Club Dance at Crescent Hall, December 13, 1917. Courtesy of the Buffalo and Erie County Historical Society.

Reverend J. Edward Nash (far right), Mayor Fuhrmann (second from far right), and others at the St. Philip's Men's Club and Colored Citizens' General Oliver Perry Centennial Week at the Elmwood Avenue Music Hall, September, 1913. Courtesy of the Buffalo and Erie County Historical Society.

and operated a settlement house in 1905 and invited the NAACP to organize in Buffalo in 1910.[56]

African Americans organized new church denominations, like Saint Luke's AME Zion, that had a progressive social agenda embedded in their programs. Along with its well-attended Sunday school classes, St. Luke operated a cooking school, headed by Mrs. John Bell, that prepared young women for the job market. Blacks established other organizations such as the Prince Hall Order of Masons and an affiliate, the Naomi Chapter #10 Order of Eastern Stars. They also founded the Twentieth Century Club and others that combined social activities with an agenda of racial uplift.[57]

The attempts of blacks to ameliorate their plight in nineteenth-century America were part of a persistent uphill struggle. Nevertheless, Buffalo African Americans met the challenge head-on, sometimes turning the law into redress and at other times utilizing public pressure and the philanthropic resources of sympathetic whites. They made some obvious strides, such as their success in dismantling the poorly equipped New York State public African schools, but their economic status declined considerably.

In 1855, Buffalo, New York was a city of foreigners. Immigration continued to be a major force in the growth and development of that industrial city until the outbreak of World War I, when it abruptly came to a halt.[58] The immigrant presence had created a well-segregated city as each group of foreign-born settled into its own ethnic enclave (see map 4). Often, the locale was determined by the types of jobs which each immigrant group was able to find. Large numbers of Italians and Irish worked at the harbors; they resided in the nearby districts, Italians on the west side and Irish in South Buffalo. Affordable housing accommodations were scarce in Buffalo and immigrants sought access in those areas where they were highly concentrated because of the availability of kinship and friendship networks.[59] African Americans experienced similar housing patterns. By 1900, there had emerged a distinct African American district located east of the downtown business district. There they found employment in the service sector.

On the eve of the twentieth century, Buffalo had a small African American population in comparison to other northern, urban centers. In 1900, for example, Chicago had a black population of 30,150 (1.9 percent of the population); Detroit had 15,816, and Cleveland had 5,988 (1.6 percent).[60] But New York, with its 60,666 blacks, had the largest concentration of urban blacks. In 1905 Buffalo's African American population was just slightly over 1,200, in a city of approximately 400,000 people.[61] It was to remain a fairly small community until after World War I. In 1915 the number of blacks increased by 33 percent to 1,600, at a time when Buffalo's population was 475,000. By 1925, Buffalo's

African American community had experienced a tremendous growth; it numbered about 9,000 out of a city of 530,000 people.[62] Yet despite this substantial increase, blacks in Buffalo still comprised a small, but significant, portion of the city's total population, about .02 percent in 1905, and just under one percent (0.9 percent) in 1925. This community was proud and had a legacy of struggle, but as early as 1900, it had developed a relationship with the white Buffalo establishment based primarily upon noblesse oblige.

Charles Johnson described the relationship between old Buffalo African American families and the old white families for whom they worked as "peculiarly friendly."[63] He noted that the whites sometimes attended African American social events which were patterned after those that the whites held. These blacks were quite familiar with the social gatherings of the aristocrats because it was their responsibility to organize and to serve at those affairs. The old black families had a presence in political campaigns, municipal celebrations, and in the reception of famous visitors to the city. Except for the Irish, whites seemed to tolerate these families.[64] Niles Carpenter reported that blacks and whites also attended some parties where everyone spoke German.[65] Such relationships led blacks to be optimistic about their citizenship as Buffalonians.

With the arrival of outsiders, established black families felt threatened and attempted to create a caste system that would protect them and their privileges from outside encroachments. They excluded from their group sleeping car porters, dining car waiters, and traveling musicians, who as transients in the city had no one to vouch for them. Johnson found that one such effort wanted to create a "blue vein" society based upon blood and color. He noted that "[this effort] met with subtle tho unexpressed opposition in the indifference of several otherwise strong pillars of the community whose veins were not readily discernible."[66]

These elite families seemed to have much more in common with the black elite of other cities than with the newcomers in their town. William Talbert and his brother Robert had married Mary and Henrietta Burnett, respectively, Oberlin College graduates and the daughters of a prominent, old family of Oberlin.[67] A study of marriage patterns in the St. Philip's Episcopal Church from 1875 to 1925 indicated that in fact most marriages occurred between Buffalonians and outsiders.[68]

Old Buffalo black families also had an unfavorable sex ratio, just as the newcomers experienced. The old families had an excess of women of marriageable age, the newcomers an excess of males. Yet despite what on the surface appears to have been a symbiotic relationship, members of the two groups did not contemplate marriage until the arrival later of southern-educated black medical doctors who were considered suitable partners. Their medical degrees had eliminated the cultural and geographical barriers which all too frequently separated blacks.[69]

These old Buffalo families maintained comfortable homes and a refined social life, an extraordinary feat when coupled with their restricted (and continually shrinking) occupational status. Johnson expressed their status thus:

> . . . the spirit of exclusiveness and prestige based on nothing which newcomers could immediately observe hangs on, nursing the memory of their past importance and the halcyon days when they were not conspicuous as Negroes and when they enjoyed without restraint all that the city enjoyed.[70]

Their relationships with the white establishment would change after the Great Migration.

African Americans began arriving in Buffalo in larger numbers at the turn of the century. But after the outbreak of the First World War, blacks rushed to Buffalo in search of jobs and the economic gains that the local industries, particularly the steel mills and railroads, offered. Young and old left the South—especially Virginia, the Carolinas, Georgia, Mississippi, Kentucky, Maryland, and the District of Columbia—and came to Buffalo.[71]

Many of them succeeded in breaking out of the service positions that they traditionally had held and gained higher incomes and more steady employment for the first time. The traditional successful black was the individual who worked as a waiter or bootblack for local hotels or elite social clubs. This phenomenon had been noted in other cities, too. One commentator observed:

> To be a janitor at some downtown store was to be highly respected. The real "elite," the "big shots," the "voices of the race," were the waiters at the Lansing Country Club and the shoe shine boys at the state capitol.[72]

By the 1920s these individuals, mainly old residents of Buffalo, had their dominance within the community challenged by the most recent arrivals, many of whom were college graduates. But a number of newcomers were "[factory] workers." One observer commented that by the mid-1920s black women sought a "Bethlehem fool or a Wickwire Mule" as suitable marriage partners.[73] This referred to the fact that the Bethlehem Steel and Wickwire Steel mills employed African Americans in large numbers where they performed arduous tasks under the most deplorable circumstances. Yet these newcomers found the prospect of higher wages and greater job security attractive.

Soon southerners became prominent in leadership positions in the Buffalo African American community. Many of these were of working-class background and several of them had established businesses that catered to their community's needs. However, blacks had not encountered strict residential segregation and would not experience wide-scale segregation until their numbers increased after the World War I migration. Then they tended to live primarily in the Ellicott district on Buffalo's east side.

As a result of more widespread segregation, African Americans increasingly were restricted to two areas of settlement within the city, the Ellicott and Masten Park districts. Both recently had been abandoned by various immigrant groups. A few of the more successful blacks bought homes on Lyth and Laurel streets in the Jefferson-Delavan area, a contiguous neighborhood.[74] The older black residential areas where all new immigrants had settled upon arrival witnessed extensive deterioration. The presence of the newcomers exacerbated these woes. Those individuals who spilled over into sections contiguous to the central community found similar conditions awaiting them. Competition for the limited housing stock and the subsequent "race" tax meant that the migrants often were compelled to pay exorbitant rents for inferior accommodations.[75] Most of the available housing lacked adequate sanitation facilities. Recreational facilities were limited and various social ills, such as crime and disease, were becoming more apparent.[76]

The migration of southern blacks into the city placed increasing demands on this small community in terms of housing, jobs, recreational facilities, and other aspects of its infrastructure. Their presence heightened the differences between blacks and whites, as well as among the black residents. Yet this tremendous influx of newcomers was not a debilitating force. Quite the contrary, southern blacks infused a renewed spirit of struggle into Buffalo's African American community, and provided that community with tools with which to wage a war for equality and human dignity at the expense of noblesse oblige.

Growing Up Black

Growing up in Buffalo was something of a mixed blessing for African Americans. The city provided opportunities for many blacks within the social norms that generally relegated them to subordinate economic and social positions in society. Furthermore, some black families benefitted from the noblesse oblige of the white families for whom they worked. Reverend Derrick Byrd of St. Luke AME Zion noted that the old African American community "served well and, enjoyed a satisfactory relationship with their patrons and employers."[1] Social worker Elizabeth Brown Talbert observed that this generally was the case until 1916 or 1917, when the black population began to increase dramatically and whites consequently began to feel the threat of a potential decline in their own economic and social status.[2] The life cycles of blacks reflected the general conditions that they experienced in the changing environment. As competition for housing and jobs increased, race relations deteriorated and the life cycles of blacks were directly influenced by these factors, as we shall see.

In 1905, black male youths in Buffalo lived at home until well into their twenties, enjoying a prolonged period of childhood and adolescence characteristic of the lives of youths in Buffalo at the time. The experience of sixteen-year-old Will Talbert in 1881 will provide clues as to what the lives of young black males in Buffalo might have entailed at the turn of the century. Talbert was born in Red Bluff, California in 1866, and his Michigan Avenue home had been in his family for over fifty years. Talbert lived in an extended family, and he was able to draw sustenance from this large network of kin and fictive kin. His family and community also provided him with a solid foundation that both shielded him from the harsh realities of racism in the city and simultaneously gave him the impetus to dream and to make his dreams a reality.

As the son of Robert Talbert, a prominent, wealthy black businessman, and Anna Harris Talbert, Will was more privileged than most children

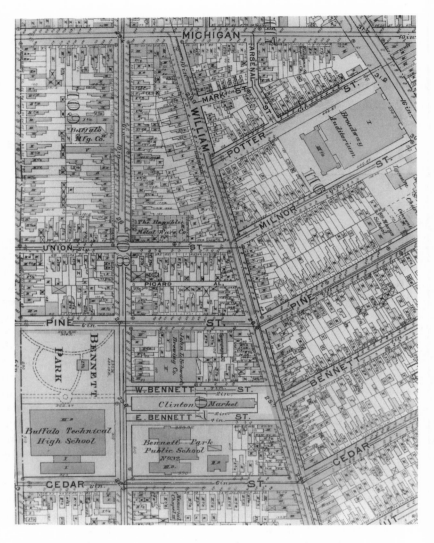

William H. Talbert's neighborhood, showing Michigan Avenue Baptist Church, Clinton Market, Memorial Chapel, and Technical High School in 1884. *G. M. Hopkins Atlas of the City of Buffalo.* Courtesy of the New York State Library.

in Buffalo, black or white. His grandfather was prominent businessman Peyton Harris, and local physician William Qualls was an uncle.[3] But like most youths in Buffalo, he was required to attend school until age sixteen, unless he had secured a work permit that would enable him to secure part-time jobs as early as age fourteen.[4] William Talbert walked the seven blocks to the Technical High School, where he studied physics, history, grammar, spelling, reading, composition, geography, civil government, and music. At the close of the school day Talbert attended "drawing school."[5] Notwithstanding the demands of his academic work, Will found the time to be mischievous, and his teachers punished him by detaining him after school for such offenses as "whispering" in class. Chastisement at school usually meant that his parents also would punish him when he arrived home. On one such occasion, Talbert related, he had to go to bed without his supper.[6]

Will Talbert had an active social life that reflected the availability of recreational and community educational resources open to black youngsters. Many of his leisure activities were connected to the African American churches and, therefore, were accessible to all youths. Such involvement highlighted the centrality of the churches in African American communities across the nation. Each week Will attended Sunday School and church. His amusements centered around programs, festivals, and concerts at the "Baptist, Episcopal, and Methodist" churches. Ice skating and sledding in Williamsville, the town just to the north of Buffalo, were regular winter events, while in the spring Talbert played ball and went sailing. On Saturday mornings he accompanied his father to the Clinton Street market.[7]

Many black youngsters also had to work to help supplement their family incomes. Although work was not essential for Will Talbert, he was an enterprising young man and worked in several positions. Moreover, situations like this imbued black youngsters with the mores and folkways that their family and community valued. His choices illustrate the kinds of job options that were available to other youngsters: He had a daily newspaper route, he shoveled snow, and he transported luggage to the train station on nearby Exchange Street. Some of his work related directly to his family's real estate business and seemed to be an internship for him to learn to manage their holdings. He wrote leases for his father and other business partners and also, as an amanuensis wrote letters for them to associates in California, Washington, D. C., and other areas. Will also spent a considerable amount of time writing letters for other people in the community, for which he earned a few pennies.[8]

Young Talbert engaged in other activities that probably reflect his class background more than widespread activities among black youths. He frequently "took tea" at friends' homes and visited ice cream parlors in the area. He attended lectures at the St. James Hall and went to dog shows when they were in town. Will also attended the performances of the Georgia Minstrel Company and plays such as "Swift and Sure." But like most young males, Talbert also enjoyed competitive sports, such as baseball and bowling.[9]

The demographic data reflect and confirm that other boys in Buffalo at the turn of the century shared some of Talbert's experiences. Until the age of sixteen, the vast majority of black boys in 1905 were enrolled in school, while a handful worked in good jobs, such as clerking or semi-skilled and skilled trades. When they reached sixteen, this changed. They were no longer under the yoke of the New York State Compulsory Education Act, which required youngsters to remain in school until age sixteen. As a result, fewer than 20 percent of black males aged sixteen to twenty years were classified as students. In fact, leaving school signalled their entry into adulthood, for most youths went to work immediately. Presumably, those who remained home contributed toward their own support. There was no brief period of idleness in their lives following their schooling.

Despite the fact that these young men had entered the world of work, they were not totally independent. Most of them continued to live in their parents' homes, where they could benefit from the emotional security their families provided as they continued to be educated in preparation for eventual departure from the fold. Black males did not even begin to leave home in fairly large numbers until age twenty. This process was virtually completed by age 26. (For a description of household relationships of black male youths at each stage, refer to Figure 2, which depicts the household relatives of young black males.)[10]

Most young males did not establish their own households once they had moved from their parents' homes. Instead, they entered what Michael Katz has called a state of semi-autonomy.[11] Many became boarders. About 26 percent of youths between the ages of 16 and 20 were boarders. As they grew older, boarding became even more attractive. These findings indicate that boarding was a significant phenomenon in the adjustment process of young black males. It afforded some of them the opportunity to live in a family setting while they made the gradual transition from childhood to manhood. Most boarders lived in households where there were few boarders. In fact, three out of five dwelled in homes where there were three boarders or fewer. This is a reflection both of the nature of housing stock in Buffalo and a propensity among blacks to board people whom they knew.

Like their own families had earlier, boarders' surrogate families also provided a modicum of security. Yet at the same time, the boarding family allowed the youths more freedom and, thus, the opportunity to escape conflicts which undoubtedly arise when young adults remain at home. They gladly paid the rents in exchange for "freedom." Further-more, boarding provided black males a chance to work and to accu-mulate funds which would enable them to get married and establish their own households later. The typical boarder was a single male. Only twelve young married couples lived as boarders; none of them had begun to raise families. A fairly common occurrence among boarders was for brothers to secure lodging within the same household; this is an indi-cation that the familial bonds remained strong, despite the fact that the youths had moved away from home.[12]

Boarders, despite the social and economic reasons for their existence, were often perceived as threats to the privacy of the family and to the chastity of unmarried daughters. DuBois wrote:

> [The result of the large numbers of strangers admitted freely into their doors] is pernicious, especially where there are growing children. The lodgers are often waiters, who are at home when the housewife is off at work, and growing daughters are thus left unprotected. . . . In such ways the privacy and intimacy of home life is destroyed, and elements of danger and demoralization are admitted.[13]

But the seriousness of the boarding problem should not be exaggerated. Black heads of households often were able to regulate the times at which they permitted boarders to enter their domiciles, and families were less likely to take in boarders during the years when their children were adolescents. Two out of five young men in their twenties headed households with boarders in 1905. This was a time when the men could use the extra money to help finance their household. Male heads of households who were ten years older presumably were raising their families, and the number of those who took in lodgers had decreased substantially. Landlords among black male heads of household in their forties increased somewhat, but only after the age of 50 did the pro-portion who took in boarders approach the figure it had been among male heads in their twenties. At this stage of their cycle, most children had already left home and were no longer potential "victims" of the people who resided in their parents' homes; lodgers also helped the aging household heads to supplement their meager wages in preparation for old age and retirement.

Establishing their own homes marked the completion of the grow-ing-up process for most males, but it is difficult to ascertain to what extent black males left the homes of their parents to set up housekeeping with their brides.[14] Economic considerations had, in many respects, com-pelled them to remain in the households of others; thus, it is not sur-prising that those black men who headed their own households were older than boarders. Those men who headed their own households also had secured more skilled positions than the boarders. This suggests that black men could increase their earning power as they aged and that the higher income enabled them to set up their own homes. The process, however, was gradual and fewer than half of male heads of household were under forty. These findings indicate the severe impact of the economic and housing conditions on black family life at the turn of the century. Difficult economic conditions did not destroy the family, but they delayed family formation. Black males tended to marry and set up housekeeping in their later years.[15] Once they were married, however, they tended to head their own homes. Few married couples were classified as servants or boarders.

A sizeable number of black men left home and became not boarders, but live-in servants; one out of five men in their early 20s lived and worked as servants, and by the time they were 29 years old, a substantial number still worked as live-in servants. While the level of skill of the servants varied, most held positions in which they were laborers or semi-skilled workers. Many worked in institutions rather than in private homes, a sign of the changing times when employers decreed white live-in servants more desirable. The typical male servant was single and members of his family did not share his household status. Thus Leonard Saunders, a 28-year-old janitor who lived in service at 58 West Genesee Street, along with his wife Catherine and their two young daughters, was unusual. Since Catherine's occupation is listed as housework, it is not certain whether she worked for her husband's employers.[16] The Saunders family was the only family that had the household status of servant. Very few young black males in 1905 lived in extended family arrangements. Perhaps they opted for other living accommodations because living with relatives tended to be tantamount to living with their parents. In a later decade, however, a substantially larger percentage of young blacks secured housing with their relatives. The processes of migration were in effect and newcomers sometimes dwelled with relatives until they could find other housing and get settled in the city.

It is significant to note that black males who had reached the age of retirement tended to live in family settings. Most of them still headed households; one lived with his grandchildren. The family unit and the respect for the old that characterized much of the African American populace meant that the elderly were recognized as household heads even when they no longer were providing income to the family. These elderly family members still nurtured and provided continuity and meaning for their young. Frequently, they also were called upon to offer childcare.[17]

The life cycles of black men in Buffalo in 1905 reveal that they enjoyed a stable, prolonged period of childhood and adolescence. However, once they reached adulthood their lives were characterized by such upheavals as boarding or living in the households of others, and late marriages. Home ownership has always been desired by blacks, yet only a few Buffalo males ever succeeded in even establishing their own households, and those who were successful were well over the age of 30. An examination of the experiences of black men in Buffalo in 1925 will illustrate how the boom ushered in by World War I and migration affected these cycles. The overall experiences of African American male youths growing up in Buffalo, New York in 1925 were similar to those who lived in the city twenty years earlier, yet there are also notable differences. More of these youths lived in households that were not headed by their parents, nearly half of those in their late teens lived in such circumstances. There was a dramatic increase in the number of these youngsters who were enrolled in school—62 percent, versus 40 percent in 1905. Once they had left school, most youths secured employment. A few youths neither worked nor attended school. Presumably, these lads had to perform tasks around their homes, but their period of idleness was brief. Black youths began to leave home earlier than they had during the pre-migration decades and they completed the process earlier. By the time they had reached their late twenties, fewer than five percent of black males in 1925 continued to reside with their parents, compared with 10 percent in 1905. The fact that these youths were able to leave home earlier than their turn-of-the-century counterparts indicates that the economic climate was more favorable for African Americans. Moreover, many of these young men undoubtedly were newcomers who had not migrated with their parents (see Figure 3).

Like those blacks who left the homes of their families in 1905, a substantial proportion of black males in 1925 did not immediately establish their own households. They, too, entered a stage of semi-autonomy, many to become boarders and live-in servants. As in 1905, heads of households in 1925 also regulated the times at which boarders were admitted into their households, in order to maximize the economic benefits and minimize the family disruption. Nearly half of those household heads who took in boarders did so during their twenties. By the time that they were in their thirties, the number of male-headed families who rented rooms to lodgers had been reduced to 43 percent as they tried to maintain a healthy atmosphere in which to raise their own children. While this figure is still large, many of those who took in boarders only accommodated people whom they knew. This was a typical pattern in Buffalo. One interviewee noted that "we never took in strangers."[18] After the age of forty, those male heads of families who took in boarders increased. In 1905, a little more than one-third of all males who admitted boarders into their homes were 25 to 40 years old. Although 1925 witnessed the establishment of a number of boarding houses, none contained more than twelve boarders and most boarders continued to live in family settings. The average household size of male-headed households had increased to 6.47. Quite a few married couples and some families, including single siblings, boarded together. However, the typical boarder in 1925 was an unattached male.

Boarding was popular for young men, but as they approached the age of 29, their numbers began to dwindle. In fact, the overall percentage of black males who boarded in 1925 was significantly lower than it had been in 1905, 32 percent versus 41 percent. This is not to argue that the boarding experience was less significant in the lives of black male youths. Quite the contrary, the social reasons for its existence continued. The decline indicates that the economic climate was more favorable for African Americans in the "Queen City" than it had been twenty years earlier. Employment opportunities for black men increased in the professional-managerial classes, as well as in the skilled trades. But, at any rate, these figures show that by 1925, despite the massive in-migration which occurred after 1916 and despite unfavorable reports about the process of acculturation elsewhere, Buffalo's black community did not witness a "floating" boarding population.[19] Their adjustment portends the development of a healthy, stable community.

As one might expect, in 1925 black males established their own households at an earlier age than in 1905, 36 percent of black men in their 20s versus 19.5 percent in 1905. By 1925, working as a live-in servant was less popular than it had been in 1905, for black men now had access to more lucrative, less servile jobs. But an impressive number of young males still found employment in hotels and major commercial establishments. While most of the servants were unattached males, a substantial number of them were married; their wives were servants also. In general, the couples had not started to raise families.

On the whole, 1925 saw an improvement in the life situations of black men in Buffalo. Black males moved away from their parents' homes earlier than in 1905 and set up their own households at a younger age. These findings can be attributed to a more favorable economic climate that allowed blacks to secure the more lucrative positions in factories which earlier had excluded them.

The life cycles of African American females can best be understood in light of the experiences of black males. The world in which these women lived was circumscribed by race, class, and gender and these factors affected their life situations. Black girls in Buffalo in 1905 enjoyed a long period of sheltered adolescence, like their male counterparts.[20] Up to the age of sixteen, at least two-thirds attended school. Another 16 percent appeared to be neither enrolled in school nor working, but they, too, probably were students, since they were bound by New York state law to attend school. After age sixteen, most girls left school, but they continued to live with their families (Figure 4). A fair number of black girls began work as chambermaids at a young age, some as early as eleven. After leaving school, however, work became the norm, and 59 percent of black girls aged sixteen to twenty held jobs, compared to 83 percent of the women in their twenties.

A surprising amount of diversification in jobs appeared among the group. They worked in professional, clerical, and skilled positions, as well as unskilled and service work. Most professional black women were teachers. The Buffalo Board of Education prohibited married women from teaching; for this reason, these female teachers were young and single, and many lived in their parents' homes. A substantial number of young females remained at home without outside work. Presumably, in this setting, their education for life continued while they performed chores in their parents' households.

Black women began to leave home in fairly large numbers between eighteen and twenty years of age, four to five years before their brothers left. Most of those who left home did so to marry and to work. Married women worked primarily in semi-skilled positions, but there were a few who found work in the nonmanual and skilled sectors, too. Most worked as domestics in institutions. A woman's ability to marry depended upon the availability of men of marriageable age and their ability to support a family. The overall sex ratio for black females was favorable in 1905; for women in their twenties, there were 126 males for every 100 females. This can be attributed to the increase in job opportunities for black male migrants and the paucity of jobs for black females. One would expect that a substantial number of these women would be wed. However, more than half of the women did not marry until the age of 28. A study of marriage patterns in St. Philip's, a black high Episcopal church in Buffalo, showed that for the period 1901 to 1925 the average age of a bride was 28.1 years.[21] Economic factors provide the clue to this observation, for we have already seen that males postponed establishing their own household until they were economically solvent. Only 25 percent of males in their late twenties had set up their own homes.

Black women in Buffalo deferred marriage until their 30s; even more significantly, the great majority of those who did marry had few or no children. By age thirty, 31 percent of black married women had children; this figure increased to 65 percent of women who had reached forty. These findings are consistent with the historically low fertility rates for Buffalo's African American women.[22] Herbert Gutman and Laurence Glasco discovered that the fertility rate for Buffalo's black community was 520 children per 1,000 fertile women in 1855, and 340 per 1,000 fertile women in 1875.[23] My own study indicates that the fertility rate in the community continued to decline, until by 1905 it was only 210 per 1,000.

The lack of children represented not only a conscious attempt on the part of blacks to regulate their family size, but also economic and health factors.[24] Males set up their households in their late 20s, because they could not afford the responsibilities of marriage and family earlier in adulthood. DuBois had observed this trend as early as 1896 when he studied Philadelphia:

> The size of families in cities is nearly always smaller than elsewhere, and the Negro family follows the rule; late marriages among them undoubtedly act as a check to population; moreover, the economic stress is so great that only a small family can survive. . . .[25]

Infant mortality rates among Buffalo blacks also were high. A study conducted by the Buffalo Federation of Churches on the ethnic sections of Buffalo in 1923 recommended that a community center which included a "well baby clinic" be established within the East Side community to lower the infant mortality rate.[26] Many women apparently remained childless out of necessity rather than choice.

Some black women left home to become boarders. Boarding was a phenomenon for young women (especially in their mid-twenties) who wished to (or had to) escape the confines of their parents' homes, or who were newcomers to Buffalo. Restrictions against the movement of women were great at the turn of the century, and boarding did not affect the black female population of Buffalo to the extent that it did the male. Still, 14 percent of adult black females were boarders. Like their male counterparts, these women lived in family settings where they could be supervised and yet were able to enjoy a modicum of freedom. Most of these women worked to support themselves, mostly as laundresses, maids, or janitresses; one woman was a proprietor of a tailor shop, while another owned a restaurant, and three women were skilled workers.

Relatively few black women left home to work as live-in domestic servants. Laurence Glasco's and Michael Katz's respective studies of Buffalo, New York and Hamilton, Ontario in the mid-nineteenth century noted that the female counterpart to the boarder was the live-in servant.[27] In Buffalo during the first quarter of this century, black women did not share a comparable experience, for employers typically did not seek black women and girls for positions as live-in servants. Few succeeded in securing jobs as servants, constituting only about 5 percent of adult black women and 3 percent of female adolescents in 1905. Glasco observed that the Irish had begun to take over the Buffalo servant class as early as 1855.[28]

Virginia Yans concluded that Italian women in Buffalo in 1905 worked in positions where they could maintain their traditional family patterns. Many of these young women worked in the cannery factories and they were assigned to crews that included their male relatives. She argues that this practice was often adhered to even if women could earn higher wages elsewhere.[29] Few African Americans had this recourse, for Italians had developed an entrepreneurial class by 1905.[30] However, although a large proportion of the black female population had to work, there was a concerted effort to keep black women out of positions where, as servants in the homes of white males, they could be subjected to sexual abuse and disrespect. DuBois expressed the sentiment that black women had to be protected from white America. He wrote passionately:

> I shall forgive the white South much in its final judgment day: I shall forgive its slavery . . . but one thing I shall never forgive, neither in this world nor the world to come: its wanton and continued and persistent insulting of the black womanhood which it sought and seeks to prostitute to its lust.[31]

DuBois urged black parents to use caution in sending their daughters into domestic service.[32] Herbert Gutman in *The Black Family in Slavery and Freedom* observed a propensity among black men during Reconstruction to keep their wives at home to avoid undesirable jobs such as domestic service or field labor.[33]

But these were neither solely Southern phenomena nor male prerogatives. Northern black women also deplored working in domestic service for a number of other compelling reasons. Elizabeth Pleck noted that Philadelphia working black women in 1919 preferred employment in a rag factory rather than domestic work, because they had their evenings and weekends free and because this schedule permitted them to spend more time with their families.[34] Married women with children equally eschewed domestic work because it deprived them of being with their children.[35] "If all else failed, a black mother entered service," Pleck wrote. She also described a greater tendency among black women to work at home.[36] Nevertheless, the realities of the labor market that restricted black female employment opportunities also often militated against them. Most black women had to work in domestic service at some time in their lives. They only could hope for day labor. And in Buffalo by the turn of the century, most live-in servant positions were in the bailiwick of immigrant women, thus allowing black women to be day workers.

The female-headed household was the exception rather than the rule among black families in Buffalo in 1905 (refer to Figure 4). Only by their late thirties did the percentage become significant; at that age, when widowhood, separation, and divorce had all taken their toll, the figure reached 25 percent. Some black women had never married, but the census data do not tell us how many actually fell into this category.

Most black children in Buffalo lived throughout their childhood in households with two parents. Fewer than 8 percent of black youths under six years of age lived in households headed by females between 1905 and 1925. As the children grew older, however, their chances of living in a female-headed household increased somewhat. By the time that the youngsters had reached young adulthood, their chances of living in a female-headed household increased further. This, obviously, was a result of the social factors that affected many communities of newcomers.

Most female household heads worked and some of these had obtained positions which paid good, steady incomes. They were cooks, caterers, and beauticians; a number of them were roominghouse proprietors. About 18 percent of female household heads were unemployed, and it is not certain how they provided for themselves and their families. Because of the propensity of census enumerations to overlook the cottage industries, it is possible that these women took in boarders or laundry, or secured money from working children. Although it was highly unusual, some women may have received money from insurance companies. In total, 37 percent of female heads of households were able to remain at home with their children.

By 1925, the economic and social climate of the African American populace of Buffalo had changed significantly. Life-cycle patterns indicate that their circumstances were more favorable than they had been in the past. African American females continued to enjoy a long period of adolescence. About 96 percent of those between the ages of eleven and fifteen lived at home with their parents and were enrolled in school.

The shift from adolescence to adulthood was more rapid in 1925, however. By the age of 21, 36 percent of young women had moved away from their parents' homes, and 62 percent had done so by the time they reached age 24 (See Figure 5). Black women also married much earlier than in 1905. Over half of the women in their early twenties were married. This sudden increase in the number of women who were married cannot be explained by looking at the sex ratios, for black women in Buffalo enjoyed favorable sex ratios in both 1905 and 1925. The answer has to lie in the economic improvement of blacks.

Just as black women married earlier in 1925, they also began to have children at an earlier age than their predecessors. In 1925 there was an increase in the fertility rate of black women, 350 for every 1,000 fertile women, compared to 210 in 1905. By age thirty, 51 percent of married black women had children in their households, and by age 40, 85 percent of married women were raising children.[37] When compared to the corresponding 1905 figures of 31 percent and 65 percent, these findings suggest that the economic climate for blacks in Buffalo had improved.

Occupational status (or, rather, the lack thereof) tends to bear this out. The community ideal appeared to retain women in the home whenever possible, and 89 percent of married black women in Buffalo were not employed outside of their homes; thus they were able to remain home with their children. This figure is about the same as for black women in 1905. However, married black women in 1925 had access to a greater variety of jobs and to better jobs. Just 4 percent of married black women were chambermaids, while virtually no one worked as a servant. In 1925, a substantial number of married black women worked in skilled jobs (24), held professional (7) and clerical (5) positions, or worked in semi-skilled jobs, including a few factory positions.

In 1925 there was an actual drop in the percentage of black women who headed their own households, and most of these women were over 40. Even more than in 1905, the two-parent family was the norm. Employed black female household heads were relegated to low-paying service positions; with the exception of one woman, none were employed in professional or clerical jobs.

In 1925 black women in Buffalo continued to board out, just as they had done in the previous decades, but the practice was not common, despite the huge wave of migrants who had entered the city. Now only 10 percent of those in their 20s boarded. Although the average household size had increased, most female boarders lived in small family situations. This was one means of aiding the adjustment process for new arrivals and a way for the young to make a transition from childhood to adulthood. The sanctions placed against women had not changed considerably and at no age level did boarding reach the proportion that it had among black males. Some female boarders who worked in 1925 found employment in skilled positions in service or in industry; the number who worked in clerical positions had increased since 1905, yet it was more likely that if a boarder worked, she secured employment as an unskilled worker, usually a laundress or domestic. Most of these women worked in institutions rather than in private homes. Most female boarders, however, did not work outside their homes. The percentage of black women who worked as live-in servants in 1925 declined; almost half of these women were in their 20s. It is quite clear that the economic prospects for black women had improved somewhat and that the immigrants had virtual control over the servant business.

In summary, the positions of females in the black community can best be understood as a result of the changes which occur in the situation of males. The occupational condition of women did not change drastically over the twenty-year period, but their life cycles changed considerably. The proportion who boarded remained about the same, but black women married and established their own households earlier than before. Thus, among those in their twenties, 25 percent remained at home in 1905, compared to only 8 percent in 1925. Similarly, only 40 percent had married by that age in 1905, compared to almost 60 percent in 1925.

The social and economic situation of African American males in Buffalo in 1905 was bleak. The men remained in the homes of their parents well into adulthood. Even after they had left home, many became boarders and the boarding period was quite long. These men, if they married at all, married late in life and had few or no children. These findings suggest that there were severe occupational and income pressures on African Americans. The neglect of family formation was an effort to compensate for these pressures.

By 1925, the black male population, despite massive in-migration, had not become a "floating" boarding population. The percentage who boarded actually decreased from that of 1905. This shows rapid adjustment to the urban environment and the potential for the development of a healthy, stable community. There was a dramatic lowering in the average age of marrying and establishing one's own household. About one-third of the twenty-year-olds in 1925 had their own households, compared to only 16 percent in 1905. Also, in 1925, only 10 percent of the men in their twenties continued to live with their parents; 20 percent had done so in 1905. These results reflect an improved economic situation—higher wages and more steady work. In addition, there probably were some improvements in housing for blacks in Buffalo. The Buffalo Negro Realty Company and other developers purchased or constructed homes for blacks during the early 1920s, but by 1930 congestion seemed to reign in the East Side neighborhoods.

Over the twenty-year period, opportunities for work for blacks increased. The migration did not affect the occupational position of most blacks; it did, however, increase the range of the occupational structure for some. Thus, about 80 percent of black men were semi-skilled operatives in 1905; by 1925, this number had dropped to about half. In 1925 the other half of the black male work force was about evenly divided between skilled and unskilled positions. The fact that many more blacks entered skilled positions suggests a tight labor market and the consequent improvement in average wages and steady work for most black males. This is the key to understanding the changes which occurred in the male life cycle. This improvement in jobs and the consequent creation of a stratified social structure had major implications for the development of a viable African American community.

To Help See One Another Through

Things don't fall apart. Things hold. Lines connect in thin ways that last and last and lives become generations made out of pictures and words just kept.[1]

For African Americans in Buffalo, family was the foundation of the community. It undergirded many of their efforts to maintain a viable community and to build the kind of city required by the demands that they faced on the eve of the twentieth century. In the urban milieu that Buffalo presented, the families of northern and southern blacks became a conduit for transmitting and reinforcing mores and folkways.

While controversy surrounds the contemporary African American family, Buffalo black families at the turn of the century formed a cohesive network and were recognized as a source of strength for their communities.[2] The black family was one of the pillars upon which individuals could draw to escape the debilitating effects of racial prejudice and discrimination, but at the same time it was a bulwark that built self-esteem and permitted them to strive to accomplish their dreams. The family also played a significant role in the migration process, for it was the singular most important factor in getting most individuals to leave the South.

Twentieth-century black families had evolved from their African and American slave antecedents. Herbert Gutman's study of African American families from 1750 to 1925 gives us clues as to the nature of their family structure during slavery and Reconstruction, and it also helps us understand the nature of African American culture and its relation to the family.[3] He described the complex naming practices slaves utilized and their strong ties to members of their community. Gutman's conclusions were threefold: (1) Slavery did not destroy African culture. The culture which the slaves brought to America was remarkably resilient, and slaves were able to adapt this culture to fit their needs in an alien, hostile environment. (2) The black family was not "destroyed" by slavery. Indeed, the African American family had sustained blacks through the unending day-to-day trials and tribulations of slavery. (3) After slavery, black people organized themselves primarily into two-parent households and continued to fulfill their needs through communal activities. Just as the African American family had sustained blacks in the nineteenth century, it perhaps became the most critical factor in enabling them to migrate from the South to the North at the turn of this century. It was also the family that enabled them to carve out an economic niche for themselves in their new environment and to build a community in cities like Buffalo.

Anthropologist Carol Stack, after studying contemporary black lower-class families in a midwestern urban setting, also noted the adaptability of black culture.[4] Hence, while the household composition of black families might have changed frequently, children experienced a remarkably stable situation. Anthropologist Patricia Guthrie, in her study of blacks on St. Helena Island, noted that the islanders had a clearly defined system for rearing children who were orphaned or born out of wedlock or whose parents were incapable of supporting them.[5] Moreover, Guthrie's study indicated that "outside" children knew the members of both their paternal family and their maternal family so that they would not commit incest.[6] Their culture provided the same kind of stability that the slaves and Stack's midwesterners had.

Students of the black experience which followed World War I contend that migration and urbanization were destructive forces which produced disorganized families and other social pathologies.[7] Gutman's study of black families in New York City in 1925, however, suggests that during the early part of this century black culture retained the resiliency which had characterized it earlier and explained the changes in their household composition as merely a part of their adaptive behavior.[8] Questions remain as to the applicability of the New York findings to other African American communities. The Buffalo data set lends itself readily to an exploration of these contentions and further substantiates their validity.

The New York State manuscript census schedules for the years 1905, 1915, and 1925 enable us to examine the ways in which black families helped to support and to shape their community. By reconstructing families and households we can make fairly strong inferences about the nature of kinship relations in an urban environment. These data offer ample opportunity to observe black families and provide a composite picture of the African American community, despite the under-enumerations and other weaknesses inherent in such canvasses.[9]

At the turn of the century, African American families in Buffalo, with few exceptions, were headed by males. In the pre-migration years of 1905 and 1915, females constituted 17 percent and 12 percent, respectively, of the heads of black families. These figures are similar to those which Glasco and Gutman observed among blacks in Buffalo in 1855 and 1875, 11 percent and 17 percent. And, in 1925, in the midst of the massive in-migration of blacks to Buffalo, only 7 percent of black families were female-headed.[10]

If the increase in the number of females who maintained their own families represents a breakdown in stability within the community, as some observers contend, this result might be attributed to the tremendous influx of African Americans into the city as a result of a wartime economy's need for laborers, as well as to the actual involvement of the United States in World War I—which, like all wars, had a deleterious effect upon the lives of Americans.[11] The change was too insignificant to warrant such an assertion. Yet, the whole question of what constitutes stability within the black community needs to be examined in this light. What impact does the sex of the head of the household in which one grew up have on the quality of life of an individual? This influence can be assessed to a certain degree by comparing the characteristics of male and female heads of household and then by examining the conditions of those who resided within their households. And if the migration experience proved to be detrimental to the viability of black institutions, how does one account for the apparent "strengthening" of the Buffalo black family in 1925 when only 7 percent of African American family heads were females? To fully understand the phenomenon of female-headed households in black families it is essential that one study the larger society to see how it, too, measures up. Future studies must compare the family structure of blacks in Buffalo to that of the white groups in Buffalo.

The family is not a static institution. It is affected by economic, social, and political considerations, and to a certain extent it affects its own environment. It is possible that children growing up in the black districts of Buffalo shared a variety of household experiences throughout their childhood. At what stage of their lives did these relations occur and to what can the changes be attributed? These are crucial questions which should be addressed. Furthermore, what effect did household composition have on children's lives?

STRUCTURE OF MALE AND FEMALE AFRICAN AMERICAN HOUSEHOLDS

Men headed 83 out of every 100 black households in 1905, while females headed 17 percent of the households.[12] While it is not surprising that most of these men were born in the United States, an unexpectedly high number gave Canada or the West Indies as their place of birth (51, or 11.8 percent). As we already have seen, heads of households were older than the general population. This delay in establishing a household no doubt resulted because the limited supply and the prohibitive cost of housing in Buffalo at the time precluded their doing so earlier.

Another prominent feature of the African American households is their size. In 1905 a distinct minority of black households, albeit a large one, supplemented their income by taking in boarders. This was especially true of male-headed households, where one-third took in boarders, usually only one or two.[13] Even fewer male-headed households had relatives present. The Buffalo data confirm earlier studies which indicate that black households had few children.[14] Nearly half of black male-headed households had no children present (45 percent), while the other families had few.

By 1915, the impact of the northern migration could already be felt in the black community, and male-headed households increased.[15] The residential distribution of the black community had contracted somewhat; blacks in 1915 resided in fewer wards than in 1905 and were more highly concentrated in those wards in which they previously were found. Men who headed their own households in 1915 were as old or older than in 1905, with even fewer men in their twenties heading their households. This reflects the selective nature of migration, for most migrants were unattached males in their 20s. These individuals would be the least likely to establish their own households, because of financial reasons, because they may have lacked familiarity with the city, and because of the paucity of housing.

The households they established were somewhat larger and more complex than in 1905. The number of male household heads who took in boarders increased from a little over one-third (36.9 percent) in 1905 to nearly half (46.1 percent) in 1915. Also, the number of boarders typically admitted into a household increased. Black male household heads not only admitted more boarders than their 1905 counterparts, but the number who shared their dwellings with relatives doubled. In most instances, only one relative lived in their home, and in no case did more than three relatives find accommodations with their kin. While many male-headed households still had no children in 1915, those that did had more than in 1905.

The black community had expanded considerably by 1925 and black male-headed households could be found in most of the city's wards. However, they were most highly concentrated in wards 6 (17.2 percent), 7 (40.1 percent), and 8 (9.7 percent), the heart of the growing black community. Male-headed households among blacks in 1925 had increased substantially; men now headed 93 percent of black households, while females headed 7 percent. This was an apparent result of the economic achievements which blacks had gained since the outbreak of World War I, when black males found Buffalo to be a suitable place to settle.

Males who headed their own homes in 1925 were on the average younger than those who managed households during the previous two decades (see Figures 2 and 3). The percentage of males who took in boarders was 45.4 percent, virtually unchanged from 1915, but well above the 1905 figures. Boarding continued to be a significant means of adjustment for recent arrivals, providing them with a modicum of freedom and security, as well as inexpensive housing. However, boarding relationships were becoming more structured and institutionalized. Fewer male household heads took single boarders into their homes (19.4 percent; down from 25 percent in 1915, and 20 percent in 1905), and the number who took in larger numbers of boarders was definitely on the rise. In 1925, there were 43 homes which housed more than seven boarders; in 1905 there had been three, and in 1915, ten.

Also in 1925, male-headed households included more relatives than ever before. Nearly one in every three households contained at least one relative (29.5 percent). While taking in relatives was also a means of acculturating newcomers to the city, these living arrangements sometimes lasted for years, which suggests that the state of the economy and the housing market were not the only considerations for black kin who shared accommodations.[16] They wanted to live together partly because of common experiences and camaraderie that extended far beyond Buffalo, spatially and temporally. (This contention will be made even more explicit when we look at black families below.)

Male-headed families in 1925 were more likely to include children than in previous years (62.7 percent). However, they still had relatively few—on the average, 1.87 children—and a 1923 study in Buffalo indicated that blacks would have to reproduce at the rate of 2.6 just to maintain their numbers. The small number of children is an indication that the migration was continuing, for migrants were the least likely individuals to have children.[17]

One can note certain patterns in the structure of black male households in Buffalo from 1905 to 1925. In 1905, few males in their twenties succeeded in setting up their own households because of the financial constraints which traditionally plagued blacks. By 1915, the proportion of black men in their 20s who had established households declined, a clear result of the migration into the city of young, single blacks who were least likely to head households. But in 1925, with two-thirds under the age of 40, black male household heads were younger than ever before. This gain is a reflection of the increased economic opportunities which black males found in Buffalo, thereby enabling them to afford the cost of rental units. Many also now brought their families from the

South. As a result of the large-scale migration, male-headed black households became more complex, with boarders, and especially relatives, on the increase.

The few women who headed black households in 1905 were a distinctly middle-aged group; four out of five were over 35 years old. Their age alone suggests that these were not "abandoned" women, but widows or singles who had never married. The demographic figures bear this out, for more than one-third of these women were over 50 years old and 60 percent were single. Female household heads in 1905 took in boarders more often than their male counterparts and they took in more boarders. Furthermore, most of these women could not rely upon others for sustained levels of support. Taking in boarders, for females, was a means of supplementing their meager wages, since they were the most economically depressed group. Female household heads in 1905 also had a slightly greater tendency to share their housing facilities with relatives than did the men. Given their age and marital status, it is not surprising that a greater proportion of women than men were without children on their premises. In 1905 the average female household head had .18 children, while male-headed households averaged 1.19 children.[18]

With migration, female-headed households comprised fewer families, but their conditions were similar to the pre-migration group. They were mature women and most were single. In fact, 75 percent were over 35 years old and over half were not married. Women were merely adapting to the traditional economic constraints of low-paying, insecure jobs. Those who were able to maintain households often had a decided advantage over those women who were compelled to board or work as servants.

In 1915, female household heads admitted more people into their homes than previously. There were more who relied upon boarders, whose rent could help improve their quality of life. And for the first time boarding houses appeared, but these paled in comparison to those in other cities. There was also a greater tendency for black females to share their households with relatives. Male household heads had an equal tendency to admit relatives, but were less likely to admit boarders.

Fewer female household heads in 1915 had children living with them than had been the case a decade earlier (39 percent versus 45.6 percent). The migration of blacks into the city partially accounts for this pattern, because in most instances, young, unmarried people were most likely to move. However, at the same time, the number of large households with children was increasing gradually.

In 1925, females comprised 7 percent of black household heads, a decline over the previous decade, and they began to head their households at a younger age. By 1925, one in three was under thirty years old, compared to 16 percent in 1915 and 6 percent in 1905. At the same time, the proportion of older female household heads declined. Female household heads were younger partly because of the massive influx of young migrants. Also, life in the city was harsh for blacks, who experienced high rates of mortality. Other social ills, such as divorce and separation, may have taken their toll, but we cannot ascertain from the census data the degree to which these may have been factors.

Partly, however, the drop in age also reflects improved opportunities for black women. Nearly two-thirds of the women heading households were not married and did not have their own children. Female household heads could use boarders as a means of obtaining income or at least supplementing funds. While fewer took in boarders than had women a decade earlier (63.3 percent versus 69.0 percent), black female household heads now took in more boarders. (The average household headed by black women took in 2.01 boarders.) Female households which admitted more than six boarders had grown to sixteen, more than three times the 1915 number, and eight times that of 1905. Also, in 1925, female household heads could rely upon a larger pool of relatives. They were almost twice as likely to have relatives present than in 1915.[19] They also had larger numbers of relatives present, although most households (62 percent) took in only one other related person. This, too, was part of the migrants' adjustment process.

More female-headed households contained children than previously. Over half (55.2 percent) had children, and those also had more: half had four or more, compared to 1905 and 1915, when the average female-headed household had .18 and 1.05 children, respectively. These results, however, should not lead one to believe that husbands and fathers were abandoning their families. As we shall see shortly, more males headed black families in Buffalo in 1925 than at any time since the middle of the nineteenth century. Moreover, illegitimacy was not a problem worth considering for African Americans in Buffalo during the first quarter of this century. Informal adoption among blacks was a common practice in the South and they carried this adaptation with them to the North. Therefore, blacks had in place a mechanism for dealing with children born out of wedlock. It would be highly unlikely that mothers with young children lived alone. However, a contemporary study conducted over a five-year period, from 1922 to 1926, indicated that illegitimacy was increasing. Between 1922 and 1926, only 1,130 black babies were born; nearly one in ten was born out of wedlock.[20]

The migration years witnessed a decrease in the age of black female household heads. For example, in 1905, 80 percent of female household heads were over 35 years old. In 1915, this figure had declined to 75 percent, and by 1925, over one-third were under thirty years old. Most of these women were not married and did not have children—60 percent in 1905, 50 percent in 1915, and 67 percent in 1925. Female household heads were younger because of the selective process of migration, which usually attracted young, single individuals. Moreover, this age differential is indicative of the increased economic opportunities available for black women and, of course, the higher mortality rates which black men experienced. Female household heads took in considerably more boarders and relatives during the migration years than they had in 1905.

KIN-RELATED HOUSEHOLDS

The nuclear family was by far the most common family type for black Buffalonians in 1905. Two in five (139) African Americans lived in nuclear families, half of which consisted of a husband, wife, and one or more children. Other nuclear family arrangements included a surprisingly large number of childless couples (39 percent), a few mothers and their children (8 percent), and even fewer fathers and their children (2 percent).

The augmented household also was an important living arrangement for Buffalo blacks in 1905. (Table 1 depicts the kin-related household

TABLE 1

KIN-RELATED HOUSEHOLD STRUCTURE OF AFRICAN AMERICANS,
BUFFALO, NEW YORK, 1905, 1915, 1925

Type of Household	1905	1915	1925
Number	344	486	2,393
Percentage			
Nuclear	40.0	42.0	42.0
Extended	3.0	6.0	12.0
Augmented	30.0	24.0	28.0
Extended-Augmented	2.0	4.0	5.0
Single	8.0	9.0	4.0
Undetermined	16.0	14.0	8.0
Households headed only by fathers[b]	2.0	2.0	2.0
Households headed only by mothers[b]	8.0	8.0	5.0
Male present households[c]	83.0	88.0	93.0

[a] Those with household status of servants, boarders, and "other" when listed individually.

[b] These figures were computed using all household classifications.

[c] These figures were computed based on all households, except where it was impossible to determine the type of household, and those headed by individuals living alone.

structure of blacks.) One-third of the black households were augmented; i.e., they took in boarders, relatives, and other nonrelated members, and altogether such living arrangements housed 30 percent of the entire black population. Taking in boarders was often an economic necessity; without them, a family might be condemned to living in the most abject poverty. This certainly was the case for many older widowed or single women who headed their own households, and who took in one or more boarders. Taking in boarders might also enable a poor family to survive or even afford a few luxuries.

Extended families in the black neighborhoods of Buffalo were a rarity in 1905. Only 3 percent of the households took in relatives. Those who did so typically were married couples without children, which is not surprising since these people would more than likely have extra space. However, on two occasions couples with children took in relatives. One of them was the Lester Dickson family, who resided at 138 Laurel Street.[21] Their address alone indicates that they were better off than the average black person in Buffalo. Lester, at the age of 35, also was somewhat better off occupationally than most other black laborers. He worked as a chef on the railroads, and his wife, Cora, who was thirty years old, like many other black wives performed housework. The Dicksons had a three-year-old son. They also differed from other couples because, in addition to having his retired parents residing with them, Joseph (75 years old) and Mary (62 years old), the Dicksons had taken in another relative, 38-year-old Edward White and his six-year-old son, Gerald. Edward worked as a waiter on the railroads. In addition to gaining extra income from Edward, the Dicksons' parents most certainly provided babysitting services, while the three younger members of the household worked. This arrangement had undoubtedly paid off already, because they were able to live in a section of Buffalo previously inhabited by only a few black professional and clerical workers.[22]

Only 28 unmarried individuals maintained separate households, and most of them were well over 30. There appeared to be sanctions militating against persons living alone. One must also consider the paucity of available housing and its prohibitive cost. Consequently, most younger single people either remained in their family of origin or became boarders in the homes of others. Herbert Gutman's findings for blacks in the San Juan Hill and Tenderloin sections of New York in 1905 were similar.[23]

Black families in 1905 had adapted to their environment in healthy, creative ways, despite the fact that fewer than half lived in simple nuclear family settings. The large number of augmented families and the extended-augmented families were attempts—apparently successful—on the part of blacks to cope with their environment. Although the nuclear family among New York City blacks in 1905 was just about as prevalent as in Buffalo, blacks in Buffalo lived in fewer augmented and extended family situations.[24] Females with children headed male-absent houses in eight out of 100 cases.

By 1915, the effect of the southern migration on black families in Buffalo was quite noticeable. The southerners had been schooled in the ways of their predecessors and their communities and when they travelled to the North, they merely established those institutions they had known in the South. Gutman painstakingly describes the nature of kinship ties, naming practices, and communal relationships among African American slaves and former slaves in *The Black Family in Slavery and Freedom*. The nuclear family was one of them, and in 1915 Buffalo's black community noted a slight increase in the nuclear family (see Table 1). Only a few black women headed nuclear families. Over half of these women resided with their unmarried adult children, an indication that they were probably widows. Adult children in black households are not unusual. Stack observed, "The most predictable residential pattern is that [black] men and women reside in one of the households of their natal kin, or in the households of those who raised them, long into their adult years. They always retain the option of returning home."[25] Guthrie noted, "[Black] adults are included in the categories 'children' and 'grandchildren' because of their genealogical connection to the household head or heads. Even though such persons have reached adulthood, they do not hold the position of family head unless they have married and their marriage remains intact, or else they have children in the household with them."[26]

The extended family was twice as prevalent in 1915 as it had been a decade earlier (6 percent of black households were extended and another 4 percent contained both relatives and boarders). Given the nature of migration and the form which black communities took in the South, it is not surprising that more of them found accommodations with their families, for relatives were able to provide invaluable aid.[27] In addition to housing, relatives helped one to become acquainted with the "ways" of the city and were often instrumental in helping blacks to obtain jobs. Indeed, a pattern whereby relatives settled in enclaves within the city begins to emerge by 1915, although census data are not the most reliable for ascertaining this trend.

William Bright owned a hotel at 167 Elm Street. Bright's brother, Oscar, and his family, including three children (six-year-old Harold, six-year-old William, and eleven-year-old Ruth), lived next door at 165 Elm. Shriver Abrams, a 32-year-old engineer, established his domicile at 9 Halbert Place with his 24-year-old wife, a domestic. They had four children, who ranged in age from one to eleven. In the same household lived Abrams' father, Jacob, who worked as a laborer in an asphalt plant; Abrams' mother, Kate, who was a domestic; and his 24-year-old sister, Grace, who worked as a maid. Ten years earlier, the elder Abrams and his wife had maintained a house with their children, Charles, Grace, and Margaret. Six females headed extended black families in Buffalo in 1915. Forty-nine-year-old Arlene Smith lived at 33 Pauline Street with five of her children. Next door lived her thirty-year-old son, Lee, and his twenty-two-year-old wife, Margaret. The patterns of residential propinquity are similar to those described by Carol Stack in her study of a contemporary midwestern city. Stack found that kin lived in apartments in the same building and also in two adjacent buildings[28].

These relationships were both an adjustment mechanism and a continuation of southern black family patterns, as the experience of Maggie Nichols Comer, the mother of Yale University child psychiatrist James P. Comer, will illustrate. Having lived in Mississippi, Arkansas, and Tennessee, she left Dyersburg, Tennessee in 1920, at age sixteen, in search of a better life in East Chicago. Her brother and half-sister had preceded her to the North and facilitated the process for her. Her brother paid her transportation costs and her half-sister and brother-in-law provided her with housing, just as they had for her two brothers. Comer contended that the family continued to play an important role in the lives of blacks and noted that southern and northern branches were intricately intertwined. Her husband's family, the Comers, lived in Comer's Quarters in Alabama, and in that community, everybody was related and attended the same church. In the North, the pattern persisted. Maggie Comer observed that the interdependence of southern and northern families reinforced their values because in addition to new family members joining the migration, those who had previously left constantly returned "home."[29] She commented:

> The fellows would work three months and run home, work three months and run home. And then they brought their wives and the wife had to go back home to see Mama. And if they got expecting a baby they had to go back home. They couldn't stay here because they was away from Mama or away from the South.[30]

Charles Johnson also reported that some managers of Buffalo factories complained that their black workers had a propensity to return to the South during the winter holiday season. This was a time when families gathered to celebrate the holiday and their bonds of consanguinity.

Family love and pride were a source of personal strength for attorney, priest, and human rights activist Pauli Murray: "Each [parent] had come from a strongly knit family of hard working people who were independent-minded, thought well of themselves, and had high ideals and strong religious values."[31] Informal adoptions and her extended family were important elements in her growing up. Murray's family members were always present and she had to show deference to them. She noted that "while this web of intricate relationships kept me under constant supervision, it also gave me an identity and an expanding world to which I belonged by right of birth."[32] It was upon this network that she drew when she decided to leave Durham, North Carolina to attend college in New York. There she lived with an aunt and uncle until she was able to support herself. Black families all over the South functioned in this manner and were the one guarantee upon which blacks at the turn of the century could rely wherever they traveled.

Augmented families had declined somewhat in significance by 1915, yet nearly one in three households still had boarders, lodgers, and nonrelatives. We have already discussed the significance of boarding as an adaptive form of behavior for blacks who moved into America's urban areas. If one looks closely at those individuals who lived as boarders, one will observe that it was not unusual for entire families to board. Thus William Washington, who worked at a pool room, and his wife, Beatrice, a proprietor of a restaurant, along with William's mother, Frances, a domestic, all found lodging at forty-year-old Sadie Washington's home at 19 Arsenal Place. It is impossible to tell whether this family was related to the head of the household, but we note again the tendency for family members to seek accommodations near each other, regardless of their household status. Of course, in some cases, individuals boarded in households headed by their friends or by people from their hometowns; in other cases, unrelated individuals migrated together, or friends lived in the same neighborhood. From the census, we cannot determine how often this happened, but certainly the Washingtons' experience was not unique and would be repeated again and again over the next few years.[33]

The number of single individuals who lived alone had increased slightly over the decade from 8 percent to 9 percent. Over half of these were males and, once again, most of them were well over thirty years old. There were a few cases in which women with children headed male-absent families (12 percent; see above). Ten years later, by 1925, with the exception of the extended family African American families in Buffalo had not varied considerably. A little more than two out of five households could be described as nuclear (1,009). The number of nuclear households including husbands, wives, and children had increased also. Mothers heading male-absent nuclear households, on the other hand, had declined by half, and only half of these women had children who were minors (29).

For blacks entering Buffalo, the extended household had become exceedingly important as a mechanism for adjustment to a new environment. Again, the proportion organizing themselves into extended households doubled over the previous decade. What is most striking about these families is the fact that nearly one in ten contained subfamilies. In those households headed by a man and his wife, for example, eleven couples, five spouses and their children, and one mother and child found housing accommodations with their relatives. Extended families now comprised one of seven such households. These extended households tended to be larger than previously.

Several of the individuals who were listed as relatives were children whose parents were absent (161). In most instances, census data alone do not permit us to determine their exact relationship to the head of the household, but, in some cases, it is quite obvious that the heads of household were acting as surrogate parents. Six-year-old Louise Gilcrist, for example, lived with Joe and Clara Hampton; the Hamptons did not have any children of their own. Louise Muckles, a fifteen-year-old student, resided with Henry and Corine Walker and their two infant children. Henry was a porter, Corine a domestic. Despite the fact that Louise was old enough to seek employment, she was still enrolled in school.

When Charles Johnson's research associates interviewed black families in Buffalo in 1923, they noted this same phenomenon. One observer wrote: "Woman had tobacco in mouth and spat often. Kitchen shabby but clean. She is raising her grandchild who is an orphan."[34] Another commented: "Very religious, a member of a 'sanctified' sect. Going into the pressing business. Caring for motherless boys."[35] Patricia Guthrie observed that blacks on St. Helena Island had informal arrangements for taking care of children when mothers and fathers were incapable of parenting because of illness, death, poverty, or simply inability to handle the situation.[36] Carol Stack found that black families in the Midwest in the 1960s knew that the collective help of kinsmen was so assured that "those who attempt social mobility must carefully evaluate their job security, even if it is at the poverty level," before they risk removing themselves from the family. The family could be counted on for food, clothing, shelter, and raising children.[37]

An examination of the composition of several extended families indicates the ways in which the family aided the adjustment process for some African Americans in Buffalo and how it generally functioned in the lives of others. Berney McCarley, a thirty-year-old steel worker, and his wife, Alice, shared their home at 335 Spring Street with their own four children, with Berney's brother, Bellos, and Bellos' wife and infant child. (There was also an unmarried female boarder in the household.) Bellos, like Berney, worked in the steel plant. Despite the fact that McCarley had relatives and a boarder, all of whom presumably were contributing to his income, his wife also worked as a domestic.

Eugene Daniel, a 32-year-old laborer in the steel plant, lived at 86 Mortimer with his wife and two young daughters. They shared their premises with his 23-year-old brother, Bishop Daniel, a laborer in the steel plant, his wife, and still another relative, 24-year-old Marshall Colby, a laborer.

Charles Thompson of 61 Union Street, a dining car waiter, his wife, Ruby, a nineteen-year-old domestic, and their infant child opened their home to Charles' 25-year-old brother, Richard (who also worked as a dining car waiter), Ruby's mother, Rose Dunn, a boarder, and an eight-year-old relative, William Kalgar.

Edward Josey, 24, a moulder's helper, resided at 606 North Division with his wife, his four-year-old son, and his twenty-year-old brother, James (also a moulder's helper), as well as his sister-in-law, a niece, and a nephew. Josey also rented quarters to a couple unrelated to his family. But one of the largest and most complex extended households was that of Thomas Woodyard of 586 North Division. Woodyard, his wife Lonie, and their son, Thomas, shared their household with his wife's family, which consisted of a mother and four sisters (ranging from five to twenty years old), Thomas' brother, Lorenzo, and Lorenzo's wife and son. Thomas was a railroad car repairer and Lorenzo was a cook.

While these cases are by no means exhaustive, they are illustrative of the significance of kinship ties for the adaptation of migrants to Buffalo.[38] First, the fact that they organized themselves into such complex families indicates that the kinship ties and the communal spirit which were endemic to the social fiber of the southern communities from which these migrants came had not eroded in the alien and sometimes hostile environment of Buffalo.[39]

Indeed, if anything, these ties may have been strengthened by the adversities the people faced. Second, despite studies by others which contend that blacks had little or no entry into the job market based on kin ties similar to those of other immigrants, these few representative cases suggest that in those areas where black workers were most highly concentrated they, too—despite their inability to secure a strong foothold in industry or at least rise beyond menial employment—utilized kinship networks to secure employment for family members.[40] Although in most instances the place of employment is not listed by the census, brothers who resided in the same household often had the same job title.

The augmented family, always significant for blacks, increased somewhat over the decade, from 24 percent in 1915 to 28 percent in 1925. Childless couples still headed most households which admitted nonrelatives, with nearly one of every two containing boarders (45 percent), but a substantial number of parents with children also took in boarders, one in four. We also note that in 1925 an increasing number of subfamilies are found among boarders—childless couples, and even parents with children.

Although most boarders lived in small family settings, a few large boarding houses also existed. Forty-year-old Etta McGhee ran a boarding house at 156 Elm Street; ten people unrelated to her found accommodations there. Her next-door neighbor, 34-year-old Josie Bruson, took in eight boarders. It was not unusual for individuals who lived in households where there were many boarders to work in the same occupation.[41] However, despite their small numbers and the limited scope of their jobs, one cannot help but notice that blacks exhibited this same occupational specialization—they were a fraternal unit. Edward Lily of 653 Eagle Street, a casting chipper, rented rooms to another laborer at the steel plant and two dock workers. Joseph Courier, a laborer at one of the local steel plants and a resident at 443 Abby, took in six boarders, all laborers at the steel mills. Sixty-year-old Kate Darls of 403 Abby had eight laborers at the steel mills renting housing facilities from her. Although it was less common, this specialization of labor was noted in those households that had a number of female boarders, as well. Fannie McDonald of 105 William Street, herself a car cleaner, had four domestics and three porters sharing her rooms.

Presumably, persons sharing the same housing facilities worked at the same establishments, thereby increasing the magnitude and, indeed, the effectiveness of their friendship network. It is quite conceivable that these people acquired jobs and/or housing accommodations because of such ties. These sample cases also substantiate Charles Johnson's observations that "the most satisfactory method for [recruiting] is to have good workers send for their friends."[42] Johnson also reported that another effective means for blacks to secure employment in Buffalo factories involved "solicitation" in their churches "through pastors or through church members."[43] In other words, it was the workers' most intimate relationships that yielded their best prospects for jobs. A closer examination of this augmented household type will further substantiate the contention that black families and friends facilitated the process of migration and urbanization. Friends who migrated into Buffalo used the same techniques relatives had favored in order to reach Buffalo and get settled once they arrived.

Bessie Williams and her husband Daniel arrived in Buffalo about 1921, after they had been involved in a labor dispute at the Jones and Laughlin Steel Mill in Alliquippa, Pennsylvania. The incident occurred following a debate sponsored by the women's auxiliary of their church to raise money to purchase carpeting for the minister's study. A question posed to the panelists was: "If a girl were stranded on an island, who should get the credit for rescuing her, the shipbuilder or the one who found her?" Daniel Williams argued that the shipbuilder should get the credit. He made an analogy to Marcus Garvey and the Black Star Line and contended that blacks should do more for themselves. Mrs. Williams describes the incident:

This debate took place on Saturday and the following Monday the minister went down to officials at the company—Oh, by the way, everybody who lived in that town worked for Jones and Laughlin Steel Company; they provided houses for workers—He told the officials that the blacks in the UNIA were plotting against the whites and trying to get the Negroes to see the racial problem and were against the ministers on the Hill. One of the officials called my husband in and told him that he had heard about the debate and he heard that his wife was secretary of the UNIA. He [the company official] told him to go up on the Hill, call a meeting of the UNIA and have his wife resign her position and asked him to leave the organization. Williams informed him that, "I won't do that and you can't dictate my wife's actions because she is not a worker in the plant." The plant official gave him two or three days to withdraw from the UNIA. At the [UNIA] meeting the men said no and said that I shouldn't resign. I speak for myself and I told them I had no intention of resigning. Officials called my husband in [a few days] later to find out his decision. He told him, "We didn't do anything." The official said, "Then dammit, you're gonna be fired." Williams said, "That's perfectly all right."

He called another meeting of the UNIA and the following day nearly 100 men [all UNIA members] marched to the plant to protest the action which they had taken regarding Williams and they demanded that they be fired, too. They were.

There was plenty of work everywhere and all of us had saved money so when we had to vacate the [company] houses, forty-four of us came to Buffalo, some to Cleveland, Detroit, Chicago, and like that, where they knew they had somebody to put them into jobs. Other friends followed us to Buffalo. We wrote back telling them that we would get them homes and jobs.[44]

Mrs. Williams had been in Pennsylvania for only two years prior to the incident which led to her departure. She and her husband were from Atlanta, Georgia; he had worked in the steel mills for some time before returning to Georgia to marry her, and immediately after their wedding, they had left for the steel mills of Alliquippa.

The Williams story was unique only in terms of the incident which precipitated their movement to Buffalo and in that such a large group of friends moved into the city simultaneously, but their story was repeated countless times by other individuals, most of whom were less vocal and who perhaps possessed less political savvy. Blacks did not just "shuffle off" to Buffalo. They were well informed about what awaited them—what kinds of jobs were available, the housing which they could expect, and the type of schooling. It was their contact with individuals in Buffalo which influenced the vast majority to migrate. It was their duty to help see one another through.

Charles Johnson interviewed a number of migrants who came to

Buffalo after the outbreak of the war. When he inquired why they had come, the migrants invariably stated that they had come "to join my family," "to visit friends and stayed," "to join friends."[45] An Urban League project resulted in the collection of letters by the post-World War I migrants. In case after case, these migrants described the intricate kinship and friendship networks which culminated in their leaving the South, as well as the continued support they received from family and friends upon their arrival. One Chicago migrant wrote the following to her friend in the South:

> My dear Sister—
>
> . . . The People are rushing here by the thousands and I know if you come and rent a big house you can get all the roomers you want. You write me exactly when you are coming. . . . I am living with my brother and his wife. My son is in California but will be home soon. . . . I can get a nice place for you to stop until you can look around and see what you want. . . . My daughter and I work for the same company—we get $1.50 a day and we pack so many sausages we don't have much time to play but it is a matter of a dollar with me and I feel that God made the path and I am walking therein.
>
> Tell your husband work is plentiful here and he won't have to loaf if he wants to work. [She also informed her friend that she would send her copies of the *Chicago Defender*.][46]

An East Chicago, Indiana migrant described for his friend in Union Springs, Alabama the wages and working conditions for blacks in the city of 30,000. He noted further:

> Doctor, I am some what impress [sic]. My family also. I rec[eived] the papers you mail me some few days ago and you no [sic] [.] I enjoyed them reading about the news down in Dixie. I often think of so much of the conversation we engage in concerning this part of the worl[d] . . . . People are coming here every day and are find[ing] employment. Nothing here but money and it is not hard to get. . . . Oh, I have children in school every day with the white children. . . . how is the lodge.[47]

A Nashville, Tennessee woman wrote her friend in the North:

> . . . what are you making and where is your son—and how do you think it would soot [sic] me up there. All of your friends said howdy and they would be glad to see you—I would love to see you and Mr. B_____. I miss you so much.
> . . . do you think that I could get a job up there if I would come up there where you are—if so write me and let me no [sic] are you keeping house now to yourself. . . .[48]

It was connections such as these that continued to influence the migration patterns of blacks to Buffalo long after the Great Migration. Maryland poet laureate Lucille Clifton's father, Samuel Sayles, moved from Virginia to Buffalo in the 1930s. Clifton described his experience thus:

> My Daddy was from Bedford Virginia [.] He came . . . when a train came through the South offering colored men jobs and a trip North. And he got on in Virginia and my [maternal] Grandpa Moore got on in Georgia.[49]

Historian Okon Uya described the re-making of African families on slave ships destined for the Americas. Uya noted that these "shipmates" responded to each other as if their bonds were predicated upon consanguinity.[50] Black migrants traveling together by train to the North may have associated qualities of respectability with those who were emboldened to leave the South, and they often forged lasting ties. Hence, Samuel Sayles was able to marry Moore's daughter with his blessings.

Connie Porter's fictional characters also used the same mechanisms to travel to the North in the 1950s and to get settled once they had arrived. Her protagonist Samuel Taylor's move from the South to suburban Lackawanna, the site of the Bethlehem Steel Company and the area of first settlement for many migrants en route to Buffalo, depicts similar patterns:

> Samuel knew what he knew of the North from men who had spent their days sharecropping, bent over in fields of cotton. These men claimed word came to them from those who had gone. A brother, an uncle, a neighbor, a friend's third cousin.
> It was true, word sometimes came, but more often they created it. As the men worked stooped in the fields, they changed the dirt that passed through their hands into flesh, breathed life into it, and proclaimed its truth.[51]

Samuel succeeded in getting a job at Capital Steel, saved his money, and after two years returned to the South, married his sweetheart, and brought her back with him—just as migrants to the town had been doing over the past generation.

If blacks were lured to the North by the pull of the letters which their relatives and other acquaintances sent South, it should not be surprising that once they arrived in northern urban centers such as Buffalo, they tried to settle as close to relatives and friends as possible. We have already seen that this is what relatives did. Although the census data alone will not permit us to ascertain the extent to which friends lived in close proximity, undoubtedly the practice was common. In fact, there is evidence that blacks from particular southern cities and/or states organized homogeneous churches based upon geographical origin.[52] Shiloh Baptist Church, for example, was established in 1916 to accommodate southern-born blacks.[53] The minister, Elijah J. Echols, had come to Buffalo from Mississippi, and so had Berney McCauley of St. John's Baptist. Their parishioners were also recent migrants who often were repulsed by the formality of the established churches in the black community and the aloofness of their members.

Naming practices provide another possible clue to the nature of family relations in Buffalo's black community. It is difficult to ascertain from census data the derivation of black children's names. However, those children who lived in certain households often shared names with their parents and other relatives. In 1905, 27 such cases were found. Most of the youngsters had the same name as their father (23); four girls had their mother's names. Such incidents increased as the migration accelerated. In 1915, 43 youngsters had their father's names, six had their mother's, and two had the name of a grandmother. The 1925 census revealed an even greater number of boys and girls who shared their mother's and father's names—32 and 165, respectively. Three had the name of uncles and one of a grandmother.

This evidence is circumstantial and can only provide us with clues to naming practices; as such it is grossly inadequate, for except when boys were listed as junior, we have no idea for whom these children were named. Yet there is no doubt that the complex naming patterns of black slaves, described by Gutman in *The Black Family in Slavery and Freedom,* persisted among their children and grandchildren, who later left the South for urban areas of the North. The naming of Lucille Clifton, whose family migrated to Buffalo from Virginia, illustrates this. Clifton relates this story which her father told her as a child:

> When you was born we was going to name you Georgia. Because my mother's name was Georgia and your Mama's mother was named Georgia too. But when I saw you there you was so pretty I told your Mama I wanted to name you Thelma for her. And she said she didn't like her name and for me to give you another name with the Thelma. So I thought about what Mammy Caline used to say about Dahomey women and I thought this child is one of us and I named you Lucille with the Thelma. Just like my sister Lucille and just like my real Grandmother Lucy. Genie, my Daddy's mother.[54]

In summary, black families provided the courage and the strength to get them to Buffalo and the armor that they would require to challenge the difficult social and economic situations that lay ahead. The extended family among Buffalo blacks was decidedly a post-migration phenomenon. Hence, the children and grandchildren of the slaves carried this adaptation with them to the North, where it afforded them the same kind of support their ancestors had experienced earlier. On the other hand, the augmented family among Buffalo blacks was a pre-migration phenomenon which can be attributed to the paucity of housing for blacks in the city, as well as the prohibitive cost of such housing.

The Buffalo data clearly indicate that the black female-headed household was the result of such social realities as high mortality rates among black men, and not social pathology within the African American community. For example, the female-headed household in Buffalo during the first quarter of the twentieth century was not an adjustment mechanism to migration and urbanization. Most female household heads were well over the age of 35 and a significant proportion of them headed households in which their unmarried adult children resided. This finding speaks to the significance of bonds between African American mothers and their children and the strengths of black families.[55] Naming patterns among twentieth-century Buffalo African Americans suggest the persistence of trends Herbert Gutman noted among black slaves.

What we see emerging here is a community of African Americans who exhibit a strong sense of family and who share similar goals and aspirations based upon their past experiences. With this solid foundation, it is not difficult to understand why these people succeeded, as we shall see, in establishing mechanisms to protect and to strengthen their community.

Work[1]

*. . . being Colored . . . was equivalent to a person
having one leg, one arm, or one eye.*[2]

By the early twentieth century, Buffalo had become a major industrial
city and the twentieth-largest city in the country. Its need for an ever-
larger unskilled labor force boded well for blacks who were migrating
into the city, especially for those who arrived after European immigration
had been halted as a result of the outbreak of the war and the subsequent
reconstruction demands.[3] Some industries had begun to tap the rich
source of southern black labor and thereby provided the impetus for
many southern blacks to migrate to the city.

The earliest labor recruiters were sent South by a large dock company
owner in 1916 to help break a strike among Buffalo longshoremen. A
black agent had been sent to Philadelphia to hire a group of "penniless"
southerners who appeared to have no prospects for employment there.[4]
Targeting over-saturated urban industrial areas also was a tactic agents
sometimes used to create competition and thus low wages. By the time
the recruits arrived in Buffalo, however, the strike was over.[5] But these
blacks never intended to break a strike. They simply responded to a
job offer when they critically needed work. Nevertheless, the mere presence of the blacks served to remind white workers that black strikebreakers were a potential threat. The steel mills of Buffalo also went
South to recruit black and white migrants to try to break the 1923
strike. Virginian Olin Wilson was one such worker and remained with
the Bethlehem Steel Company until his retirement.

In another instance, black workers were hired to replace striking
white employees at the National Aniline Chemical Company in the
spring of 1934. Etta Hein, strike sympathizer and YWCA administrator,

wrote Buffalo congressman James M. Mead to seek his help in settling the strike. She summed up the feelings of many of the strikers:

> I was fortunate to see that a body of blacks under heavy guard, of police, that are being paid by hundreds of the men out on strike, as taxpayers, were marched proudly into the plant before the very eyes of the white men, doing picket duty outside of the plant. Think of it, the race that we whites has [sic] fought for to release them from the auction block, are not [sic] guarded by the police and allowed to take the white men's bread away. What chance has the white man to win back his job, if a practice of this kind is allowed to exist? The purest in heart cannot keep a desperate thought away and that was my feeling, I was almost on the verge of doing most anything to seek revenge.[6]

Remarkably, Hein failed to acknowledge that the African American workers also were taxpayers. Her observations are also revealing because she noted her embarrassment for harboring such feelings at a time when the YWCA had launched a campaign to ameliorate race relations.[7] If many black Buffalonians were optimistic about their future in northern cities, Hein's assessment and a careful scrutiny of their economic status will indicate that few of their hopes translated into reality because of prejudice and discrimination in the job market.[8] By the 1930s, whites typically characterized black workers as strikebreakers, the enemies of labor, despite the fact that there was little basis in reality for their opinions. Their negative views were heightened after the economy began to contract during the latter half of the 1920s. Sam Abbott, chair of the Workers Alliance of the Unemployed in Erie County, reported as late as 1937 that Buffalo corporations transported African Americans

TABLE 2

IMMIGRATION TO BUFFALO

Year	Number of Arrivals
1915	1,383
1916	549
1917	701
1918	1,051
1919	1,383

Source: Charles Johnson, "The Buffalo Negro Study," 1923. National Urban League, unpublished manuscript, State University of New York at Buffalo Archives.

to the city because they were "primarily interested in the Negro people. . . for the sake of giving them jobs [to]. . . break the strike of workers out to better themselves."[9]

BLACK MEN IN THE WORLD OF WORK

Blacks comprised less than 1 percent of the city's population in 1905, yet they constituted a significant segment of the city's labor market. Virtually all black males had jobs, but outside the key industries. Some were unskilled municipal workers, but most were concentrated in service jobs as hotel waiters (34, or 5.2 percent), porters or bell hops (43, or 6.6 percent), Pullman porters (32, or 4.9 percent), railroad waiters (34, or 4.2 percent), and chefs on the railroad (28, or 4.3 percent). Their status was circumscribed by the kinds of industries Buffalo offered, as well as the general lower-class status to which blacks virtually had been relegated by the turn of the century.[10] Buffalo was second only to Chicago as a rail center, and the Buffalo Statler, especially, and other hotels hired blacks for service jobs. (Many of the blacks who worked at the Statler resided in nearby Bean Alley.) Thus, a fairly substantial number of black males found steady jobs working for the railroads and the hotels. They performed both highly skilled and unskilled tasks.

Black males performed a number of unskilled tasks that included washing at garages, laundry work, and janitorial work. Only five black males were listed as servants. A few black men found other service positions, including pantrymen and three butlers. Black males also worked as carriers, peddlers, street laborers, lumber shovers, and a church sexton. But the census recorded only three who worked as laborers in factories in 1905. These workers comprised 10 percent of employed black males.

Black males in 1905 found themselves employed in several semi-skilled and skilled positions, such as bartender, masseur, fireman, chauffeur, mason, carpenter, painter, paperhanger, plasterer, tailor, dry cleaner, shoemaker, and moulder. Seven black men worked in skilled jobs in factories. In all there were 44 blacks employed in skilled positions; they comprised 9 percent of black male workers. It is interesting to note that over half (23) of these men worked in the construction industry.

Although black males worked in various skilled positions, the number was regrettably small, especially in comparison with the status of black workers who had resided in Buffalo a generation earlier. Thus, in 1875, 16 (8.5 percent) of black males were barbers. This occupational decline was experienced by other craftsmen, too. Eight men, or 4.3 percent, worked in the building crafts in 1875, whereas, in 1905, twenty men, comprising 3.1 percent of their population, worked in the building trades. In 1855 eleven black sailors made up 8 percent of black male workers; by 1905, black men had been excluded completely from this job. The decline was noted for blacks in other northern cities as well.[11] At the turn of the century the immigrant populations had replaced blacks in many of their traditional occupations.

The decline in occupational status for black males was not the whole story. In some occupations, blacks actually *made* gains. A case in point are the eleven black males who were proprietors in 1905. The 1855 and 1875 censuses did not record any black male proprietors. Now the Buffalo East Side community supported two hotel keepers, three restaurateurs, two nightclubs, one caterer, two cigar stores, and one secondhand store. The proprietors comprised 2 percent of black male workers.[12]

Black males also made modest gains in the clerical sector. Three males were employed as store clerks, including one in a "fancy" store. Two worked for local banks, seven were listed as office clerks, and one was a collector. One each worked as postal clerk, office clerk, and railroad clerk; there was one black male bookkeeper. These workers made up 3 percent of black male workers. If the Italians are representative of immigrant workers, the immigrants surpassed blacks in their ability to acquire clerical jobs. One hundred forty-eight, or 4 percent, of Italian males worked in clerical positions, as compared to 3.1 percent of black males.[13]

Some black males were employed in the professional sector. Most were musicians (23 percent); two of them taught music. One black man worked as an engineer. Only one clergyman was listed by the census recorder. Undoubtedly there were more; however, most black congregations could not adequately support their ministers, compelling them to secure additional employment. In 1905, there were also two jockeys who resided in Buffalo. James Weldon Johnson observed that black horsemen during the latter part of the nineteenth century were prominent at all of the major horse races.[14] By the turn of the century, black jockeys were a passing breed. Johnson attributed their decline to the fact that many of them earned between $10,000 and $20,000 annually.[15] Organized forces thus sought to replace them with whites.

Baseball was becoming a popular sport at the turn of the century, and Buffalo produced two professional black ball players. There were also two black publishers, of whom one was the South African nationalist Francis Peregrino, who edited a newspaper called the *Spectator*. There was one realtor. There were two black attorneys, but black doctors, lawyers, social workers, and teachers were conspicuous by their absence. Professionals comprised 5.3 percent of black males and 6 percent of black workers, but if musicians and athletes are excluded, only six, or 1.1 percent, of black males worked in the professions.[16]

In 1915, black males in Buffalo benefitted only marginally from the city's continued economic growth. Work was available to them, the variety of jobs increased significantly, and the jobs increasingly were at a semi-skilled rather than an unskilled level. Yet, they continued to be excluded from the truly dynamic sectors of the city's economy—the docks, the steel mills, and the construction industries—and were confined largely to the low-paying service jobs that traditionally had been reserved for blacks. At the same time, the sheer increase in the size of the black community provided increased opportunities for entrepreneurs and professionals.

The availability of work continued to attract black migrants to the city. Over the decade from 1905 to 1915, the number of adult black males increased substantially. And they found jobs. The census of 1915 lists 96 percent of these men with jobs; only a handful of them, however, were in the city's main growth areas, the mills and factories. Sixteen black men were employed in local plants, and these were apparently exceptional individuals—eleven were skilled workers and another four were foremen. Black males also were unable to find work along the city's bustling wharves, docks, and canals. Only seventeen black men worked as longshoremen, dockhands, or in other capacities on ships or at the Buffalo harbor. Few were able to penetrate the city's construction industry, working primarily as moulders, masons, electricians, carpenters, and painters. The same was true of white-collar employment, where only eight black men found jobs as clerks, bookkeepers, and collectors. African American males employed in these clerical positions in 1915 increased, but their overall participation remained at their 1905 level of three percent.

The majority of black men continued to work primarily in the service trades. A few lucky ones were self-employed as, for example, barbers and tailors. Most, however, were not, and worked for railroads, hotels, and restaurants. Railroads and hotels, which in 1905 accounted for 47 percent of employed black men, still employed 33 percent in 1915. The railroads hired black men as chefs, dining-car waiters, and attendants; hotels hired them as bellboys, elevator operators, cooks, and waiters. Other important service positions filled by black men included bartenders, pantrymen, waiters, and elevator operators in stores, restaurants, and similar establishments.

Black proprietors in 1915 almost doubled as a few enterprising individuals succeeded in capturing a segment of the market that resulted from the increased black population. They included hotel keepers, a rooming house proprietor, restaurateurs and cafe club owners, caterers, and tailors.

The greatest proportional expansion in job opportunities for black males in 1915 occurred in the professional sector.[17] Now 9 percent of black males were professionals. A little more than two-thirds of black male professionals were entertainers. The musicians still dominated with

25, including two teachers, followed by thirteen baseball players and two actors. But significantly, the community now supported four doctors, eight clergymen, one teacher, one architect, and two engineers.

By 1925, the occupational profile of black men had changed dramatically in Buffalo. America's entry into World War I heated up the economy of cities like Buffalo, and the continued prosperity of the 1920s kept employment at record levels. The perils of wartime shipping had drastically cut the number of foreign immigrants who would have filled those jobs in industry, and the passage of immigrant restrictive legislation in the 1920s kept their numbers to a minimum. The result was a severe employment vacuum in the mills and factories. The vacuum was so strong that it partially overcame the racism which had excluded blacks from industrial work in the North and pulled them into this dynamic sector of the economy for the first time in significant numbers.

Immigration prior to World War I had filled the need for semi-skilled operatives in the Buffalo automobile, manufacturing, and steel mills. However, immigration declined significantly with the outbreak of the war. In Buffalo immigration fell from 1,383 in 1915 to 701 in 1917.[18] Furthermore, with the resumption of immigration beginning in 1918, fewer than two-thirds of new arrivals were males eligible for employment. These events accelerated the migration of black males to Buffalo and had a positive effect on the employment opportunities for some black men, as well as on the general status of blacks in the community. The number of black males increased fivefold, from 854 in 1915 to 4,832 in 1925. Only 2 percent of adult males were either unemployed or listed no jobs. Black males experienced significant gains in all sectors of employment except the semi-skilled, and they performed more than 300 different job classifications.[19]

A sizeable number of African American men (34 percent) worked as semi-skilled operatives. The railroads and local hotels employed nearly half of these men. This was a tremendous increase over the decade. These were good jobs that offered better pay, often free travel, and permitted blacks to come into contact with diverse groups of people with various perspectives on contemporary issues. Indeed, many of the leadership cadre of the post–World War I black community had antecedents among this group. But they performed the same service jobs — such as bellhops or redcaps (173), dining car waiters (166), railroad chefs (76), and railroad waiters (42), as had their predecessors. The percentage of black men who performed semi-skilled maritime functions had increased also. Sixty, or 5 percent, held such jobs. (This figure does not include 23 other men who "worked on the ships or harbor" and whose skills could not be determined.) Large numbers of semi-skilled black males also worked as chauffeurs (142, or 11 percent), janitors (59, or 5 percent), and chefs (75, or 6 percent). However, only a handful of black men found employment as servants or valets.

By 1925, the local factories had enlarged their black male labor force. Over 200 men, representing 18 percent of black male semi-operatives, found employment in plants, with a considerable number working in the steel plants. A decade earlier, only five black males had worked as semi-skilled operatives in factories. This change in practice occurred partly as the result of a 1923 strike in the steel mills which resulted in the recruitment of blacks. Previously, most unions in Buffalo had excluded blacks. Some, such as the Curb Setters and Asphalt Pavers, operated under a closed-shop agreement with the city. Others, like the Tug Firemen, maintained a closed-shop agreement which excluded blacks because in performing their duties it would be "necessary for blacks and whites to live and work in close quarters."[20]

Some African Americans desired union affiliations and others brought their organizing skills from other regions to Buffalo. The Colored Musicians Union had been organized in Buffalo in 1917, the result of racial exclusionary policies of the local musicians union. Lloyd Plummer, secretary of the Colored Musicians Union, observed that "the union was conceived in discrimination; our local was. The cause of it is discrimination. Previous to 1917 there was one local here where there were no colored members."[21] Plummer described the formation of the union to the members of the New York State hearings on the conditions of urban blacks:

> The white musicians had demonstrated outside of Fleischmann's, a prosperous night spot on North Division Street that hired black performers, because they were not members of Local #43, an affiliate of the AF of L. When Fleischmann took the [black] musicians to the union hall and offered to pay their membership dues, the union rejected their applications[22]

There also were reports that Local #43 tried to dissuade proprietors who specifically asked for black musicians.[23] The American Federation of Labor did not organize African American workers. Thus, excluded from the unions and prey to their racist policies, blacks were logical candidates for strikebreakers. These very practices, however, forced some unions to review their racial policies. After the steel strike of 1923 was resolved, blacks retained their positions.[24] By 1936 Olin Wilson, hired by Bethlehem Steel in 1923, had become an organizer of the Steel Workers Organizing Committee (SWOC), an affiliate of the Congress of Industrial Organization.[25] He had been recruited by Charlie Payne, whom the SWOC had sent from Charleston, West Virginia to organize steel workers in the Buffalo area. Wilson became president of the local that met in the Elks building in Buffalo, and he served several terms.[26]

In spite of their tenuous relations with the unions, African Americans were making an impact on the industrial scene. Three firms which had utilized black help commented that they did "good hard work," further observing that blacks were suited for "hot work." This gave blacks an advantage in securing jobs working in the areas of blast furnaces, hot presses, hot rolling, and other such positions, where they could earn on an average of 50 cents per hour, starting wage.[27] Olin Wilson worked in various positions in these areas at the Bethlehem Steel Mill. Time at work varied from 40 to 60 hours per week.[28] Assigning jobs based on perceived "racial" or "ethnic" characteristics seemed to be widespread. In a study conducted by Niles Carpenter, University of Buffalo sociologist, those firms reporting on Italian workers had noted their preference for "outside work" and their ability to perform inadequately on "inside jobs."[29] Hence, many Italians worked at the harbors.

Those black males who earned a living working as laborers and skilled workers were about equally divided, 666 and 671 respectively. Nearly one-third (31 percent) of these laborers found jobs in the local factories, with the steel plants predominating. The plants employing the largest numbers in 1920 were the Bethlehem Steel Company (1,164); Pullman Car Shops (350); American Radiator Company (305); Pratt and Letchworth Company (196); American Brass Company (183); American Car Foundry Company (120); Jacob Dold Packing Company (112); and Wickwire Steel Corporation (80). Here workers were able to earn a minimum of 40 to 50 cents per hour starting wage, which could go as high as 42 to 60 cents, depending on the position.[30] Dockworkers comprised the third largest industry in which black laborers worked, yet there were only 32, or 5 percent, in this category. General laborers among black males had increased significantly from 8 to 18 percent over the previous decade, substantiating the contention that Buffalo was a fruitful place for unskilled blacks to relocate.

Just as the number of laborers increased, so did African American skilled workers. Whereas they comprised only 10 percent of the black male work force in 1915, in 1925 they amounted to 18 percent. A remarkable number found employment in Buffalo factories (246, or 37 percent). These men worked as masons (24, or 10 percent), moulders (84, or 34 percent), moulders' helpers (21, or 9 percent), mechanics (50, or 20 percent), tinsmiths (6, or 2 percent), brass mill laborers (26, or 11 percent), and so forth. The steel mills employed also many of these workers, who could then earn $30 to $50 weekly.[31]

The building trades employed the second largest group of skilled black male workers (188, or 29 percent). They were carpenters (39, or 21 percent), painters (36, or 19 percent), bricklayers or masons (21, or 11 percent), paperhangers (15, or 8 percent), plasterers (18) and plasterers' helpers (3) (a total of 21, or 11 percent), plumbers (12) and plumbers' helpers (3) (15, or 8 percent). The number of barbers had more than quadrupled since the previous decade, as this lucrative field expanded to meet the needs of newcomers. There were a number of black craftsmen, including shoemakers, blacksmiths, cabinetmakers, and tailors. (All but one owned their own shops.) A number of black skilled workers were employed in the transportation industry; some worked for garages, and in some instances the railroad companies hired others as brakemen and mechanics. Two of the five African Americans who worked on ships were captains. The food industry also hired a number of black males (38, or 6 percent). Most were meat packers (19) or butchers (11); there were also four bakers in the group. The progress which black workers had made in the skilled trades assured higher income and more steady employment for a number of blacks, an improvement that would also have significant ramifications for the developing black community.

By 1925 a few (139, or 4 percent) black men worked in nonmanual positions. The largest number worked in clerical positions (30, or 4 percent). According to the 1920 census, half of clerical jobs were held by males in Buffalo (14,151 or 50 percent), and 19 percent of all men worked in the clerical sectors. However, clerical workers comprised only 1 percent of black male workers in 1925. Clerks predominated in this field—29 (store clerks are excluded). The number of male bookkeepers remained the same as in the previous decade (2). Although the total number of black clerks increased, their position in the overall market declined.

In 1925, 22 men owned their own retail businesses. There were now four hotel keepers, two grocers, five rooming house proprietors, two coal dealers, and five owners of cigar stores; one man owned a fish market and one operated a hardware store. Besides these black proprietors, two others managed their own collecting agencies and one was a "junk" dealer. Thirteen men were employed as salesmen. Proprietors comprised 1 percent of black workers; most of their businesses were small and catered to African Americans. Four realtors and two insurance agents capitalized upon the market provided by the black community, too.

The number of black men who worked as professionals had increased since 1915, although they, too, lost ground in the black labor force (4 percent). The types of professions in which they engaged, with a few notable exceptions, remained virtually the same as earlier. Musicians formed the largest group (38), followed by clergymen (28). There were more undertakers, and fewer ball players and jockeys. Little Harlem, the night club on Michigan Avenue that was the center of black cultural life, also made Buffalo a good place for actors to move, and a few did so. But the greatest change occurred in the number of men who were pharmacists (12) and engineers (9). Ten years earlier, there had been only two engineers, and no pharmacists.

Data compiled from the 1920 census indicate that 7 percent of whites of native parents, 5 percent of those of foreign or mixed parentage, and 2 percent of those of foreign parentage were professionals. The same data reveal that 3 percent of black males were professionals. So while blacks compared favorably with the foreign-born or those of mixed parentage, they lagged far behind native whites and continued to do so throughout the decade.

Earlier in the century, African Americans had been highly concentrated in the domestic field, but by the 1920s, they had become prominent in certain other industries. Johnson noted in his study of black workers that blacks, though comprising less than 1 percent (.9) of the population of Buffalo, exceeded earlier numbers in more than 40 major occupations. For example, black clergymen, stationary firemen, furnacemen, and chauffeurs comprised more than twice their earlier proportion; there were four times as many music teachers and craftsmen, eight times as many semi-skilled workers in rolling mills and as janitors, and more than twenty times as many domestic servants and rolling mills laborers.[32]

Toward the latter part of the decade, employment for black males became a special problem. The country was on the verge of economic disaster and blacks bore the brunt of it.[33] By 1930, it was quite obvious that the employment gains brought on by World War I and the migration of blacks North were seriously jeopardized. A 1930 study of unemployment in Buffalo, conducted by the New York State Labor Department and the Buffalo Foundation, revealed that the black unemployment rate of 25.8 percent was the highest among different populations in the city. Only 15.8 percent of white males were unemployed and 18.2 percent of foreign-born males. Fewer than half (42.5 percent) of black males worked full time, while the rates for whites and the foreign-born were 64.2 percent and 53.8 percent, respectively.[34]

The career of Joseph Brown typifies the experience of many migrants who came to Buffalo. Brown, a native Virginian, had arrived in Buffalo in 1922. Recruiters from Bethlehem Steel had come to Virginia and offered Brown employment and transportation to any of their sites, and he accepted their offer on numerous occasions—so frequently, in fact, that the recruiter recognized him and suspected that he would not work in their Buffalo plant; Brown convinced him otherwise. Brown said that the transportation passes had permitted him to travel outside of Virginia and also allowed him to ascertain what working conditions for blacks were like in those other parts of the country.[35] The train that Brown traveled on when he left Virginia permanently took him directly to the Bethlehem Steel Mill in Lackawanna. Workers departed the train and reported to an office to secure housing and job assignments. Brown got his assignments, walked out of the door and took a "jitney" cab to Buffalo where friends awaited his arrival, and never returned to the Bethlehem Steel plant in Lackawanna.[36]

Brown's later decision to walk away from the Bethlehem Steel Company seemed to be fairly typical, for Bethlehem Steel was one of those factories that paid lower wages. In 1923 one firm brought 3,700 blacks from Richmond, Virginia alone. The factory was unsuccessful in keeping them, since its hourly wages were three to ten cents less than what other plants paid for comparable jobs.[37] Another recruiter brought to Buffalo a group of blacks from Norfolk, Virginia who were earning good wages of 45 cents per hour with promises of 70 cents per hour as skilled workers, along with housing and transportation. When the company reneged on the labor agent's offer, the workers left the company after earning enough money to tide them over until they found suitable employment.[38]

Joseph Brown later found a job at the American Brass Company, where he earned $1,700 annually. Although higher than wages earned by those who worked in service positions (for example, porters earned only $25 per week, for an annual salary of $1,300), this income was modest.[39] After seven years of employment at American Brass, he left his job to open a grocery store. His effort failed, and he faced two years of unemployment. Finally, in 1931, he found a job working in the less secure building trades, where he earned $900 a year. This position lasted for only one year, however, and once again Brown faced unemployment. This time he was out of work for a year. The next position which he accepted, working on state highways, lasted six months and paid only $360. However, Brown was fortunate to find positions with other construction firms throughout the decade; most of his jobs lasted for only one or two years and were terminated because of a reduction in the labor force. His income never again reached its 1922 level or, for that matter, that of his first construction job back in 1931. By 1940, Brown was unemployed again. For a brief period in the 1940s Brown found employment as a sheriff in Erie County.[40]

Olin Wilson also was one of those workers hired by Bethlehem Steel in 1923. Wilson had learned from newspaper accounts in Richmond that Bethlehem was recruiting. However, he had to travel to Norfolk to meet the company's special agent. When he expressed interest in a job at Bethlehem Steel, the agent told him of opportunities in Bridgeport, Connecticut, Pennsylvania, and Buffalo. Wilson already had acquired some information about these sites: friends who had gone to Bridgeport the previous fall had returned to Virginia before Christmas, with horror stories about their living conditions, so Wilson rejected that option. On the other hand, he had been told that Buffalo offered an ideal environment to raise a family. This information was critical, for he and his wife were expecting a child. So like Joseph Brown had earlier, Olin Wilson boarded the special railroad car that the Bethlehem Steel Company had provided in Norfolk and disembarked when he arrived in Lackawanna. Wilson lived in the plant until his family arrived two months later and then they moved into company housing in the village.[41] Unlike Brown, he remained with the company until he retired.

It was difficult for most blacks to succeed in Buffalo, regardless of their economic status. For those who did, success frequently resulted from holding down two or more jobs or from the additional incomes that other household members contributed. Poet Lucille Sayles Clifton, who grew up in Buffalo, related the following story that illustrates African Americans' work ethic and their relentless efforts to succeed economically:

> A lady down the street from us had a civil service job, just nothing,
> just a file clerk or like that, but Daddy used to tell me when she
> would pass by, "Lue, you keep being a good girl and you can be just
> like her." She married a man who was a chiropractor and published
> a little newspaper. He also had a shoe repair shop and he used to fix
> the shoes himself. He would be in there late at night tacking shoes
> together with a tack hammer.[42]

When William Jackson accepted appointment as executive secretary of the future black YMCA in 1923, he commented on the paucity of job options for young men from middle-class families. He noted the large numbers of young black men who were compelled to work for the railroad.[43] And the story of the black physician—such as Dr. E. E. Nelson—who worked for the railroads until he had earned enough money to establish a medical practice became all too familiar.

Just as class had little effect upon the type of job that migrant workers found initially, length of residence in the city also was not a major factor in determining one's success in climbing the socioeconomic ladder. The case of Thomas Payne, a prominent longtime resident, confirms this. In 1925, although he was 65 years old and had worked as a file clerk for at least twenty years, Thomas Payne was still employed as a file clerk. We have already seen that the status of Joseph Brown deteriorated over time.

The old African American families of Buffalo had come primarily from the upper South, long before the Civil War began. Working mainly in service occupations, they were famous caterers and the attachés and confidantes of the city's wealthy white families.[44] They comprised the staff of all of the hotels, oyster houses, and restaurants. The skilled craftsmen who joined their ranks were mainly escaped slaves who brought their skills with them from the South.

The migration of southern blacks to Buffalo after 1916 changed the job picture for blacks, because for the first time, these workers opened up industrial positions for large numbers of African Americans. By 1931, 98 percent of black workers were southern-born. Notwithstanding the advances that blacks made in the workplace, their complaints of discrimination and even persecution on the job were widespread. A case in point involved a black man who worked as a wheel turner, a highly skilled position, who produced an average of 22 pairs of wheels a day, with a peak production of 27. His white colleagues, who only averaged seventeen, organized to force the black man to quit his job. Fearing for his safety, the African American secured a gun permit and carried his revolver to work with him. While whites protested that he was armed, he did not have any more trouble.[45] Olin Wilson also suggested that fear of retaliation was a barrier to African Americans' quest for better jobs or promotions at the Bethlehem Steel Company:

> There were some Negroes who could do the work [skilled jobs], but they didn't want to because of the fear they had of what might happen. Then there were those who were willing to take a chance at it, but nobody encouraged them to. I called it an inter-woven kind of thing because while one said go ahead, the other said you better not.[46]

Carpenter found that 85.7 percent of the blacks whom he interviewed were dissatisfied with their work environment. Race friction occurred frequently on the shop floor, and black laborers also reported instances where they were denied the promotions or supervisory roles that they had earned. Olin Wilson described such an encounter in the blacksmith shop at the Bethlehem Steel factory early on:

> I didn't like swinging a sledge hammer for a man who didn't know as much about putting steel together as I had already learned. I didn't want to tell him because that was not my business. I was there to help him, not to tell him. So I quit [that position].[47]

By 1937, after fourteen years on the job, Wilson worked as a crane operator. But even so, his position was not certain. Wilson recalled that

> the regular [white] crane operators knows [sic] where he is going when he comes in the plant each day, but in the section where I work . . . we [blacks] have to come down and wait until the foreman assigns us and . . . I am only a substitute. I am subject to go in a dozen different directions and as to which, the will of the foreman will be the deciding factor for that day.[48]

Some black workers indicated that employment agents and factory personnel divisions had refused to hire or promote them, opting instead to select white workers. Furthermore, blacks reported that securing job training opportunities increasingly was made more difficult because white faculty and students created a hostile environment for them in existing courses.

Despite the apparent gains in their employment status, African American males in Buffalo also were cognizant of the fact that other ethnic groups were surpassing them at all levels of employment. Foreigners comprised a large percentage of unskilled factory labor and theirs was the largest semi-skilled group in local plants. The children of immigrant groups experienced even greater occupational mobility, dominating supervisory positions as foremen and superintendents. The native-born whites controlled the professional and clerical jobs. Blacks, on the other hand, were able to maintain significant proportions only in labor and domestic service.[49]

Niles Carpenter's study of color and nationality in Buffalo paints a similar picture. He observed that the Irish and the Germans, by far, held most of the high-status jobs in the city because they were well established and were better connected socially than the new arrivals. The Polish and the Italians brought agricultural skills with them that were similar to those of many blacks from the South. However, unlike blacks, they were able to penetrate and control certain skilled and unskilled industrial jobs. The Italians were concentrated in construction and other "outdoor" jobs, while the Polish were more evenly distributed throughout the industries. These immigrants all made advances more quickly than blacks and achieved higher positions in less time. The discrimination that these eastern and southern European immigrants experienced proved not to have a long-term impact upon their ability to gain a footing in the growth industries of the city. For blacks this process would remain an uphill struggle because color and nationality were important determinants of who succeeded and who did not.[50]

Black males in Buffalo entered the twentieth century with a ray of hope as far as their economic status was concerned. First, although the gains they made were marginal at best, when compared with those of other ethnic groups, their outlook was not unrealistic, for the increasing black population necessitated an increase in goods and services, many of which would be provided by blacks themselves. Second, wartime necessity created jobs for black men in industry. This was the key ingredient, in that their changing occupational status could help to steer them upon a course that would allow them to establish a viable, modern community. Furthermore, a larger black populace would provide the troops needed to vocalize their grievances and would be more capable of resisting the discrimination and prejudice blacks faced in Buffalo. The increased incomes would permit blacks to help finance organizations that addressed their grievances in Buffalo.

The advances that black men made in industry are only half the story. Their involvement in labor unions, the quality of their work experience, and their ability to take care of their families and community organizations is the other part. They attributed the major impediment to their progress to discrimination on the part of employers, foremen, and workers, and also to the fact that a disproportionate amount of their income had to be devoted to housing.[51] This situation led Mary Talbert to remark that the black man "faces a closed door to opportunity that compels him to knock hard and long if he would enter."[52] Nevertheless, African American males were not disillusioned and one of the major thrusts of their protests during the 1920s and 1930s focused on the issue of jobs. Individual blacks, as well as organized groups, were at the forefront of this struggle.

Thus, it was not accidental that the Buffalo branch of the National Association for the Advancement of Colored People was granted a charter by the national office in January of 1915. This was merely the first of many attempts by blacks to organize to alleviate their plight. They established the Michigan Avenue YMCA in 1923. The Buffalo branch of the National Urban League, founded in 1927 to address social and economic concerns, later became the primary voice of blacks in Buffalo.

BLACK WOMEN IN THE WORLD OF WORK

The economic outlook for African American women in Buffalo at the turn of the century was dismal, with few jobs and a limited range of options. In 1905, the range of occupations available to black women was much more severely restricted than those for black males. Black women worked in only 27 job categories, most of which were unskilled service positions. The limited range of jobs available to black women resulted from their race, gender, and class. First, there was a paucity of job opportunities in Buffalo for all females, especially for those who lacked special skills. Second, training institutions in the city did not admit black women into their programs. Finally, employers and supervisors in certain businesses did not desire to hire black women because they perceived that whites did not wish to work with them.[53]

Despite these restrictions, two-thirds of the black women in Buffalo in 1905 found it necessary to work outside the home. The options available to them were the ones which were physically most taxing and which offered the least remuneration and job security: most found employment in unskilled positions. But even here black women found themselves working in narrowly defined fields. Over half of them (298, or 54.1 percent) worked as chambermaids and domestics in private homes and hospitals. Most of the rest worked as servants (19), laundresses (11), janitresses, porters, waitresses, and day workers. Only 11 black women,

Mary Burnett Talbert and her secretary in Talbert's office, with daughter
Sarah May Talbert Keelan and granddaughter Yvette Keelan, circa 1922.
Courtesy of the Buffalo and Erie Courty Historical Society.

Bricklayers rebuilding checkerwork in open-hearth regenerative chambers,
Bethlehem Steel Mills (1929). Courtesy of the Hamburg Historical Society.

Rolling Mills Crew, Bethlehem Steel Mills, 1929. Courtesy of the
Hamburg Historical Society.

Black porters and maintenance workers pictured with ushers from
the Shea's Buffalo Theater. Included, in the first row, second from
left, is a Mr. Scott, chief of maintenance and clean-up, 1929.
Courtesy of the Buffalo and Erie County Historical Society.

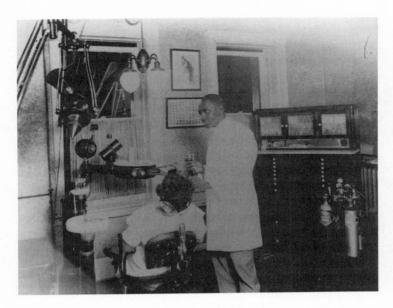

Dr. Elisha Gilbert in his office at 259 William Street, circa 1930. Courtesy of the Buffalo and Erie County Historical Society.

Ann Montgomery (in center wearing corsage), proprietor of the Little Harlem nightclub, with well wishers at the New York Central Terminal on Padereski Drive, 1938. Courtesy of the Buffalo and Erie County Historical Society.

Brown Bomber Cab Company, circa 1939. Left to right: James Daniels, Lamar Keaton, Cecil Green, Elijah Gibson. Courtesy of the Buffalo and Erie County Historical Society.

comprising a mere 2 percent of their population, were successful in owning and operating businesses designed to serve blacks. Six women were rooming house proprietors. One each owned a restaurant and tailor shop. All of these establishments were small and the proprietors were unable to significantly affect the employment situation in their community, but these women did provide some alternative housing in a tight market, and they served as role models for some.

A few black women were engaged in skilled trades, working as hotel cooks, seamstresses, beauticians, milliners' helpers, and practical nurses. One woman was employed as a waitress in a hotel, considered here to be skilled work; one was employed in a supervisory position, as boss of a labor gang. Only two females worked in clerical positions. All three of the professional black women in Buffalo in 1905 were teachers. The 1905 employment data indicate that the economic outlook for black females was dismal. Severely restricted job options and competition for the available jobs assured meager wages.

By 1915, the percentage of black women working outside the home had increased from two-thirds to three-fourths. Job opportunities for black females had expanded significantly over those of their 1905 sisters. They now were found in 41 categories, up from 27. Despite the dramatic increase in job classifications, the types of industries in which these women found themselves remained virtually unchanged. Unskilled positions still dominated. Most black females still worked as chambermaids in hospitals and general housekeepers. The number of black female laundresses increased, and the number of black women servants in 1915 declined significantly. One black woman worked as a matron, and another listed her occupation as day worker. These findings suggest that by 1915 Polish and Italian women had displaced black females as servants. The percentage of black women employed in relatively skilled positions increased slightly in 1915, to 4.2 percent. They were listed in the census with occupational titles such as beautician, hotel cook, driver, seamstress, iron contractor, finisher, bartender, practical nurse, and cook on a boat, a semi-skilled job.

By 1915 the black population of Buffalo had almost doubled in size, a change reflected in the increased number of female proprietors whose businesses were geared to serve the black community. Twenty-three women or 3.3 percent operated businesses. The increase in rooming houses accounts for most of the rising number of businesswomen (2.9 percent). The other three female proprietors were caterers. The year 1915 also saw a slight increase in the number of black women who found employment as clerical workers. Two bookkeepers, two bookbinders, one saleswoman, and two clerical workers made up about 1 percent of black female workers. More black women worked as school teachers, but certainly fewer than their population would warrant. One black woman was a professional actress. This brought the number of black women who worked as professionals to four, comprising a little less than half of 1 percent of their population.

These findings indicate the overall condition of black women in the world of work was still dismal. However, there were some gains. The number of black females who secured work had risen substantially since 1905.[54] For the first time black women secured jobs in industry. Clerical workers increased. This change portended the development of a more "normal" class structure within the black community and higher income and more steady employment for a few black families. However, despite these improvements in their employment situation, black women were still plagued by discrimination in the job market and were primarily restricted to the lowest-paying positions.

After the large-scale migration, the most notable feature in the employment picture for black women in Buffalo in 1925 was the dramatic decline in the number of women who were gainfully employed. Slightly

less than 20 percent (19.5 percent) were working. This finding is a-
stounding in view of the huge numbers that found it necessary to work
in the earlier decades. How can one account for this factor? One explanation could be that the employment picture for black males improved remarkably over the previous years; i.e., black men gained more
steady, higher-paying jobs, thereby permitting black females to remain
at home. Charles Johnson, sociologist and director of research for the
National Urban League, noted in his study of black migration in 1918
that 300,000 fewer black women reported working than had been the
case during the previous decade and suggested that the drop was a
result of black males' economic advancement.[55] The fact that a considerable number of men in Buffalo found employment in factories suggests this as a plausible explanation, too. By 1925, approximately 16
percent of black males worked in local factories. But the demobilization
of the armed forces and the accompanying economic slump are equally
plausible explanations, for women lost their jobs to make positions available for men. Moreover, while most women were employed in clerical
positions, black women were unsuccessful in penetrating this field. (See
Figures 6 through 11 for a comparison of the impact of ethnicity on
women's work.) Furthermore, the fact that a considerable number of
women who worked in home industries were overlooked by the census
recorder, because of a tendency to list only the occupations of those
women who secured employment outside of their homes, should explain
matters further.

Despite the massive increase the city experienced in its black population following the war, the employment patterns for black females in
1925 were quite similar to those noted for 1905 and 1915.[56] Although
the postwar period found African American females in Buffalo employed
in a greater variety of jobs than ever before (78 classifications), domestic
work still dominated their employment picture. Of a sample of 100
women who were placed in jobs in 1925 by a black employment agency,
91 were placed in domestic service, two in factory positions, and seven
in hotel and restaurant work.[57] The New York State manuscript census
for 1925 reveals that almost 55 percent of all working black females in
Buffalo still were employed in domestic work. This is a slight increase
over the previous decade's findings. In 1925, there were chambermaids,
laundresses, house servants, janitresses, porters, a matron, and those
who "worked at" local hotels.

Although black women were virtually restricted to domestic jobs, they
faced increased competition in that field from immigrant women, especially Scandinavians, Poles, Czechs, Finns, and Slovaks.[58] The superintendent of the State Employment Bureau in Buffalo revealed that 75
percent of those individuals who requested domestic help in 1923 expressed a desire for whites.[59] Even women who worked in transportation

or other industries were usually hired to perform domestic types of service. Nearly a dozen were employed in garages as washers and laborers. For the first time the railroads employed black female car cleaners, and black women also found daywork positions with the city government.

In his 1923 study Charles Johnson observed that "opportunities for Negro women are ridiculously low."[60] Johnson found of the approximately 2,900 females working in 45 plants, only 54 were black.[61] He discovered that some manufacturers refused to consider the employment of black women because they believed it would create an extraordinary overhead cost, since their racial practices would require separate accommodations and working spaces. Social activist Mary White Ovington, in her study of black female workers in New York, discovered that "despite her efforts and occasional successes, the colored girl . . . meets with severer race prejudice than the colored man, and is more persistently kept from attractive work."[62]

By 1925, Buffalo industries had begun to employ black women in greater numbers, although there were still very few black females in the local plants and none in the major ones. Here, too, they performed domestic types of jobs. Seventeen worked as charwomen. Eleven women were classified as laborers in four companies: a cement factory, a steel mill, a construction company, and a refrigerator company. One woman worked as an attendant in a factory. Other types of unskilled work dominated the employment picture of black females in the self-styled "City of Good Neighbors."

Such a paucity of black females in industry and the narrow range of jobs to which they were confined substantiate the fact that the restrictions which prevailed earlier were still widespread. In his 1925 study Niles Carpenter confirmed Johnson's earlier observations. He attributed the failure of black women to gain a foothold in industry to the unwillingness of employers to "introduce anything of an experimental nature such as the employment of colored help would be, which might upset the morale of his working force or lessen the quality and economy of production."[63] His findings confirm that the employment picture for black women remained grim.

Often companies lacked racial policies governing the hiring of black women altogether, and their supervisors instead imposed their own racial views and perceptions upon the workplace. Educational background or class status had virtually no impact upon the ability of African American women to secure jobs. When Beatrice Eve, a West Indian student at Bryn Mawr, returned home to Buffalo in the summer of 1926, she sought employment in the garment industry. After her efforts proved futile, she solicited aid from V. Freda Seigworth, YWCA industrial secretary. When Seigworth contacted the personnel manager at Barmon's clothing factory on Eve's behalf, she was told, "I've been in the sewing room for twenty years and wouldn't want to take 'one [African American]' on now."[64] Eve had an excellent record at school and had worked in the garment industry in New York. She even had been a member of the International Ladies Garment Workers Union. Disappointed with the results of her recruitment efforts, Seigworth contacted Arnold T. Hill, industrial relations secretary of the National Urban League, for help. She informed Hill that "the Industrial Relations Association of Employment Managers seem friendly to the use of colored labor. Claude Peale of the American Radiator Company, as you know, is favorable. However, there is almost no one concerned about colored women."[65]

The Buffalo Urban League noted that such efforts by Seigworth represented a new "attitude" on the part of the YWCA in its treatment of African American women. Beginning in 1926 the "Y" initiated practices designed "to crystallize sentiment in favor of Negro girls." The YWCA hired two African Americans as clerks in the Central Association and lobbied in support of black women in the garment industry. Consequently, some dress manufacturers hired several black women. The Y organized these young women into clubs to enhance their understanding of industrial problems and admitted them as members of the YWCA. The Urban League report praised the YWCA for its new policies, but the League concluded that its efforts had only scratched the surface of the problem.[66]

There was a remarkable increase in the number of black women who secured employment in the skilled trades in 1925. In fact, of employed black women, 129 (17 percent) now held skilled positions. Even here most of them worked in the tertiary sector; there were seamstresses, tailors, and a dyer. A number of other personal care positions opened up for black women. The number of black hairdressers increased, and four women operated their own shops. For the first time, black women were hired as elevator operators. One woman was an inspector, another was a telephone operator, and two others secured employment as bookbinders. In addition, black women found positions as practical nurses; getting them admitted into nurse training programs, however, would remain an uphill battle.

The number of black women professionals grew, but still, too few black women found employment in the professions. The community could take pride in its librarian, seven school teachers, several music teachers, actresses, its one social worker, and accountant. In 1925, the number of female proprietors increased considerably. Thirteen percent of black female workers managed their own businesses, including Ann Montgomery of the Little Harlem Nightclub. While one woman managed a restaurant, and there were several caterers, most proprietors ran rooming houses. The nature of these businesses precluded their hiring vast numbers of workers, hence they had virtually no impact on the overall employment situation of blacks. Yet the presence of such businesses revealed the influence of migration, for blacks increasingly supplied some of the goods and services that their community needed. Black women still were underrepresented in the clerical sector, with only two bookkeepers and an office clerk.

It is quite apparent from the forgoing that employment opportunities for black females were dismal. A look at the wages of a selected group of these women will further substantiate their economic disadvantage. Domestics earned between $8 and $12 per week, while office maids earned $12 to $15. Those women who did laundry in their homes earned $3 to $12 weekly. The two women who had factory jobs earned a minimum of $11.50 per week, with income going as high as $13.50. One clerk who "passed" for white earned $12.[67] All of these salaries were low. In December 1921, a study by the New York State Factory Investigating Commission fixed the minimum wage by which a woman could maintain herself in "decency" at $15.55 per week for Buffalo. Undoubtedly, for later years the minimum income which women needed to earn increased considerably.

A nationwide study of the positions working women obtained will further substantiate the fact that the employment picture for black females in Buffalo was bleak, but quite similar to that of black women throughout the United States, who were on the bottom of the socio-economic ladder. Nationwide, 39 percent of black females worked in agricultural pursuits, while 12.7 percent of all women worked in such positions. Nearly 43 percent of black women were employed in domestic and personal service; 25.6 percent of all women worked as domestics. Only .2 percent of black women were successful in acquiring clerical positions; 16.7 percent of women nationwide held clerical jobs.

Length of residence in the city had little effect on job opportunities for black females in Buffalo during the first quarter of the twentieth century. Most black women in Buffalo were destined to remain in the same job classification, as we will note when we trace a number of their careers through the New York State manuscript census. Kittie Bright, a 21-year-old bride, worked as a domestic in 1905. Although by 1915 she and her husband had established their own household, she still worked as a domestic. Kittie Bright was not in Buffalo in 1925, although her husband and children were listed in the 1925 census. Eighteen-year-old Nellie Barnett found employment as a domestic in 1905; she lived with her parents at the time. Ten years later, then a boarder, Barnett still worked as a domestic (the 1925 census did not list Barnett). Emily Walker, 28 years old in 1905, was a domestic, too. She retained her position in 1915, and by 1925, she no longer worked.

Another black woman, Lu Tarrance, was 31 in 1915, married, and employed as a domestic. By 1925, she no longer was employed (Tarrance was not in Buffalo in 1905). In all of these instances, African American women secured the jobs traditionally associated with black female employment. Marriage for those who were advancing in years sometimes brought an end to their careers, but these women never experienced occupational mobility.

The career of Clara Payne, the daughter of Buffalo city clerk Thomas Payne, is a notable exception to the foregoing observations. The 43-year-old woman worked as a domestic in 1905. Ten years later, when she was 53, Payne worked as a caterer, and by 1925, at the age of 63, she was a social worker. Payne experienced tremendous job mobility even though she had passed the age when most individuals would expect to launch a new career. Her mobility partially resulted from the in-migration of southern blacks into the city and the concomitant problems which, although ever present, became more highly visible. In response, the black community exerted pressure on the city government to employ black social workers. But by the late 1930s this field was still largely closed to African American women because of a lingering policy of discrimination against blacks in municipal employment, be it appointive or civil service.[68] Florence Morris, 26, of 40 Northland, was another exception. One of the few fortunate black women who, by 1925, had secured a higher-paying position in a factory, Morris worked as a machine hand. Payne and Morris worked in "middle class" jobs in their community and resided in an area where some African Americans had found access to better housing.[69]

The economic plight of black women in Buffalo at the turn of the century was dismal, but they made some marginal gains in the clerical and professional sectors and a few secured better-paying jobs in industry. Moreover, their job options expanded somewhat. For these reasons, black women shared the optimism of black men, who in most instances had migrated to Buffalo. Black women continued to migrate to the city in large numbers and many became involved in the various social improvement organizations which were established after the First World War.

One would expect that the socioeconomic status of these workers affected the growth and development of the black community of Buffalo. A most obvious case is housing. As early as February 1919, housing officials noted that the Buffalo community offered a paucity of affordable housing for laborers.[70] As migrants in Buffalo continued to swell the African American populace, the demand for housing in the black community became critical. Blacks tended to move into the older areas of the city, flanked on one side by the downtown business district and

on the other by a light manufacturing district.[71] This area of first settlement had experienced repeated recent southern- and eastern-Euro-
pean immigrant arrivals. Decay and overcrowding were inevitable.

The housing situation in the areas of first settlement was deplorable
and several observers and agencies attested to its quality. William Jackson, the recently appointed secretary of the proposed black YMCA,
contended that the housing situation for blacks in Buffalo should be
given utmost priority. He noted that there were inadequate provisions
for caring for young men who had migrated to the city in the homes
of "decent colored people."[72] More than a decade later, William Evans,
executive director of the Buffalo branch of the National Urban League,
suggested that this grave problem was much more widespread.[73]

In 1912, the Buffalo Foundation conducted a study of 429 households
to ascertain the extent of housing deprivation African Americans endured.[74] Only 12 (3 percent) of the families canvassed actually owned
their own homes. More than two-thirds of the families in the sample
paid $20 or more for rent. Scholars conducting the survey considered
these figures to be moderately high, but in keeping with the law of
supply and demand. The study concluded that blacks were forced to
rent homes in a limited number of areas because of racial prejudice
and discrimination, circumstances which increased the demand and
limited the supply. Thus, they were compelled to pay dearly in comparison to their wages for the accommodations they received. The foundation also reported that blacks paid higher rentals than had the whites
whom they succeeded.[75]

The increased earnings of blacks by the middle of the decade improved the housing status for a few fortunate ones, but blacks generally
had difficulty in securing adequate housing regardless of their income
levels. In his testimony before the New York State Temporary Commission on the Condition of the Urban Colored Population (TCCUCP)
in 1937, William Evans noted that "there seems to be well-organized
public sentiment [in Buffalo] which works just as effectively as if [prop-
erty owners' covenants] did actually exist."[76] By the 1930s, the housing
shortage was so grave that the Buffalo Municipal Housing Administration
could no longer ignore it. The agency sought federal funds to construct
low-income housing units.[77] Racial and ethnic segregation was so taken
for granted in Buffalo that the Housing Authority recommended that
consideration be given to three housing projects, one in the Italian
neighborhood, one in the black community, and one in the Polish
area. The Willert Park municipal housing project on Jefferson Avenue,
in the heart of the African American community, was completed in
1937.[78] Housing remained one of the community's critical problems,
and such organizations as the Buffalo Urban League launched several
largely futile campaigns to improve housing for blacks.

BLACK BUSINESS ENTERPRISES

Dr. Ivorite Scruggs, a prominent black physician, lamented the fact that blacks owned so few businesses in Buffalo in the 1920s, especially in view of the size of the black population. His concern was echoed by a number of black spokespersons nationwide, as well as locally. The most prevalent businesses in the black community of Buffalo at the turn of the twentieth century were catering establishments, restaurants, hotels, barber shops, beauty parlors, and pool rooms, most of which served a black clientele. Black businessmen found these types of enterprises appealing because they had a wealth of experience in those areas. In most instances they required little capital initially and many of them grew out of the service jobs blacks typically performed. Another compelling consideration for blacks who founded businesses catering to their own was the fact that they faced virtually no competition from groups outside of the black community. Other northern cities witnessed the development of similar black business establishments in conjunction with their increased migration North.[79]

With the growth of its population and the arrival of a small cadre of more affluent and better-educated blacks in the 1920s, Buffalo's east side witnessed the establishment of several new businesses and businesses that represented a new type of professional development among black businessmen in Buffalo. These, too, were dependent upon the black community for patronage. Although many met with limited success, each operation was viewed as an experiment in race pride, and black spokesmen urged the African American community to support these "race" enterprises.

The businesses founded by blacks in Buffalo were primarily service establishments which catered to the needs of the African American populace, just as in other northern cities at the time. The Talbert family had operated a lucrative real estate business in the city since the nineteenth century. The Sims and Towne New and Used Furniture Store on Michigan Avenue was one of the oldest business establishments in the black community.[80] The Jones Brothers Mortuary not only had an office at 66 William Street but, after four years of service, located a branch on Wasson Avenue in nearby Lackawanna.[81] Helen and J. Elwood Smith operated a mortuary on the East Side, too. Rosa Montgomery, a recent graduate of the Maloney School of Beauty Culture, announced the opening of her beauty parlor at 268 Spring Street in the summer of 1925.[82]

In 1929, Dr. Ivorite Scruggs purchased the largest piece of real estate owned by blacks in Buffalo when he and his wife Ruth bought from the Lakefront Realty Company a three-story apartment building located at Peckham Street and Jefferson Avenue. Dan Montgomery operated a successful hotel and supper club on Exchange Street, where many nationally acclaimed black artists performed. Montgomery's place also was an important meeting site for black intellectuals. Ann Montgomery's Little Harlem, on Michigan and Elm Streets, was renowned in literary and entertainment circles and attracted prominent "Harlem Renaissance" personalities in the 1920s and 1930s.

Robert Joplin, proprietor of the McAvoy Theatre, which opened in September 1921, planned to promote "high class pictures and up to date vaudeville," thereby attracting prominent performers to the Broadway and Madison establishment. Joplin intended for his business to satisfy the entertainment needs of a black clientele, and he further planned to serve the black community by employing "colored girl ushers, colored orchestra, and colored operator."[83]

During the 1920s Buffalo's African American population supported nine black newspapers. The *Buffalo American* was one of the most important.[84] Reverend Sidney O. B. Johnson, pharmacist Charles Patrick, and NAACP secretary Marshall Brown, all newcomers to Buffalo, edited, published, or managed the newspaper. Like other black newspapers, the *Buffalo American* was concerned about newsworthy events and advertising. It informed its constituents about the conditions that African peoples experienced throughout the world, but especially in the South and in those areas controlled by imperialist powers, such as in Haiti. It hailed the establishment of every "race" business enterprise and publicized the achievements of African Americans. But beyond these important accomplishments, the *Buffalo American* helped to forge a collective identity among blacks that was predicated upon their history and race, as well as their adherence to the concepts of self-help and racial solidarity. The *Buffalo American* also employed a few blacks in white collar positions and gave them first-hand experience working for the press.[85]

By the 1920s, several black professionals had begun to practice in Buffalo. Attorneys Clarence Mahoney and Julian Evans opened offices on William Street. Robert Burrell, a future president of the NAACP, established his legal business in the Brisbane Building downtown. Ophthalmologist Yerby Jones, a native Buffalonian and graduate of the University of Buffalo Medical School, began his career in an office in the home of his parents, at 428 Jefferson Avenue. Other black physicians— Ivorite Scruggs, Ezekial Nelson, Theodore Kakaza, and H. H. Lewis— established practices on the near East Side also. Charles H. Patrick, pharmacist and proprietor of the Ruth-Patrick Drug Company, operated the largest store of that nature in Buffalo. Dr. Elisha Gilbert opened his dental office at 259 William Street in the 1930s.

John Brent, a black architect, was a notable exception to this pattern. Brent had worked for several white architectural firms before he received the commission to design a new structure for the Michigan Avenue

YMCA. After he secured this lucrative contract, he resigned to establish his own firm. Cornelius Ford, a prominent livestock dealer, had a career pattern which differed substantially from those of other black business-men, too. From the time of his arrival in Buffalo in 1906, Ford forged a successful partnership which had as one of its customers Armour and Company, at the time the world's largest meat packing company.[86] He was the sole black member of the Livestock Association and frequently consulted with dealers across the nation. Ford's achievement in business was considered to be a "fine model for other members of the race." Yet, successful though the firm may have been, its impact on the black community was limited, for Ford was in a position to employ only a few blacks, and virtually all of his clientele was white.

The transitory nature of black business enterprises, as well as their low volume, precluded their playing a major role in the economic de-velopment of the black community. In an attempt to alleviate these problems, a number of cooperative economic endeavors got underway in the 1920s and 1930s. These co-ops resulted in part from the con-temporary black thought that racial solidarity and self-help were the most expeditious means of addressing the critical issues which affected black Americans. This philosophy was an outgrowth of the teachings of the late Booker T. Washington, and also had its antecedents in slave and post–Civil War African American communities across the nation. Moreover, during the 1920s many black intellectuals had come under the tutelage of Marcus Garvey and his Universal Negro Improvement Association, which advocated economic development of black commu-nities by blacks. W. E. B. DuBois, editor of the *Crisis*, used this NAACP publication as a forum to spread his own views on black economic cooperation after World War I, for he fervently believed that the es-tablishment of cooperatives was a means for blacks to ward off or at least to diminish the debilitating effects of economic depressions, while increasing the general viability of their communities. B. M. Ruddy, of Memphis, an adherent of DuBois' philosophy, explained:

> The good results of co-operation among colored people do not lie alone in the return of savings. They show, also, new opportunities for the earning of a livelihood, and the chance offered our colored youth to become acquainted with business methods. For naturally in enter-prises of this sort colored property is used wherever possible, colored management, and colored clerks, typists, book-keepers, and the like, are employed. . . . Colored people are furnishing their own with work and money for services received and the recipients are handing the money back for re-distribution to the original colored sources.[87]

Black Buffalonians, imbued with this contemporary economic phi-losophy, also organized a number of cooperative enterprises during this period. One of the earliest was the Douglas Grocery Company, Inc., founded in the summer of 1920 and located at 149 Clinton Street.[88] It was capitalized at $10,000. Among the first to subscribe were Reverend J. Edward Nash, pastor of the Michigan Avenue Baptist Church; James A. Gant, a 35-year-old fireman of 227 Clinton Street; and Irene L. Allen, a housewife who resided at 526 Linwood Avenue with her chauffeur husband, Virgil, and their six-year-old son, George. Most of the organizers were working-class men. Shares could be secured for ten dollars each, and by the July 8, 1920, mass meeting held at the Michigan Avenue Baptist Church, subscribers had already contributed half of the necessary funds. At the end of the meeting, more than $1,500 in shares were sold.[89]

The Douglas Grocery Board of Directors was composed of a number of civic-minded black men who viewed their enterprise and the community support which it had engendered as a "noble example of race pride." Certainly, the enthusiastic response from the community must have reinforced their belief. W. R. Wilson, president; Alfred A. Boykin, vice president; Howard B. Phillips, secretary; Lewis W. Holley, who worked as a bookbinder; Leonard S. Sayres, a chauffeur; R. H. Broyles; A. H. Cavitt, Pullman porter; R. W. Coan, Pullman porter; and Joseph Nichols, carpenter, comprised this board.[90] The board planned to open a chain of supermarkets. The opening of the company's first store, located at 132 William Street, occurred on September 6, 1920.[91] A feature in the black weekly *Buffalo American* called attention to this accomplishment and concluded:

> [This store] will bear close inspection at anytime as to the way in which it is conducted, cleanliness, politeness, reasonableness in prices, equal competition; and above all the direct application of business principles to business. . . . visit this store of your Race.[92]

The Douglas Grocery, Incorporated, operated successfully for several years.

Another joint effort among black Buffalonians resulted in the incorporation of the Buffalo Negro Realty Company (BNRC) on May 24, 1920. Its establishment was an attempt to alleviate the serious housing shortage blacks faced. The company not only bought and sold existing homes which had been renovated, but constructed new homes as well. Samuel A. Waddell, president, conceived of the idea and laid the organizational plans. Waddell was born in South America and educated in British Guiana. He had resided in Buffalo for only eight years, during which time he had learned the real estate field and had become a member of the Buffalo Real Estate Association. Vice President Joseph Moon, a native Virginian, had worked as a foreman at the Lackawanna Steel Company for 22 years. Moon was a man of "careful calculation, alert to opportune investments, service, [and] straightforward." Several of these directors were associated with other progressive movements in the city. The Reverend Sidney O. B. Johnson, minister of the Lloyd Memorial Congregational Church, a social activist and later editor of the *Buffalo American*, was elected secretary of the Buffalo Negro Realty Company. Pharmacist Charles H. Patrick, longtime proprietor of one of the city's largest drug stores, the Ruth-Patrick Drug Company, served as treasurer of the new corporation. Director Edward Gaffie, a native Buffalonian, had worked as stationary engineer at the city of Buffalo pumping station for ten years. In addition to his knowledge of real estate appraisals, Gaffie possessed special skills regarding construction and wholesale business transactions. Joseph Martin, another director, who owned several pieces of property and was closely associated with another real estate firm in the city, was able to contribute his special skills and knowledge to the new company.[93] A native of Baltimore, Martin had been a resident of Buffalo for twenty years. The Reverend A. L. Wilson, another director, had had previous experience in real estate before joining the firm.

Just one month after its incorporation, the company purchased two houses on Jefferson Avenue, close to Ferry Street. At the time of the purchase, the homes were occupied by whites, but the BNRC planned to lease them to "respectable" black families during the first week of August.[94] On August 23, 1920, the company acquired another renovated house, a two-family brick structure on South Division Street.[95] These properties were located in the area that comprised the nucleus of the growing African American community.

To help finance these acquisitions, the company sold shares of stock at $100 per share; an investor could purchase a share by depositing $10 and paying the remainder on the installment plan. Twenty-four stockholders in the Buffalo Negro Realty Corporation received dividend checks of 6 percent only two years after the company's founding. This was considered a major feat, for no other "financial investment company of Colored men [in Buffalo] has successfully conducted business to a dividend paying basis."[96] The BNRC continued to conduct a lucrative business in the 1920s.

In 1931, the Young Negro Cooperative League Movement, which was founded by George Schuyler—a socialist and a journalist for the *Pittsburgh Courier*—influenced local blacks to organize their first successful large-scale enterprise in Buffalo, a grocery store. Weekly receipts totalled $850 and the Citizens Cooperative League employed four full-time cashiers and four part-time clerks.[97] While this organization was shortlived, it was the forerunner of the Buffalo Cooperative Economic Society, which was incorporated in 1935 as a result of the untiring efforts of Dr. Ezekial Nelson who, while working for the railroads in the 1920s, had travelled frequently to New York, where he came under the influence of Marcus Garvey's philosophy and his UNIA.[98]

The leadership which guided the formation of the Buffalo Cooperative Economic Society was convinced that the philosophy surrounding its founding was relevant to the circumstances confronting twentieth-century African Americans. Since community support was essential, Dr. Nelson and other members of the society conducted seminars on such topics as "Economic Status of the American Negro," "Importance of Self-Help and Cooperative Economics to the Negro," "Techniques of Operating a Business," and "The Value of Cooperative Credit Unions to the Negro."[99] After only four years in existence, the BCES had opened a market and a federal credit union. Its zeal and sound business practices certainly contributed to the nearly thirty-year longevity which the BCES enjoyed.

All of these efforts, whether individual or cooperative, were a source of racial pride. These business concerns employed a few blacks in positions such as clerks, typists, and bookkeepers, jobs that only a minuscule number of African Americans had succeeded in securing outside of the community because of job discrimination. These efforts made members of the black community cognizant of their status in relation both to blacks in other parts of the United States and to whites in Buffalo and helped to increase support for community self-help organizations. That these endeavors were largely marginal in terms of their financial successes can be attributed to the fact that African Americans lacked significant economic power. Nowhere in the country did they wield significant political, economic, or social power, power which would have provided them with some leverage to change the economic landscape dramatically for African Americans in Buffalo.

Racism was pervasive in Buffalo in the 1920s and 1930s, just as it was around the country. Its influence was significant and carried over into the relationship blacks had with local financiers. African Americans were unable to secure long-term financing for mortgages for homes, and their chances of acquiring loans to establish businesses or to expand them were even more remote. Participation in the various co-ops was contingent upon the personal fortunes of the individual members. Nevertheless, their efforts indicate a recognition that creating business establishments was also an essential dimension of their self-determinationist goals of community-building.

PART II

Blacks Organize to Improve Their Status: Institutional Development

Philanthropy and Uplift

Our city as a human problem is not unlike other cities. Parts of it by birth, talent and good fortune are lifted into a position of power and resourcefulness. Other parts by inheritance and tradition are foreign to the ideals and opportunities of a full and free American life. One-half does not know the other half. Yet the two halves rise or fall together. There is a solidarity in the life of a city. If one half suffers the other half suffers also. The weal of one is the weal of the other.[1]

The huge migration of blacks to northern, urban centers changed the landscape of the cities and the lives of all blacks who resided there. Their movement made more apparent the racism in northern backyards, and African Americans seemed to lose altogether the gains that they had made during Reconstruction and to be destined to remain second-class citizens. While noblesse oblige had governed the relationship between old Buffalo black families and whites, it proved inadequate for the new population of southern-born blacks, for as the black population expanded, the white population increased its tactics of discrimination and segregation. Generally, the conditions of blacks in Buffalo seemed to decline. Mary Burnett Talbert described post–World War I Buffalo as "a hard nut to crack." She further observed that the employment situation for blacks in Buffalo was deplorable and that blacks in the 1920s could best be described as "having little or none."[2]

Talbert, a graduate of Oberlin College, had moved to Buffalo after her marriage in 1891, and she had become a part of the old guard of black Buffalonians that included her husband, William, a prominent real estate broker and city bookkeeper; livestock dealer Cornelius Ford; and the Reverend J. Edward Nash, among others. Talbert's relationship to the Buffalo community was dwarfed by the national stature that she had attained as president of the National Association of Colored Women (NACW) and as NAACP vice president. In fact, as the African American population increased because of the Great Migration and as social conditions in the black areas deteriorated, neither the mayor nor members of the city council appointed any of these spokespersons to policy-making positions that would permit them to address the problems that the city faced. Occasionally, city officials called upon them to serve in advisory positions, but the prejudice against African Americans was so great and their numbers were so few that they were virtually ignored by the government.[3] This increased the pressure upon the organizations within the black neighborhoods.

To counteract these developments black organizations had to reassess their goals and objectives. Likewise, the increase in the black population of Buffalo forced a reorganization of many existing "social units" and the establishment of several new ones. Black social organizations were confronted with the dual problem of improving the conditions for the African American community and ameliorating the racial situation in the city at large. The Michigan Avenue YMCA represented this new thinking and was in a unique position to deal adequately with many of the more important social concerns of the Buffalo black community, and an examination of the Michigan Avenue YMCA from 1922 to 1940 sheds much light on the black community and the efforts of black organizations to fulfill what was considered to be their "mission" in the community. It should be noted from the outset that the Michigan Avenue YMCA conceived of itself as a "self-help organization." The Y's facilities for community meetings were the best available to African Americans in Buffalo. Prior to the construction of its new building, many of the Michigan Avenue YMCA's public lectures were held at local churches, especially Shiloh Baptist Church. However, the churches, because of religious antagonisms, were often not the most suitable accommodations for interfaith meetings. The opening of the YMCA provided numerous black social and religious organizations with facilities for educational activities. Black Buffalonians took great pride in the Y because they collectively had worked to create it.

From the turn of the century, Alfred H. Whitford, general secretary of the Young Men's Christian Association of Buffalo, was aware of the existence of a multiplicity of problems within the city's black community.[4] When Julius Rosenwald, president of Sears and Roebuck Company, renewed his 1912 offer of $25,000 to any Y branch that would undertake the construction of a building project designed specifically for the use of the African American population, Whitford was pleased. He believed that the YMCA activities could be extended to the black community with contributions from Rosenwald, as well as local philanthropists. In his annual report for 1922, Whitford exhorted the Christian community to carry out its mission by working in the black community of Buffalo:

> The city churches of Buffalo are alive to the expansion program of their denomination and support missions located in the needy sections of their country and also in foreign lands and yet collectively fail to get together to help a neglected needy group who are forced to live in an undesirable, congested section between Michigan and Jefferson, and south of Broadway.[5]

In July 1922, the Buffalo Federation of Churches conducted a survey of the black sections of Buffalo.[6] Whitford included the results in his annual report because they were "of interest to all who are interested in the advancement of the colored race."[7] The report pointed out that housing conditions between Broadway and Michigan, and west of Jefferson and east of Michigan, were among the most deplorable for blacks in the city. It noted further that there were no public recreational facilities available for men and boys in that area. The federation saw the need for a night school for young black males who were recent southern migrants and too old to be placed in regular classes in the public schools; it also proposed the establishment of a branch library for the black community. While a third of the population, 2,279 persons, were members of the various Protestant denominations, these churches were indebted up to more than one-third of their value; white churches usually carried a debt of less than half this amount. Such indebtedness virtually precluded any possibility of the black churches' establishing a recreational center to meet the needs of members. The only facilities available both day and night to the black male population were the "vicious places" that tended to demoralize even the "good citizens."

Whitford argued that if whites "who care for others would make possible a Negro Community Center for men, women, and children located in the residential section near Jefferson Street, it would be a good investment for Buffalo; moreover, it would safeguard their [blacks'] interests and strengthen their churches."[8] While pointing out the relatively low cost of buildings for black YMCA's throughout the country, Whitford also emphasized the extensive use to which the Y facilities in black communities had been put. Buffalo, he maintained, had been derelict in meeting its obligation to the growing black community. Whitford concluded with a request for funds to be designated for work specifically in the black community.

The Young Men's Christian Association began its organizational activities in Buffalo in 1852. From the beginning, most Y activities focused on religion. However, the Board of Directors was committed to improving the physical, intellectual, and social conditions of youths, and the board implemented programs designed to fill these practical needs: for example, the Y worked closely with local industries in devising its educational programs. The board continued this policy into the twentieth century. By the eve of World War I, there were the Central YMCA, the Genesee and West Side branches, plus several railroad divisions which had been established to accommodate the young men whom the railroads employed. A. H. Whitford and the Board of Directors believed that it was their duty to alleviate social problems in the city. In 1910, the Y opened the Men's Hotel in downtown Buffalo to accommodate the young, single men who were flocking to the city. After the war, the central administration embarked upon a massive expansion policy which included buildings for the North and South Buffalo Community branches. Other community branches were proposed, one in the Kensington and Riverside sections, a Seaman's branch in lower Main Street, a University of Buffalo branch, and a boys' branch in the vicinity of Broadway and Fillmore.[9]

The Whitford report of December 1922 appears to have generated little support within the Buffalo YMCA organization, for there is no indication that any arrangements were being planned to organize activities among blacks. Sometime later a group of 150 "representative" black men petitioned the Board of Directors to begin Y work among the men and boys of their community.[10] In direct response to their petition, the Board of Directors of the Buffalo Association announced that it had placed into its budget for the next year provisions which would allow for the organization and maintenance of a "colored" branch of the Young Men's Christian Association. This branch would serve the needs of blacks in Buffalo as well as those who resided in the nearby town of Lackawanna. Under the capable leadership of A.H. Whitford, the Buffalo Association embarked upon their plan during the summer of 1923.[11]

The association appointed William H. Jackson of South Carolina to head the committee which would explore the prospects of establishing a branch of the Y to serve a population that was "needy" and "meriting" a helping hand. Jackson, a veteran YMCA man and churchman, was a good choice for this position and brought a wealth of experience to the post. After he received his bachelor of arts degree from Lincoln University in 1901, Jackson taught school in Florida and Georgia. For five years he served as executive secretary of the Center Avenue Branch YMCA in Springfield, Ohio, and for the next fifteen years he was superintendent of the Presbyterian Sunday School Mission in the southern region. As Sunday School Mission Superintendent, he took specialized courses in religious training at Lake Geneva, Wisconsin and also spent two summers studying in the Department of Sociology at Columbia University. At the conclusion of his fifteen-year tenure as superintendent, he returned to Orangeburg, South Carolina to continue teaching. It was from this latter post that Whitford summoned Jackson to Buffalo in 1923.[12]

By September 1, Jackson had an office in the Central Branch YMCA on Pearl Street, from which he would map out a viable program for black youths. With the aid of M. T. Green, T. C. Holcolm, and Leonard Sayres, Jackson called together the Lincoln Club of Youths of St. Luke's AME Zion Church. The St. Luke AME Zion Church was located at 585 Michigan Avenue and had established a number of highly acclaimed educational programs that stressed the training of blacks so that they would become experts "in the lines of their possibilities, rather than [educating them] above and beyond."[13] Several other youngsters from the black community joined the Lincoln Club to form what later became the core of the Michigan Avenue YMCA Boys Club.[14]

In trying to get the YMCA program off the ground, Jackson believed it was advantageous to surround himself with influential business and professional men from within the black community. The original members of the Board of Managers, the governing body of the Michigan Avenue Branch, were Rudolph S. Lane, chairman; John E. Brent; Justice Taylor; R. W. Coan; C. A. Sims; and Dr. I. L. Scruggs.[15] Some of these men and many of those who later joined them as managers were recent arrivals to Buffalo who had established themselves in the professional sectors of the local black community.[16]

John E. Brent came to Buffalo from his native Washington, D.C., after having attended Tuskegee Institute, where he studied carpentry and architecture. He was graduated from Tuskegee in 1907, and after a short teaching career in the D.C. public schools, Brent went to Philadelphia, where he enrolled in the School of Architecture of Drexel Institute. He graduated from Drexel in June 1913 and shortly thereafter moved to Buffalo, where he worked for a number of architectural firms. Brent served as a member of the "vestry" or ruling body of St. Philip's Episcopal Church, and was active in many social and benevolent organizations in the "Queen City," including the NAACP (as a past president). His experience and knowledge would prove to be beneficial in the development of the new branch.[17]

Dr. Ivorite Scruggs, a native of Mississippi who had spent his boyhood in Memphis, Tennessee, came to Buffalo in 1921. He had received a bachelor of science degree from Howard University in 1915 and a medical degree from Howard in 1919. Scruggs was an outstanding civic leader, and in recognition of his services was later appointed as a member of the Board of Directors of the Metropolitan YMCA of Buffalo, the first African American in the history of the United States to be appointed to such a position.[18]

Several other men from within the black community shared their skills in the establishment of the Michigan Avenue YMCA.[19] The most prominent were Cornelius Ford,[20] a livestock dealer, and Dr. J. Edward Nash,[21] pastor of the Michigan Avenue Baptist Church from 1892 until his retirement in 1953. Nash had been in Buffalo perhaps longer than any of the other founders of the Y. He was familiar with the problems of blacks in Buffalo and had worked to alleviate their plight through participation in many community organizations, including the local branch of the NAACP and later the National Urban League.

Professionals were not the only ones who were instrumental in the establishment of the black branch of the YMCA. The Michigan Avenue Branch's first member was a machine operator named Welton Townsend, who was recruited right on the street by Jackson. Townsend was interested in Jackson's project, gave him a $1 membership fee, and later became a member of the new YMCA's policy-making body, the Board of Managers. Other working men, both skilled and unskilled, were involved in the Y from an early date. Peter Lomax, a porter, and Ninde Davis, a laborer, were other early members of the Board of Managers.[22]

The diverse backgrounds and experiences the organizers brought to the planning committee were important to the initial success of the Michigan Avenue YMCA. The programs they instituted reflected their strengths, and the Michigan Avenue Y in turn became one of the most prestigious, respected institutions within the black community. Indeed, it became a model for other associations among blacks.[23]

The first major problem confronting managers was securing adequate facilities. In 1923, the Metropolitan YMCA rented the former home of St. Luke's AME Zion on Michigan Avenue as a temporary home for the new branch because of its accessibility to the black populace. This temporary space proved inadequate almost from the start.

The fact that the YMCA facility was designed exclusively for the black population did not create an issue. Blacks in Buffalo had been experiencing an increase in restrictions on their personal freedom since before the war.[24] A segregated facility merely fitted into the emerging pattern. Moreover, those individuals who were making arrangements for the new facility were either migrants from the South or individuals who had spent a substantial number of their early years in the South. The influence of the late Booker T. Washington was strong among them. Brent had studied at Tuskegee, Jackson had studied and taught in the segregated school systems of the South, and Scruggs had received his medical degree from Howard University. Nash and Ford had reached maturity in the South and had studied at the missionary schools established for African Americans during the latter half of the nineteenth century. Each of these individuals was keenly aware of the advantages that could accrue to the community through the YMCA programs they envisioned for blacks in the Buffalo area.

William Jackson contended that "education is one of the chief needs of the colored citizens today," especially for the southern migrants who were entering the city to seek work in the factories. Although blacks were permitted to attend the educational classes at the central Y, most interested blacks were loath to attend classes and seek advice from instructors because of their poor skills and the larger white attendance in what the migrants perceived to be a hostile environment. Jackson believed the best solution to this problem would be a special branch devoted to the needs of African Americans.[25]

An editorial in the *Buffalo American,* a black newspaper, observed: "Young men by the hundreds are coming to the city and the great need for a YMCA has been felt for some time by those who are far-seeing and desirous of the Race's uplift."[26] But Dr. Ivorite Scruggs, at the first anniversary celebration of the Michigan Avenue YMCA in 1925, captured the spirit of the founders of the Y and their pragmatism when he expressed his sentiments regarding the all-black institution. Scruggs cautioned:

> We must choose between fear of segregation on the one hand and on the other, racial progress; we must choose between developing the best within us in our own institutions, built along the lines of other groups and a means of self-expression for us, or merely content ourselves with becoming a minor part of institutions fostered by other groups.
>
> . . . This is the adjustment period. In the years to come we will have furnished a foundation upon which to develop a superstructure of our own civilization. We must build so that the edifice will be strong and inspiring.[27]

From the beginning, the Michigan Avenue YMCA was dedicated to the welfare of black youths in Buffalo. The program of activities grew each year, attracting large numbers to the facility. The YMCA building served as a social center for African Americans. Observers noted that "these limited quarters have become a bee-hive of activity; practically the only social center for the exclusive use of colored people."[28] The membership reflected the growing importance of the Michigan Avenue Y. By December 1924, the branch boasted 265 members, sixty of whom were boys.[29] The Sunday meetings had an average attendance of 55. Sixty-six students were enrolled in the two Bible classes and the daily attendance at the rooms averaged 45. During its first year, the Michigan Avenue YMCA sponsored a two-week camping trip at the YMCA's Camp Weona for 25 youngsters. Shiloh Baptist Church was the site of a mass meeting sponsored by the Michigan Avenue YMCA in conjunction with the National YMCA Conference, which convened in Buffalo in 1924.

Its speakers series was quite successful. Over 500 persons came to hear Major Robert R. Moton, president of Tuskegee Institute, urge the audience to "take up the sword of intelligence, industry and education in the battle for the inherent and enfranchised privileges of the Negro throughout the United States."[30]

The work of the organizers was initially very successful and "thoroughly appreciated by the colored citizens." In 1923, the Metropolitan YMCA purchased a huge lot near the corner of Michigan and Cypress, along with the original building for use of blacks.[31] Also in 1923, Sears magnate Julius Rosenwald issued a momentous challenge to the Buffalo community. He let it be known that he would donate $25,000 toward the building fund if the Buffalo community could raise $125,000 for the construction of the Michigan Avenue YMCA by December 18, 1925.[32] A fund-raising drive for the Michigan Avenue YMCA was initiated in the Fall of 1924, and was extremely successful. The editor of a white daily newspaper, *The Courier*, publicized this important achievement and exhorted whites in Buffalo to follow the example of blacks in meeting their quota during the annual YMCA fund-raising drive:

> An example of such giving appears to be present in the gifts for the proposed "Y" branch for Negroes. The honor of advancing the hand of the clock at Lafayette Square yesterday fell to Rudolph S. Lane, Negro captain of the Michigan Avenue team, highest for the day. That is an honor in which the Negro citizens of Buffalo can justly take pride, for it marks their high interest in the things for which the YMCA stands and is seeking to promote in still greater degrees. Also it is a good sign that the value of the "Y" work is appreciated. Buffalo cannot afford to let slip this opportunity to make the "Y" more efficient than ever.[33]

After the Buffalo community had raised its quota of $125,000, Whitford indicated that he received Julius Rosenwald's donation on Christmas Eve, 1924.[34]

The problem of an adequate physical plant for the Michigan Avenue YMCA, however, was still prominent when George B. Mathews, Buffalo industrialist and owner of the *Buffalo Courier*, invited Whitford to his home in early June of the following year to discuss an interest in the welfare of black citizens. Whitford later informed the Board of Directors at a meeting held on June 30 that Mathews agreed to donate $100,000 to the YMCA to be used as a trust fund "to carry on and extend the educational, recreational, and settlement work among the Negro population of Buffalo and vicinity."[35] The grant stipulated, however, that larger facilities than those already planned were to be provided in the projected new building. The board accepted both the gift and the circumstances under which it was given. The trust became known as the

"Booker T. Washington Foundation" and was the largest donation ever made for the support of the Y's work among African Americans in the United States.[36] It was merely the first of many gifts that George and Jenny Mathews would contribute to the support of the Michigan Avenue YMCA. By the time of his death twenty years later, Mathews' contributions totalled over $500,000.[37]

The Metropolitan Y had included a new building for the black community in its five-year plan for the years 1922-1927.[38] However, the Mathews' contribution, along with the Rosenwald grant and the successful fund-raising drive of the Michigan Avenue Y in 1924, guaranteed the construction of a new building to house the Y much sooner than previously planned.[39] Before the Mathews' donation, foundation support for the Michigan Avenue Y totalled about $440,000.

After reviewing the credentials of potential architects for the new structure, Secretary General Whitford, upon the approval of the Board of Directors, commissioned John Brent, an original organizer of the Michigan Avenue YMCA, to perform the task. He was only the second black architect to receive an assignment to design a YMCA for blacks. Brent subsequently resigned from his post at Oakley and Schallmore to establish his own firm, and the Michigan Avenue YMCA was his first large-scale commission.[40] Plans for the proposed four-story structure got under way immediately. They included classrooms, separate men's and boys' departments with social rooms, billiard rooms, a library, locker rooms, and a standard-size gymnasium and swimming pool. The plans called for a 54-room dormitory and a cafeteria with a seating capacity of eighty. Space for a barber shop and a tailor shop were also incorporated into the design. The building was to be constructed for $200,000, but it actually was erected at a cost of $285,000.[41]

The new Georgian-style colonial Michigan Avenue YMCA was opened and dedicated amidst great pageantry and splendor on Sunday, April 15, 1928. Three thousand people visited the structure during the day, and a total of 5,000 for the week. More than 1,500 people attended the dedication ceremonies, over which Rudolph S. Lane, chairman of the Michigan Avenue Board of Managers, presided. Local and national dignitaries attended the ceremonies, including George and Jenny Mathews and Julius Rosenwald. YMCA secretaries Thomas Taylor of New York City, A. L. Comither of Brooklyn, Charles E. Trye of Cleveland, Thomas A. Bulling of Rochester, George Arthur of Chicago, and B. W. Overton of Cincinnati were among the YMCA officials present. Julius Rosenwald congratulated John Brent on "the completeness and architectural beauty of the building both inside and out." He summoned Brent to the platform to congratulate him personally on the "beautiful and successful building he had created for the colored group in Buffalo."[42]

People from all over the community rallied to the support of the

The Michigan Avenue YMCA, and the site of the proposed new building. The Sims-Towne Used Furniture store is on the right. Courtesy of the University at Buffalo, SUNY Archives.

The new Georgian, colonial-style Michigan Avenue YMCA, designed by John Brent. Courtesy of the University at Buffalo, SUNY Archives.

Board of Managers, Michigan Avenue YMCA. Standing, John Brent, architect; far left, Rudolph Lane; second from right, Cornelius Ford; far right, William Jackson, executive secretary. Courtesy of the University at Buffalo, SUNY Archives.

Campaign Workers, Michigan Avenue YMCA, Buffalo, N.Y., December 6, 1931. Courtesy of the University at Buffalo, SUNY Archives.

Game Room, Michigan Avenue YMCA. Courtesy of the University at Buffalo, SUNY Archives.

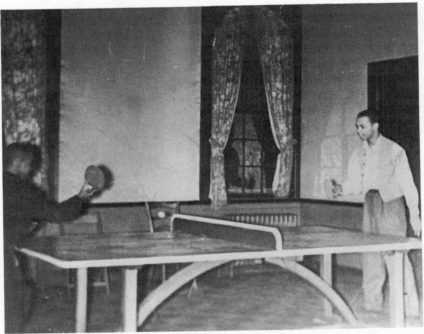

Game Room, Michigan Avenue YMCA. Courtesy of the University at Buffalo, SUNY Archives.

Cafeteria, Michigan Avenue YMCA. Courtesy of the University at Buffalo, SUNY Archives.

Finance Committee, Michigan Avenue YMCA. Standing far left, Dr. Ivorite Scruggs; center, William Jackson. Courtesy of the University of Buffalo, SUNY Archives.

Camp Wales Hollow, Michigan Avenue YMCA. This forty-acre
site was the gift of George and Jenny Matthews. Courtesy of
the University at Buffalo, SUNY Archives.

Youth Group, Michigan Avenue YMCA. Courtesy of the
University at Buffalo, SUNY Archives.

Third Western New York Youth Conference, Michigan Avenue
Branch YMCA. Courtesy of the University at Buffalo, SUNY
Archives.

Michigan Avenue YMCA and it became the most important social center
for the black community. The Y became an arena in which individuals
of varying political persuasions—from Garveyites to Democrats—could
come together in harmony. The membership was made up not only of
persons from the various Protestant denominations and social groups
within the black community, but also of those individuals who lacked
other organizational affiliations.[43] These participants, like the organizers,
perceived the YMCA as a self-help project—a means of ameliorating
the race's condition and displaying the achievements of African Americans in science, sports, education, the arts, and other areas.[44] More
importantly, black Buffalonians believed that it provided a forum in
which black youths could receive recognition for their accomplishments
in fields which were not readily accessible to them and a means by
which young men and women could build character.

The Michigan Avenue YMCA was certainly the finest structure and
the best-equipped social center available to the black community when
it opened in 1928. To make certain that the Y was accessible to most

members of the black community, the usual fees were reduced with foundation support. Men paid an annual fee of $2 for a basic, or "social," membership which entitled them to use the reading room and the game rooms, to rent rooms in the dormitory, and to participate in religious activities; a $5 membership included all of the aforementioned plus the right to use the physical educational facilities; a full senior membership for $7 permitted them to have complete use of the YMCA and to be assigned a locker on the premises.[45]

Membership for boys varied according to age. Children from age nine to twelve paid an annual membership fee of $2; those thirteen to sixteen paid $3. High school students and working young men were charged a $4 membership fee. Those who were enrolled in the Young Men's Division paid an annual fee of $5. These charges and fees were less than those at other YMCA branches in Buffalo.[46] At the same time, a number of subsidized memberships were offered to youths who could not afford these membership fees. These memberships were made available from individual contributions or through donations from various black and white civic groups or from foundation monies set aside for this purpose.[47] During the economic crisis of the 1930s, the number of subsidized memberships increased substantially.

In the new building, the Board of Management continued the policies which it had instituted previously. The building was staffed by experienced professional, clerical, and service personnel who often served as role models for the youths.[48] Each YMCA program was designed to fulfill the goals of building character, educating, and assuring the physical development of black youths. In essence, its programs were intended for physical and mental improvement.[49] The Y's mission was carried out by the various committees which operated within the larger structure. There were six major subdivisions within the organization: the Physical Education Department, the Religious Work Committee, the Boys Work Committee, the Girls Work Committee, the Education Committee, and the Health Week Committee.

The YMCA's traditional concern for developing the physical prowess of youth meant that the Michigan Avenue YMCA was also concerned about the "physical" development of black youth. During the first year in the new building, the physical education program was the best attended of all the programs offered. Activities scheduled for every day of the week (except Sunday) included gymnastic classes, volleyball, basketball, tumbling, and wrestling. The department's offerings were designed specifically for "mass appeal." This policy fitted into the scheme of the founders and managers of the Y. The Physical Education Committee described the Physical Department as "a laboratory where a practical demonstration of moral development as well as physical development is conducted."[50] The committee brochure continued: "In the Gym the boys and young men are taught to play the game of life squarely and manly, through play. There is no better way to train characters than through well supervised play."[51] In addition, the program provided an excellent "public relations forum," for it displayed well-disciplined youths who enjoyed using the facilities and exhibited the various skills which they had acquired at the Y and its conferences and celebrations.[52] For example, basketball was an extremely popular sport, and in 1927 the Michigan Avenue Y teams were victorious in 41 out of 45 games. These and other group activities were used as a vehicle for maintaining and improving relationships among various sectors of the community and throughout Erie County. Seventeen Inter-Church Basketball League games were played at the Y.[53]

Herman Daves and his assistant in the Physical Department, Leon Hall, organized and supervised activities which included "leadership training" for the youth of the black community. Each of eight clubs which met regularly at the Y had its own set of officers who were responsible for arranging and directing the club's annual program. The Boys Department program usually included educational and recreational activities. Bible instruction, literary programs, social and business meetings, and movies of a "socially redeeming character" were part of the regular calendar of events. A number of youth groups held conferences at the Y, among which were the Hi-Y Clubs and the Older Boys Clubs. The conferences pursued such themes as "Employment and Youth," "Health and Hygiene," and "Black Youth in Higher Education." From the very beginning, these conferences focused on issues of significance to youths in Buffalo and from the surrounding area.[54] Indeed, the Michigan Avenue YMCA was intended to be the funnel through which black youths could filter into the mainstream of the Buffalo community.[55]

The organizers of the Michigan Avenue YMCA were quite aware of the social background of the youngsters they served. Most of the youngsters came from homes of little means and lived in the worst sections of the city. By 1924, most blacks were southerners and while parents were most encouraging, they often lacked the resources to provide their children with the tools for improving their economic status. Although their children would learn the basics in the public schools, the Michigan Avenue YMCA provided enrichment educational programs and helped to boost self-esteem. The organizers firmly believed that the family was the "center of Christian living" and that their ultimate success in promoting youth, "the hope of tomorrow" for the community, was to a great extent contingent upon the entire family's participation in and support of the Y's overall program—thus, the committees regularly planned activities involving parents as much as possible.[56] There were "Father and Son" and "Mother and Son" banquets. Tickets for the banquets were available for a nominal fee of 75 cents for both parent and son. But since this cost sometimes represented the wages of an hour and a half, subsidized tickets were also available to ensure that those parents who wanted to attend could accompany their sons. There was also a special "Parents Night," when parents were given the opportunity to observe the physical skills their children had learned during the year. The swimming exhibition and Ping-Pong and billiards tournaments, which were sponsored by the Boys Department, provided family entertainment and attracted large numbers to the YMCA. Moreover, these projects did much to enhance the self-concepts and self-images of the youths. Nearly 3,000 boys attended some 187 meetings in 1927, the most popular of which were the Sunday afternoon religious and social activities.[57]

Although religion pervaded all of the activities of the Michigan Avenue Y, specific programs were designed to meet the religious needs of the members. Charles Sims, Peter Lomax, and Justice Taylor of the Religious Work Committee scheduled Bible study sessions every Sunday morning. These sessions were planned primarily for the men who lived in the dormitory. The Sunday afternoon meetings, however, were open to the public and consisted of a lecture followed by a general discussion. The usual topics were contemporary concerns such as the problem of young people and the church, or themes selected from the Bible.[58] Through these programs the youths had a forum in which to discuss problems in a wide variety of areas. Once a month, high school girls were even invited to these discussions. The Religious Work Committee also scheduled movies on Tuesday, Friday, and Saturday evenings, with the intention of keeping the youngsters off the street and away from the "vicious places" of the city.

The task of creating and implementing a program which would not only affect the social conditions of African Americans in Buffalo, but which also would have significant ramifications for their economic situation was assigned to the Education Committee in 1928: Secretary Jackson, Ninde Davis, attorney C. M. Maloney, and J. Herman Daves. The Y scheduled several classes during the 1928–1929 fiscal year and students could enroll by paying the $2 registration fee.[59] The curriculum of the Education Department also reflected the philosophy of the managers and founders. These men were generally pragmatists and, thus, the courses were designed to meet the immediate and long-term needs of the black community. At first glance the course offerings were somewhat conservative, but since the chief goal of the Michigan Avenue YMCA was to elevate the black community, the managers usually sought the most efficacious methods for solving immediate contemporary problems. Music appreciation was the only "academic" subject offered. Students who enrolled in this course underwent a rigorous six-month training program which was intended "to prepare persons for successful singing for positions in church choirs and through them to advance the cause of *artistic* singing" (emphasis added).[60] Students in the music institute frequently performed in public concerts. These musical performances and concerts guaranteed that the Michigan Avenue Y would continue to attract the attention of potential benefactors, both black and white.

The Metropolitan YMCA in Buffalo had established vocational courses including auto mechanics, accounting, and plumbing in the branches in 1900.[61] Yet these fields, which required greater skills and commanded higher wages, were not taught at the Michigan Avenue Y. Only two vocational courses were offered at the black branch of the Y in 1928, furnace operation and household management, because individuals who completed them generally were able to secure immediate employment. Males enrolled in the "Essentials of Furnace Operation," a four-month course designed to promote safety and economy for those persons interested in operating steam boilers. Topics for discussion included: how to start a good fire; dampers; fire doors; coal; how or when to put on or take off the draft; fluctuations of furnace temperatures; and steam pressure.[62] The four-month course in household management, or "domestic science," included topics on household values, house management–arithmetical problems, housewifery, renovation, menu planning, preparation of food, table service, child care, budgets and home life, and hospitality.[63] The course was justified by the Education Committee because of the marketability of the skills which were taught. It was extremely difficult for black women to secure employment outside of the domestic area; if most black women were to work as domestics, then let them be the best that money could buy. Black women would then monopolize this business and at least minimize foreign competition. The advertisement for the course reflected this sentiment:

> Positions requiring special skills in the household industries are multiplying. The skilled household assistant who is capable of assuming responsibility for the wise administration of the household activities, as well as for their performance, is demanded in the modern home, and training in the home economics is imperative for one who would fill such a position.
>
> There is an increasing demand for the intelligent young woman trained in child care to act as children's nurse. Homemaking training offers an opportunity for development of special talents and for active participation in the *progress* of the race (emphasis added).[64]

The Michigan Y also served as an employment agency for black workers, and William Jackson was successful in placing many individuals in positions requiring skills acquired from courses taught at the Y.[65]

In the 1920s, the Metropolitan Branch YMCA of Buffalo had expanded, but when the Great Depression hit the city, the Buffalo Association was compelled to curtail many of its programs. The Y's emphasis shifted to that of conserving financial resources and in some instances guaranteeing the survival of the branches. Although the endowment funds of the Y were not immediately jeopardized, the operating budget was deficient from 1929 through 1942, when the Board of Directors consented to become a part of the War Chest Fund.[66] (Throughout the entire period of economic decline, the Buffalo Association had avoided this fate because it feared that it would be conceived as a charity organization by the public, thereby threatening its basic goals.) To help ease its financial burden, the board initially decided to terminate personnel. The physical directors in the branches were the first individuals to be cut, and part-time employees replaced them. This stop-gap measure was inadequate to solve the YMCA's financial crisis, and the board cut the salaries of its entire staff; simultaneously, it sought to negotiate new settlement agreements on the loans it owed to several local financiers. Although these negotiations were successful, the Central YMCA discontinued some of its projects. Its educational program was one of the first to be suspended, and finally in 1931, the Association closed three of its branches: West Side, South Buffalo, and Humboldt.[67] However, the YMCA was able to continue its programs in most of the branches mainly because they were well organized and each experienced volunteer assistance.[68] The Michigan Avenue YMCA also averted retrenchment because of its special endowment funds. Nevertheless, membership declined, and in an attempt to stem this trend, in 1933 the Association reduced membership fees considerably in all of its branches. Boys at the Michigan Avenue YMCA paid 50 cents in annual fees plus 5 cents per month; men were assessed a fee of $3 per year. In the other branches, fees were reduced to $2 and $3 annually for boys and $12 and $14 for men.[69]

In the face of such cutbacks, it is remarkable that by the 1931-1932 fiscal year the course offerings of the Michigan Avenue YMCA had been expanded greatly. The music appreciation course saw the greatest revision. The title of the course was changed to the YMCA Institute of Music and included sight-reading, vocal training, organ, and a capella choir for women. The Y sponsored its own quintette, composed of members of the Institute of Music. Special courses on piano and violin were scheduled, too. The Sunday afternoon tea provided the setting for a music appreciation hour which allowed young people to display their unique musical talents.[70] Although no YWCA was established for blacks in Buffalo, classes were set up for women and girls at the black YMCA.[71] A sewing course designed primarily for female heads of households taught the making of garments and remodeling and repairing older clothes: "We feel certain with every housewife having knowledge of how to do those things, she and her children will have more clothes, better clothes, and a larger bank account."[72] The Needle Art Club, which had been organized for girls ranging from age nine to fifteen during the

1929-1930 fiscal year, was quite popular. This course was designed to teach girls to appreciate "the beauty of art" and to give them the advantage of "making a home beautiful as they grow into womanhood."[73] A public speaking course (taught by Reverend J. Edward Nash) and English grammar (with Otis Davenport Jackson as the primary instructor) were also added to the academic program.

While the program of the Education Committee provided opportunities for blacks to advance, it did not provide courses in the skilled trades from which blacks virtually had been excluded. This policy prevailed throughout the 1930s and the 1940s because of the basic utilitarian outlook of the Board of Managers of the Michigan Avenue Y. The outlook was not unique to this Y. It had been a part of the initial YMCA policy and the practical character of the Y expanded after the turn of the century.[74]

Certainly this prevailing philosophy resulted in the establishment of the vocational schools at the Metropolitan Y.[75] The managers of the black branch not only had to be aware of YMCA principles, but they also had to be cognizant of the social reality Buffalo presented—i.e., in addition to the declining economy, African Americans had to deal with the traditional prejudice and discrimination which confronted them in the city.[76]

During the 1936-1937 fiscal year, the Education Committee set up a college catalogue library and counseling service for those individuals who wished to pursue a college education. By 1939, there was a concern among committee members about the lack of guidance programs for the hundreds of black youths who were graduating from high school with little knowledge of what the future held for them.[77] The committee believed that a guidance program would help black youths "steer clear of the pitfalls of the passing generation" of high school graduates.[78] Moreover, in October 1937, Secretary Jackson announced that courses in shorthand and typing would be formed because of the increasing opportunities in business for black women. It was all the more necessary that these courses become a part of the YMCA curriculum, for business schools in Buffalo refused to admit black women.[79] This problem confronted black women whenever they sought to improve their educational skills and thereby enhance their access to a greater variety of jobs. One student reported that her attempt to enroll in the State Normal School elicited the following comment from an admissions counselor: "We only admit students whom we can place and being Colored is like having one eye, one arm, or one leg."[80] It was equally difficult for blacks to gain admission to the nurses' training programs that the local hospitals conducted, and this state of affairs seriously jeopardized black community efforts to move forward economically. In response, the YMCA provided crucial training programs so that some women would be prepared to assume positions in fields from which they traditionally had been barred. Students who enrolled in the business courses at the Y were required to pay only a small fee for the rental of the typewriters.[81]

One of the most popular and elaborate educational programs implemented by the Education Committee was a series of public forums beginning in the 1929–1930 fiscal year. Although the forums ostensibly were directed at the adult members of the Y, they were open to the public. One could purchase an admission ticket for the season for $1.25 or pay 50 cents for each session. Prominent figures were invited to participate in the forums, and the list of those who spoke reads like a "Who's Who in Black America." Between 1930 and 1936, among the individuals who participated in the Annual Forums were: Dr. Mordecai Johnson, president of Howard University; Dr. W. E. B. DuBois, editor of the *Crisis;* Congressman Oscar Depriest; Mary McLeod Bethune, president of Bethune-Cookman College; Nannie Burroughs, president of the National Training School for Women and Girls; Walter White, executive secretary of the NAACP; and Mary Church Terrell, first president of the National Association of Colored Women.[82]

Most of these lecturers, like the founders and managers of the Michigan Avenue YMCA, were associated with the South, particularly through their educational backgrounds. Most of them depended upon the black community for their livelihood and either worked within the community or performed services organized explicitly to serve that community. They, too, were imbued with the philosophy of self-help and racial solidarity. C. C. Spaulding, president of the North Carolina Mutual Insurance Company of Durham, lectured on "Negro Achievement in Business." During one of his visits to Buffalo, in 1935, W. E. B. DuBois addressed the topic "Italy and Ethiopia." The Italian attack on Ethiopia was a major concern of black Americans, and blacks throughout the country rallied to aid the Ethiopian cause through financial contributions and by helping to influence public opinion.[83] Their support represented both self-help and racial pride.

The lectures often presented goals toward which the youth of the black community could strive. President Johnson of Howard University, in his address "Religion and Poverty," delivered at the tenth anniversary celebration of the Michigan Avenue YMCA, exhorted the community: "The message that religion gives to the poor man is the message God gave to Ezekial; 'Son of man, stand upon your own feet. . . .' God makes no promise to take care of you unless you stand up on your own feet."[84] Johnson also asked Orthodox Christians to consider "dispassionately and constructively all adverse criticisms against religion, admit its shortcomings, and seek improvements in the light of present-day needs." The public forums were a means for providing increased self-awareness within the black community. Patrons of the YMCA were well represented at the forums, along with hundreds of people from the local community. Newspaper accounts frequently referred to the well-attended performances and lectures, and noted the interracial composition of the audiences.[85]

The Michigan Avenue YMCA was involved in numerous other programs designed to advance the social, economic, and intellectual conditions of blacks in Buffalo. Often professionals and organizations from the larger Buffalo community joined with black individuals and groups to present social programs. In the 1930s, the association established the "Negro Health Week" lectures. Dr. I. L. Scruggs presided over the Negro Health Week program and—joined by Dr. Marvin Israel and Dr. Nat Kutzman from the larger Buffalo community, Dr. Yerby Jones, and Dr. Theodore Kakaza, South African emigre and former president of the local branch (or "unit") of the Universal Negro Improvement Association—presented a series of lectures dealing with such topics as "Health Problems in Your Family," "Dental Hygiene," "Communicable Diseases," "Heart Disease," and "Personal Hygiene."[86] Twenty other organizations joined the Y in sponsoring the health lecture series, including the Prince Hall Masons, the Adult Education Center, the Buffalo Department of Health, Public School 32, the Memorial Center and Urban League, Inc., the City Federation of Women's Clubs, and the Book Lover's Club.[87] Sessions were held at the Michigan Avenue YMCA and other social and community centers throughout the city.[88]

The Michigan Avenue YMCA addressed many of the social needs of its black constituents through its guidance program, its health program, its course offerings, its physical education department, its dormitory, and most important, its educational programs. Under the capable leadership of William Jackson, it was considered quite successful by local residents. Jackson's dedication to the Y led one contemporary to remark, "W. H. Jackson, Executive Secretary of the 'Y' Branch, has done more for the Negro race in Buffalo than any other colored man. . . ."[89] The leadership ability demonstrated by Secretary Jackson and his aides was recognized by individuals inside and outside of Buffalo. NAACP Director of Branches William Pickens contacted Jackson in an attempt to gain his assistance in reorganizing the floundering Buffalo chapter during the early years of the Great Depression.[90]

The men and women who were instrumental in the establishment and direction of the Michigan Avenue YMCA had a vision for the black people of Buffalo. They conceived of the Y as a force in elevating or improving the social, cultural, intellectual, and educational conditions of that community. They moved with what, at times, appeared to be a "messianic fervor" in planning and promoting activities which would improve the social environment within the community and, at the same time, ameliorate race relations within the city. Indeed, in an environment plagued by discrimination and segregation, with limited opportunities to climb the social or occupational ladder, the Y provided an opportunity for some black youths, such as Russell Service and Arthur Griffa, to achieve professional status within the Y.[91] Leroy Coles, longtime executive secretary of the Buffalo Urban League, and the late Daniel Acker, a president of the NAACP, grew up as members of the Michigan Avenue YMCA.[92] Many youths were placed in jobs in industry and private homes as a result of the recommendations they received from the Y. Still others were encouraged to attend college through the career guidance program offered at the Michigan Avenue YMCA.

The Michigan Avenue Y was generally at the forefront of social activities in the black community. Its tournaments, forums, and later the newspaper it published presented favorable images of African Americans to the populace of Buffalo. The expansion of its programs and facilities, the increase in attendance at its functions, and the long list of successful persons today who grew up as members of the Michigan Avenue Y all attest to its achievements.[93] The self-help emphasis of the Y and the efficiency ethic of the 1920s led to the creation of an educational program that became an important source of "racial pride" for black Buffalonians. The success of the Michigan Avenue YMCA in meeting its challenges can be attributed primarily to the men and women who provided shrewd leadership in mobilizing and bringing into the Y diverse groups from within the Buffalo community, as well as the veteran professionals who were called upon to guide its projects. Moreover, the programs they established attracted a large endowment fund which guaranteed that the Michigan Avenue YMCA's programs would continue to serve Buffalo's African American community.[94] The Michigan Avenue YMCA was an important phase in the African Americans' quest for community and self-determination and just one more weapon in an arsenal that would be used to build a modern community for the black citizens of Buffalo.

Not Alms,
but Opportunity

Although the Michigan Avenue YMCA effectively addressed certain problems experienced by African Americans in Buffalo, there were other areas it left untouched. Housing was among the foremost problems, for the Y was designed to provide housing only for transients. Unemployment, which reached mammoth proportions among blacks in Buffalo by the end of the decade, was another pressing concern. And while the Y's director, William Jackson, had succeeded in placing a few youngsters in service positions, this barely scratched the surface of the problem. There was no effective vehicle for educating the black population about disease prevention, and few agencies did anything to solve the problems of those who suffered from various illnesses. All of these issues critically affected the lives of black Buffalonians during this era. The hardships African Americans endured all were exacerbated by the continuing influx of blacks to the city and the racial hostility that greeted them. A number of race-conscious blacks and civic-minded whites recognized the necessity of alleviating the plight of Buffalo's black populace, for they realized that the community's prosperity was dependent upon the success of each of its components.

The National Urban League had been organized in 1911 as a result of the merger of the Committee for Improving Industrial Conditions of Negroes in New York, the National League for the Protection of Colored Women, and the Committee on Urban Conditions among Negroes in New York.[1] The various units which comprised the league had been dedicated to solving the immediate problems of urban blacks. The newly formed league would continue in this vein.

There was some sentiment in Buffalo that a branch of the Urban League should be established to explore ways of solving the critical issues facing the local black community. Specifically, its object was "to ensure for Negroes in work and in play, in study, in health, and in living conditions, depending upon the needs of the community, the greatest possible degree of equality and opportunity in accordance with the faith which gave birth and meaning to the United States of America."[2] Charles S. Johnson, director of research for the National Urban League, was commissioned to make a thorough investigation of the plight of black Buffalonians. Johnson completed his study in 1923, and concluded that the situation of Buffalo's African American populace was deplorable and was deteriorating rapidly.[3] Moreover, Johnson noted that Buffalo would be a fruitful field in which to carry out the league's work.

All of the services in which the Memorial Center and Urban League of Buffalo engaged under the leadership of William Evans had a significant impact on the lives of black and white Buffalonians. Its professional staff of paid and volunteer workers, its keen sensitivity and responsibility to the black community, and the judicious and expeditious manner in which it sought solutions to social and economic issues confronting blacks won it community support and respect. The league's accessibility and harmonious relationships with the community reinforced the black community's persistent demands for it to push further in certain directions and to initiate programs in others. A contemporary remarked that William Evans, executive secretary of the Buffalo Urban League, was one of two individuals who had contributed most to the African American community of Buffalo.

Interest in establishing a branch of the League in Buffalo stalled after Johnson's report; there was no follow-up from the Buffalo group.[4] Not until 1926, as migrants continued to pour into the city and as support services to blacks remained woefully inadequate, was interest in the Urban League rekindled. In September, T. Arnold Hill, industrial relations secretary of the National Urban League, asked Reverend Sidney O. B. Johnson, pastor of Lloyd Memorial Congregational Church, to lend his support to the league's efforts to organize in Buffalo. Hill stressed the importance of soliciting the aid of influential business persons and philanthropists. Shortly thereafter, a committee of key individuals was formed to drum up support. This was essential because Buffalo would have to provide funds for the operation of the league, as well as pay an annual membership fee of 2 percent of its budget to the National Urban League.[5]

A little over a week after he had sought Johnson's support, Hill arrived in Buffalo to ascertain local sentiment regarding a branch of the league. Hill devoted considerable time to interviewing social workers, "who because of their interest in social problems or their sympathy for Negroes" directed him to possible contributors.[6] Interviewing the social workers proved to be beneficial, indeed. Following their advice, Hill was able to concentrate his efforts on the managers of local industries, including the three largest employers of blacks. Not only were these industrialists prospective contributors to the league, but many had expressed an interest in the general social plight of African Americans in the city. Some of these local executives suggested that Hill contact their main offices in New York City, since decisions were made at that level. Their support would prove to be essential in organizing a local chapter of the Urban League.

Hill communicated with several other Buffalonians who had previously been involved in issues related to blacks. One was Eric L. Hedstrom, a businessman who had recently embarked upon a project designed to construct housing for blacks and who chaired the committee of the Federation of Churches which had begun to investigate the problems of African Americans in Buffalo. Another, a Mr. Emerson—general manager of the Standard Oil Company and an active member of the local Presbyterian Church, which sponsored the Memorial Chapel, a settlement house with a large black clientele—proved to be of great assistance. Attorney Albrecht was contacted; he had handled the trust fund George Mathews had established for the Michigan Avenue YMCA. Reverend Alfred Priddis, assistant to the bishop of the Episcopal Church, promised financial support from his church. At his conference with W. H. Crosby of the Iron Company and Mr. Peake of the American Radiator Company, both expressed a desire to see "Negroes integrated into the community." A. H. Whitford recommended that Hill discuss plans for the Urban League with attorney John Sprague, a friend of the late Booker T. Washington. Other prominent figures in professional and social circles of Buffalo were also referred to Hill.[7]

Hill's visit to Buffalo culminated in a joint meeting with those persons with whom he had spoken or who had expressed interest in the Urban League. David Adie presided over this meeting. The Reverends Elijah Echols, Sidney O. B. Johnson, and J. Edward Nash, along with social worker Clara Payne, represented the black community. From the outset, the Urban League was designed to be an interracial organization whose intent was not only to alleviate the harsh economic conditions which blacks experienced, but also to ameliorate race relations in general. T. Arnold Hill explained:

> The Urban League is a coordinating agency; its aim is to get things done, to work with all agencies. It is directive, has on hand a body of information and fact. It is interracial, has a colored executive secretary and both races on the board; [the League] tries to eradicate discordant elements in the community. It works on city problems—housing, industry, recreation, etc., whatever is not being taken care of already.[8]

Groundbreaking of the Michigan Avenue Baptist Church.
Among those present: Reverend J. Edward Nash, Sr., third
from right, with Frances and Jesse Nash, Jr. Courtesy of the
Buffalo and Erie County Historical Society.

Reverend Sidney O. B.
Johnson, pastor of the
Lloyd Memorial Congre-
gational Church. Cour-
tesy of the Mamie John-
son Family Collection.

Members of the league were required to pay a minimum annual dues of $1, which entitled them to elect members to the Board of Directors. The board, in turn, appointed committees which carried out the routine operations of the league. A salaried executive secretary supervised the overall activities.

Some members of the organizing committee expressed grave doubts as to the feasibility of the Buffalo community raising the $6,000 which would guarantee the league's survival for at least one year. Their fears were exacerbated further when David Adie proposed that blacks contribute 25 percent of the needed funds as an indication that they favored the league's establishment.[9] Reverend Johnson questioned the propriety of expecting blacks to contribute such a large proportion of the budget:

> We need the League to open up industrial opportunities. Is it right to try to get 25% of [the League's] support from negroes, when [the] benefit of better interracial conditions will be felt by the whole community?[10]

Will Mosher Clark, principal of Public School 32, concurred with Johnson. However, he believed that the funding of the League should be a matter of "self-help and not charity." Reverend Nash expressed some misgivings about the response of the organizing committee should the Buffalo Council of Social Agencies fail to endorse the Urban League as one of its projects. This, in essence, meant that the survival of the league would be contingent solely upon individual contributions. These were questions left to be resolved at the future meetings.[11]

But the most crucial question affecting the status of the Buffalo Urban League was raised by several key white figures, including Virginia Schoellkopf, philanthropist and wife of the Hudson Power Plant magnate, who questioned the necessity of establishing a branch of the league, for it was her understanding that the Urban League would only duplicate the services currently being rendered by the Michigan Avenue YMCA. A. H. Whitford and William Jackson of the YMCA allayed her fears by assuring her that the work of the YMCA was outside of that performed by the Urban League.

Blacks, on the other hand, were supportive of the efforts to establish a league branch, although prior to the October meeting a number of prominent black clergymen opposed its establishment because they believed it would jeopardize the social service programs sponsored by their own churches.[12] But after David Adie and Hill addressed it, the black ministers' council unanimously voted to approve the formation of the league and urged that their vote be registered with the Buffalo Council of Social Agencies.[13] The ministers' support virtually guaranteed the support of their congregations. Hill commented that their action was "perhaps the most encouraging during his entire visit." The organizing committee voted to continue to map out plans for a local chapter. Hill left with the intention of returning to Buffalo after the first of the year to conclude his work with the founding committee.

The economic crisis during the late 1920s undoubtedly had some bearing on the number of blacks who were employed in the city's factories. Nevertheless, the proportion of blacks working in major industries was about the same as it had been in 1923, when Johnson completed his study of Buffalo blacks. This situation influenced many blacks to advocate on behalf of the league because they envisioned it as a possible solution to one of their community's most critical issues. Thus, community groups and "Friends of the League" sponsored a number of projects, such as dinners, teas, concerts, and fashion shows, within the community to raise funds. The Shiloh Baptist Church was a leading supporter. Reverend Echols had previously announced that the Men's Brotherhood at Shiloh had voted unanimously in favor of the league and pledged to provide some financial backing. St. Luke's AME Zion and the white Universalist Unitarian churches actively championed the league.[14] Social services agencies, such as the Council of Social Agencies, the Children's Aid Society, and the YWCA, also advocated the league.[15] The aid of all these groups and other organizations in the black community assured that the league would be a reality in 1926.

The work of the organizing committee continued. A specific program designed to achieve the goals established by the National Urban League was drawn up for the Buffalo chapter. The league's major goals were to help black migrants adjust to their new, urban environment and to mollify race relations. The gravest concerns of blacks in Buffalo were employment, housing, and health. The new organization intended to focus on these issues and to serve as a "clearinghouse and correlating agency for the social service work among the colored people in Buffalo."[16] It proposed to strengthen those activities currently under way and to develop new mechanisms for dealing with the foregoing problems when necessary. The industrial program was designed to place workers in positions which provided an opportunity for advancement. The health department aimed to conduct a massive educational program which would inform African Americans about preventive care or symptoms and notify them of available clinics and health facilities. The housing division planned to work with the municipal housing department and with agencies that regulated housing so that more sound, sanitary structures would be made available to blacks.

The bylaws of the National Urban League provided that an interracial board of at least fifteen dedicated and knowledgeable men and women be established to govern the league. It was recommended that seven or eight African Americans serve on the board. Board members were to be selected solely upon their ability to implement the league's programs.[17] A special committee of five appointed by the Buffalo Council of Social Agencies was authorized to select the board members, five of whom would serve for one year; the others would serve for three years. The ten remaining board members would elect five members for a three-year term, establishing a rotating membership which would allow for continuity. An alternative provision allowed for the general membership to elect persons to fill the expired term. The committee devised an austerity budget for the Buffalo chapter that allowed only two salaried employees—an executive secretary at a salary of $3,000, and a stenographer at $1,200. The remaining $1,800 was allocated for operating expenses and travel.

In 1927, David Adie, then secretary of the founding committee, summoned interested persons to a February 2 meeting at the Charity Organization Society on Franklin Street where, under the direction of T. A. Hill, they actually initiated organizational procedures for a local branch of the Urban League. In a matter of ten days their task was accomplished. The Buffalo Urban League, in addition to serving blacks in Buffalo, would map out a program which would embrace all of Erie County, especially the industrial suburb of Lackawanna. The local press hailed its establishment as a landmark in race relations in the "Queen City."[18] The new branch of the Urban League was scheduled to open shop early in the spring after an executive secretary had been appointed.

Despite the interest, the Urban League's future remained tenuous during the early months, as was quite evident at the first Board of Directors meeting, held on February 11, 1927. Douglas Falconer, chairman of the organizing committee and of the temporary organization, presided. He explained that the eight remaining vacancies on the Board of Directors would be filled gradually as suitable individuals who were willing to serve were identified. While the organizers felt that industry should be well represented on the board, Falconer announced that diverse interests should be considered also, yet the organizers had not been successful in delineating these interests. For these reasons, Falconer argued that permanent elections should be postponed and only temporary officers appointed.[19]

Interracial conflict seemed to underlie the disorganization and became even more apparent when Irene J. Graham of the YWCA informed Hill that the local branch of the league was in a "critical" state. Graham attributed the problem to ignorance of the league's goals on the part of the "so carefully chosen directors." Moreover, she revealed that the board members were not overwhelmingly enthusiastic about conducting important interviews in Hill's presence. These board members now showed the same disdain for Clara Payne and the other blacks.[20] During

William L. Evans, Executive Secretary of the Buffalo Urban League, 1927–1963. Evans Family Collection. Courtesy of Mrs. Theresa G. Evans.

this time, it was not unusual for even liberal whites to ignore the opinions of the black community leaders whom they ostensibly supported. Other such incidents impeded the league's progress. However, once the executive secretary arrived on the scene, the energy of all factions was channelled into enthusiastic support.

William L. Evans, former industrial work secretary of the Chicago Urban League, arrived in Buffalo to assume the position of executive secretary of the Buffalo Urban League on June 1, 1927. He was well suited for this position. A native of Louisville, Kentucky, Evans had earned a bachelor of arts degree from Fisk University, and he had studied engineering and architecture at Columbia University. Evans continued his schooling, and in 1935 he earned a masters in sociology from the University of Buffalo.[21] He came to Buffalo armed with a wealth of knowledge and experience which included teaching, urban planning, and addressing the labor problems of urban blacks.[22] This broad range of study and experience, coupled with his astute leadership abilities, enabled Evans to effectively direct the local league's projects.

Evans found an executive board of 24 members awaiting his arrival. The board comprised a number of business and professional members, as well as influential lay people. The Board of Directors was composed primarily of native-born white male Protestants (eleven), most of whom were prominent businessmen—such as C. M. Ramsdell, vice president of the Manufacturers and Traders Trust Company; attorney John Sprague; and stockbroker Carl Bowman. However, other members, like Unitarian minister Palfrey Perkins, the board's first president, Dr. Don Tullis of the Council of Churches, and Alfred Priddis of the Episcopal Church, were renowned in religious circles. Rabbi Joseph L. Fink served as a member of the Urban League's first Board of Directors, too. Of the six white female board members, Virginia Schoellkopf and Mary Hedstrom were married to influential business executives and were committed to social reform and philanthropy; three represented the Lafayette Presbyterian Church, including the former head worker of the Memorial Center, Eleanor Emerson; Freda Seigworth, director of Industrial Relations for the Young Women's Christian Association, was also a board member.

The six black members of the executive board were prominent in other social organizations within the black community also. Black board members were Reverend Elijah Echols of Shiloh Baptist Church, vice president of the League; social workers Elizabeth Talbert (secretary) and Clara Payne; social activist Lucy Bethel, wife of the prominent minister of Saint Luke's AME Zion Church and chair of the Ladies Auxiliary; and physicians John L. Waters and Ivorite Scruggs.[23] Other members of the first Board of Directors were David C. Adie, secretary, Buffalo Council of Social Agencies; Will Mosher Clark, principal of Public School 32; Douglas Falconer, executive director of the Children's Aid Society; Claude Peake, a local industrialist; and George Neumann, a University of Buffalo sociology professor. The Lafayette Presbyterian representatives on the board were Mrs. Frank Messenger and Mrs. J. G. Meidenbauer.[24]

The proposed budget of $6,000 was a minimum figure and proved to be insufficient. The actual cost of operating the Buffalo Urban League during the first year was $9,000. By the time Evans arrived, only $4,000 had been raised. Local blacks had donated only $875.98 of their $1,000 pledge. The Ladies Auxiliary, a group of black women whose chief function was to promote Urban League endeavors and to study the community's social problems, set out to raise the balance due.[25] Virginia Schoellkopf, chairman of the Finance Committee, donated the balance, thus guaranteeing that the branch would be fiscally solvent. Schoellkopf continued to underwrite the league's budget until it was admitted to the Joint Charities, the forerunner of the United Fund, in 1929.[26]

The Urban League and the Memorial Chapel were united in 1929. The circumstances which led to the merger are worth noting and entail a discussion of Memorial Chapel. In 1865, the Lafayette Avenue Presbyterian Church established the Memorial Chapel, a social center designed to accommodate German children, especially those who lacked

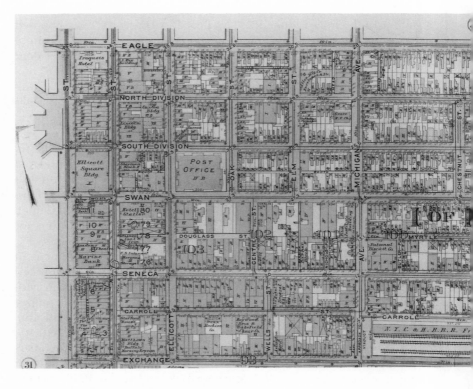

This 1917 map outlines what would become the core of the
African American community by the 1930s. Century Atlas
Company of Greater Buffalo. Courtesy of the New York State
Library.

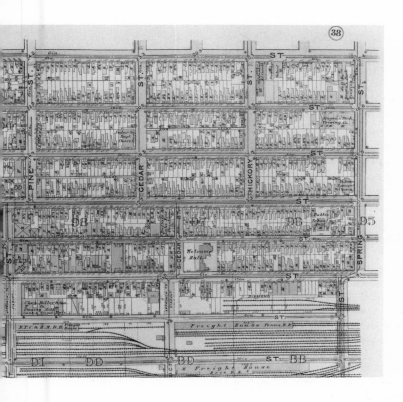

an English-speaking Sunday school. Located in the area just east of the downtown business district, the center soon attracted other immigrant groups and with the post–World War I migration of blacks to Buffalo, its clientele became distinctly biracial. Its culturally diverse programs attempted to dissolve racial hostilities and interethnic conflict within the neighborhood. Memorial Chapel provided classes in crafts, home economics, and some academic subjects.

By the latter part of the 1920s, both the Urban League and the Memorial Center sought funding from the Joint Charities of Buffalo. The charity organization suggested that a merger would lead to greater efficiency, since the goals and objectives of the two groups were similar and they served virtually the same clientele. The boards of directors of the two agencies agreed to merge. In 1929, the Memorial Center and Urban League constructed a constitution which pledged

> To bring about coordination among the existing agencies and organizations for improving the industrial, economic, social, and spiritual condition of Negroes; to develop other agencies and organizations where necessary; to remove the causes of interracial friction and to promote the forces that make for harmony; and through its social center to attempt to meet the needs of the immediate neighborhood in making possible fuller and happier life in the community and every individual in it. To conduct and promote activities (interracial and otherwise) in the fields of education and recreation; to develop community leadership; to act as an interpreter by providing a place where people of different backgrounds, races, and opportunities may meet one another in a natural human relationship, leading to a fuller mutual understanding and sympathy, and in general to promote, encourage, assist, and engage in any and all kinds of work for improving conditions within the city of Buffalo . . . and to do any and all things necessary or incidental to the carrying on of such work.[27]

This document remained the basis for their collaboration on various social issues which affected the community until 1947, when the Urban League dissolved the partnership.[28]

During its first year in operation, the league headquarters on William Street was bustling with activity, and it earned nearly $5,100 from membership fees alone.[29] Although the league was established to work with the migrant black population, its membership, consisting of sixteen nationalities, reflected the diverse ethnic backgrounds of the community in which its headquarters was located.[30] Blacks, by far, comprised the largest segment of the membership, followed by Italians and Jews, and significant numbers of Syrians, Germans, and WASPs.[31]

The league's initial program consisted of 21 projects designed to be all-encompassing: employment and related activities, health, criminal justice, family and welfare, housing, and education. A study of each of these programs will elucidate the Urban League's role in social uplift in Buffalo's black neighborhoods and how it helped both to define and support their notion of community.

Employment concerns were the most critical issues confronting the newly established league. The general secretary and the members of the Board of Directors were gravely concerned about the resultant economic plight of black Buffalonians, for the industrial situation in Buffalo was worse than in most cities.[32] By 1931, most blacks had been in Buffalo fewer than ten years and most of them had experienced a three-year period of unemployment.[33] The Board of Directors of the League and the executive secretary believed that unemployment lay at the root of many of the other social ills prevalent in the community at the time.[34]

The Industrial Department of the league began several projects to improve employment prospects. Evans had served as industrial work secretary for the Chicago Urban League from 1919 to 1926, the Urban League's first Industrial Work Secretary.[35] He arrived at the Urban League headquarters in Buffalo on June 1, 1927 with a definite notion of how best to address this problem of unemployment. His solution included a twofold plan to improve the working conditions of African Americans and simultaneously to increase black employment.

To achieve the latter, the league sponsored a series of forums and conferences with local industries. League officials hoped that through "gentle persuasion" industrialists would begin to experiment with the use of African American labor. Many employers had failed to hire blacks in some instances because of their own preconceived notions of inadequate black performance on the job, and in other instances because of the racist attitudes of white workers.[36] Evans did not limit his propaganda campaign solely to entrepreneurs. He also addressed community groups, and during his first year as executive secretary he lectured some 56 community groups on such topics as "Industrial Efficiency," "Creating Business from Negro Resources," "Industrial Opportunities for Colored People," and "Using Educational Facilities." These lectures generally were well attended; the average attendance among white organizations was 74. Blacks also poured out in record numbers in response to the league's efforts.[37]

The league's involvement in the unemployment issue did not yield immediate results. Between July and October of 1928, 113 persons registered for employment at the league's office, bringing the total who had applied for work to 158. At the same time, employers submitted 31 requests for female workers; 24 were actually placed. In the case of males there were only seven requests and six placements. Women were readily placed because they were hired as domestics and it was socially acceptable to employ black women in such positions. Evans noted that

"September showed a rather unusual activity for domestic workers, probably due to the fact that housekeepers returned at that time from their summer homes."[38] A substantial increase in the number of married women with children applied for work at the league's offices in 1929. These mothers found it necessary to provide for their families, since their husbands had been unsuccessful in securing employment.[39] This trend continued throughout the decade.

The Urban League sponsored its first industrial conference in December 1929. Calling together representatives from industry, the New York State Employment Service, and the Industrial Aid Bureau, the league gained support and petitioned Public Works Commissioner Fisk to give preference "to local workers rather than [disreputable] transients from Hotel DeGink" and Canadian nationals. The league urged the city to speed up the job-creation process and reported that the mayor had announced that he was initiating a policy that would end racial discrimination in the Industrial Aid Bureau.[40]

Evans reported that a black woman was hired as manager of the Sinclair Service Station at Michigan Avenue and Sycamore Street; this was the only instance in which a major white corporation employed a black person in a managerial position. Despite the fact that this occurrence was unprecedented, it portended a new trend of hiring black managers to operate white-owned businesses which catered to blacks. Undoubtedly, the Sinclair Oil Company was motivated by a desire to undercut its competition, especially the two black men who had opened a service station at the corner of Sycamore and Oak streets, and who had the support and patronage of those blacks who considered their enterprise an example of the progress of the race.[41] During the fall of 1931, Standard Oil placed black attendants in several other service stations catering mainly to blacks. Mixed crews of blacks and whites were experimented with at two stations, and twelve black youths were hired as car washers in a downtown station.[42]

The league's attempt to secure positions for blacks as taxicab drivers in companies owned and operated by whites was also unsuccessful. Owners contended that their insurance companies would cancel their policies if they employed black chauffeurs. They agreed, however, to hire blacks in other capacities, such as cleaners, mechanics, and garage attendants. Another company, the Forty Cent Taxicab Company, founded by a Mr. Kleinfelder, hired African American drivers only, in an obvious attempt to corner the market in the black areas of the city where nationalistic tendencies often were manifested by campaigns to "buy black" and to support those businesses which employed blacks. The black-owned My-Cab Company had been forced into bankruptcy when its insurance policy was canceled because it hired black drivers only. Through persistent harassment, the local police also helped to bring about the company's demise. In view of the My-Cab Company's fate, Evans and his staff watched the "innovation," as evidenced by Kleinfelder's enterprise, with "interest." The Brown Bomber Taxi Company later provided service to the East Side community. Some corporations refused to even consider the employment of "colored people on any account." The DuPont Rayon Company personified this group. Its manager, Mr. DuPont, even refused to grant Evans an interview.[43]

The following year, the league's fortunes improved somewhat and the young organization could list among its accomplishments the placement of 77 individuals in the job market; six were placed in skilled positions, earning more than $50 per week.[44] These men worked with people of diverse ethnic backgrounds and their performance on the job had been exemplary, thus enhancing the league's credibility with employers. Arrangements made between the league and the International Railway Company not only included the hiring of blacks but also provisions for their promotion. Although these achievements may appear to be modest, in view of the depth of deprivation blacks experienced in the "City of Good Neighbors" at the time, they were significant. Evans observed:

> We have made some important placements industrially, such as wire drawers, auto mechanics and domestics. While these placements have not been conspicuous, they are important in view of the fact that the Negro group is still seriously restricted in the line of employment in Buffalo.[45]

Also during 1929, the league succeeded in having five African American candidates admitted to take the civil service test for the position of probation officer. Although all passed the examination, none of the five placed in the top ten and thus were not appointed to the post. Despite these results, a precedent had been set, and the fields in which blacks could be employed were expanded further. However, Elizabeth Talbert, who had taken the examination and been placed on the civil service list, gave another account of this situation when she testified before the New York State Temporary Commission on the Condition of the Urban Colored Population in 1937. She informed the commission that the government agencies in Buffalo only made appointments until they reached the level of the black candidates. Thereafter they made temporary appointments until the list had expired.[46] At the same hearing Reverend Sidney O. B. Johnson testified that there were fewer than fifty African American civil servants at all government levels.[47] Johnson also suggested that subterfuge on the part of the government agencies had led to this sad state of affairs. He further added that "as a matter of truth, because of our [African Americans'] lack of political solidarity or strength, hitherto we have not been able to get anything in the way of appointments out of these city departments."[48] In 1931, the league placed 27 men with a public utility company in semi-skilled positions. The experiment proved to be successful, and other blacks were added to the payroll. The same year a black man was hired as manager of a pharmacy in the black community.

The Industrial Department carried on a number of other activities which aided black workers. It maintained a list of the salaries paid for specific jobs, and thus was able to monitor the wages paid to its clientele and to offer guidance in matters relating to salaries. Urban League officials acted as ombudsmen by investigating all complaints involving the unfair dismissal or treatment of African American workers, and disseminated information on workmen's compensation.[49] These services helped make resources available to blacks who had not explored fully other means, either because they lacked familiarity with the avenues which provided such services or because they were repelled by the overt racism of other agencies.

In 1929, the Urban League board ordered an investigation of the working conditions of the Red Caps at the New York Central terminal after they revealed that their wages had been terminated and that the company had employed an anti-union policy which made it virtually impossible to redress their grievances. The league's study indicated not only that the men had not been paid wages, but also that they had to pay 25 cents a day to the chief porter, who increased his staff to 100 men. Although the Red Caps were not considered employees, they were subjected to discipline and regulations on hours of work, and they had to provide their own uniforms. Previously they had received monthly wages of $45. The Urban League forwarded their petition to the station master and the chairman of the Railroad Labor Board. However, the Red Caps' grievances were only redressed in 1933, when the United Transport Workers organized them and became their bargaining agent.[50]

The Industrial Division's program was perhaps the most ambitious of all the Buffalo League's undertakings. Its successes were contingent upon both the cooperation of industrialists and upon the state of the local economy. As early as September 1929, Evans observed that the industrial program was "far from satisfactory."[51] In all of his correspondence to the national office, he deplored the fact that unemployment was increasing. As the city was steadily engulfed by the Depression, conditions for black workers worsened. Evans noted, "The problem grows more acute daily here, and in my opinion there are probably 3,000 Colored workers of the 35,000 unemployed in Buffalo."[52] Eight hundred persons registered for employment in 1931; only 98 were placed in permanent and temporary work.[53] Blacks often were displaced by white workers, even in such traditionally "black" jobs as domestic service.[54] The general secretary observed that this process seemed to be occurring rapidly: "Our office has seen a steady decline [in requests] for Negro maids, chauffeurs, butlers, cooks, waiters, housemen, porters and janitors."[55] Even the Municipal Industrial Department discriminated against blacks through its hiring practices, despite earlier pronouncements to the contrary. It was easier for African Americans to receive doles than to secure employment. The Man-A-Block Plan demonstrated the kind of response blacks could expect from local government agencies which controlled hiring for relief projects: it denied them jobs.[56] Evans and his staff protested the hiring practices of this agency and Chairman Myron Forbes assured Evans that his administrators would no longer deny African Americans work because of race. However, this agreement was reached too late to benefit blacks, for the Man-A-Block project was short-lived.

The Buffalo Maintenance Division refused to employ blacks for trimming trees and shoveling snow, even in those districts where there was a substantial black population.[57] This policy continued to plague blacks throughout the decade. Evans cited as the culprit the absence of African American interviewers in the Industrial Aid Department, a disadvantage which initiated the practice of rank discrimination. He indicated how the policy affected black employment:

> The practice was to have two days in which men could report, the men on the west side reporting on one day [mainly white], and those on the east side reporting another day. The men on the east side were largely negro [*sic*] men. In the snow shoveling period, the weather was so arranged that it didn't snow except on the days the whites reported, so that the negroes [*sic*] didn't have jobs on the days they reported. It [snow] was measured on the part of the Industrial Aid employees, so that the negroes [*sic*] didn't get any work.[58]

Domestic workers faced increasing exploitation as the city became more deeply engulfed in the Depression. Some employers sought only to give them food and shelter, instead of wages, or they offered them the low pay of $2 per week. The league sought to end this practice by arranging a conference of all non-fee employment services and secured their support for a minimum wage of $8 a week for experienced domestic workers and $5 for novices.[59]

While the Buffalo Urban League certainly took the initiative in dealing with issues which plagued the community, it also responded to the pressure that workers and others from the local black community exerted on it to help solve what it considered its gravest problems.[60] Evans admitted that his staff and facilities were inadequate to effectively deal with all of the community's problems: "At times the feeling of utter helplessness and futility of effort has been almost overwhelming as the procession of troubled souls file in and out begging for a chance to be self-supporting." Evans further observed, "At no time has the demand for charity exceeded the plea for opportunity."[61]

The state of the economy compelled the National Urban League and its affiliates to reassess their goals. Given the racist industrial policies of many firms, the league's recruitment activities—always marginal in terms of their success—dwindled to a virtual standstill. At this juncture, league officials could only hope that blacks would not be discriminated against in the distribution of government services and relief, including jobs, food, clothing, and other such aid. The national office asked league officials to accept every invitation to serve on "recovery" committees and to volunteer their services in order to assure that these committees would be sensitive to and begin to address the needs of blacks.

In this vein, William Evans served on the Mayor's Committee on Stabilization, established in 1930 to supervise hiring practices and to create positions. This committee was chaired by Alfred H. Schoellkopf, president of the Industrial Committee of the Buffalo Chamber of Commerce and husband of NUL board member Virginia Schoellkopf.[62] In 1938 Mayor Thomas L. Holling appointed Evans to a four-year term on the City Planning Commission. During his tenure the Kleinhans Music Hall and the Memorial Auditorium were planned.[63] Evans and his staff served on several other committees which affected the lives of black Buffalonians.[64] Moreover, Urban League officials were not totally dependent upon local governmental actions; they also sought assistance from government officials at the state and federal levels, where they believed they would receive more equitable treatment.[65] In expressing his desire to have Frances Perkins, state industrial commissioner at Albany, investigate the conditions in Buffalo, Evans lamented, ". . . we would appreciate any assistance from anywhere on our unemployment situation in Buffalo."[66] The Urban League was acting in concert with the desires of the black workers, who also echoed this sentiment throughout the decade. M. H. Moultrie, of 208 Waverly Street, was one who sought assistance from Commissioner Perkins to secure employment, too. He wrote:

> The government has given the Curtis Aro-Plain company a large order for gov Plains but the Negro is excluded in their factory Can their be something don about this Please exvise us. . . . We need work to and as American Citisen Arnt we entitle to jobs where the gov is spending mony for the defens of this country.[67]

The Buffalo League continued to pursue all options to secure jobs for African Americans. It compiled records on contractors who attempted to secure state contracts. In addition to working with the State Industrial

Committee and the Temporary Commission on the Condition of the Urban Colored Population, New York affiliates went on record in support of several legislative bills which affected state agencies and tax-free enterprises. One measure extended the merit system more equitably by providing that appointing officers must state in the public record the reasons for passing over any individual on a certified list of qualified applicants for positions. Another bill stipulated that utility companies and public works contractors who applied discriminatory hiring practices should be faced with fines or subject to imprisonment. This same provision penalized labor unions which denied persons membership or equal treatment based upon race, creed, or color. The league's support of this legislation represented its first attempt at legal advocacy. The legislature, however, did not pass any of these bills into law until the World War II era.

On the other hand, the Works Progress Administration (WPA) and the National Youth Administration (NYA) provided the Urban League its first opportunity to use legal sanctions to combat discrimination in employment, for government policy stipulated that the use of federal funds was conditional upon full integration without regard to race, creed, or national origin. Despite the traditional discrimination against African Americans in the Buffalo area, the Urban League insisted on a nondiscriminatory policy. Consequently, it received projects that employed over thirty workers at Memorial Center in homemaking, marketing, buying, dietetics, food service, and garment-making. The NYA set up special projects that accommodated over 100 youths at the Urban League. Evans served on the local NYA Board. The league also housed two orchestras and the Buffalo Philharmonic Orchestra until Kleinhans Music Hall was completed. Nevertheless, the league still had to monitor racist practices on WPA and other government-funded projects, insisting that the WPA philharmonic orchestra project include African American musicians. It also investigated discrimination against African American nurses at the Buffalo City Hospital and the Johnson Park Youth Center.[68]

Evans believed that the Emergency Advisory Councils programs ought to be extended. These were committees of well-established blacks who tried to pressure New Deal agencies into addressing the problems of blacks. These committees also instructed blacks on the functions of governmental agencies.[69]

In spite of the Depression, the Buffalo Urban League, like other branches, continued its educational program designed for African American workers. The league now intended to imbue blacks with the knowledge which they would need to fight for their jobs. John T. Clark, of the national league, explained their job programs:

> Our labor program involves Negroes working in all types of Industry and it is our hope that even those employed in the hotels, apartment

houses, or "what not," might be gotten together to carefully go after protecting their jobs during a crisis of this kind when the competition for jobs is so critical.[70]

So, at the same time that the league was negotiating for jobs and overseeing relief activities, black workers themselves would be making efforts to retain their positions. Union activities among blacks in Buffalo had always been limited. In fact, there were only a dozen carpenters and bricklayers who were union members by May 1934.[71] This project proved to be exceedingly challenging, with limited results, not because of a lack of enthusiasm on the part of blacks, but because of the entrenched racist practices of white union officials and union members.

Throughout the Depression, William Evans and his staff struggled to deal with the unemployment issue and continually explored new means of solving this crisis. They attended the regional conferences of the league and participated in the organizing sessions to make certain that Buffalo's unique problems were addressed.[72] Despite all their efforts, the Industrial Department's program remained the weakest link in the league's program.

The Buffalo community received the league's other programs with enthusiasm and the league met with considerable success in those areas where whites were least threatened. Its health program reflected concern for the high mortality rate of blacks in Buffalo. Based on a population of 10,000 in 1928, the death rate for African Americans was 21, almost double that of the general population.[73] Such a high death rate indicated that African Americans in Buffalo suffered from a general ignorance of child care practices and access to affordable health care. The staff of the Buffalo League began to plan health programs during the 1929 fiscal year. An educational program which would make blacks better prepared to use preventive health care measures was the focus of the league's health program.[74] The league also provided services for epileptic children and for the hospitalization of persons who otherwise refused medical treatment. In 1931, a "well baby" clinic, where mothers could bring their offspring for regular physical examinations and inoculations, was added to the program.

One of the league's more successful health projects was its milk program, which was established for undernourished children in public schools. League officials were the first to officially recognize this problem when they donated $100 to Public Schools 32 and 75 (two-thirds of black students attended School 32). The Buffalo Board of Education subsequently established a milk fund of $16,000 and extended the service to all public schools.[75] Staff members of the Urban League carefully supervised sanitation conditions in the black neighborhoods and frequently consulted with the Health Department regarding this matter.[76] Although the lives of black Buffalonians were improved greatly because of the league's projects, Evans reported in 1932 that health and housing problems "have grown so acute" in the last three years that they could only be handled when the league acquired additional facilities and staff to implement them. Unfortunately, the needed expansion did not occur until the World War II era and the return of economic prosperity.

In 1928 a record number of African American arrests occurred in Buffalo. Desperate social and economic conditions and racism led to the incarceration of 936, or 7.8 percent, of the black populace during the year. The investigations into their causes indicated, according to league officials, that only minor infractions of the law, in most cases, had led to the arrests. Among these were violations of the vagrancy laws of Buffalo.[77] Evans used the TCCUCP to explain the disparities and the unequal treatment meted out to blacks in the criminal justice system— from a refusal to hire black probation officers and police to unfair sentencing in the justice system.[78] Another challenge facing the African American population was the systematic exclusion of them from the jury pool. Until 1933 it virtually was unheard of that a black served on either trial or grand juries in Erie County. Upon inquiring about this miscarriage of justice, the Urban League submitted a list of fifty registered voters to the commissioner of jurors; twenty-five were accepted.[79]

The Urban League embarked upon a project to alleviate "vice conditions" in black neighborhoods and to improve relationships between the community and the white policemen who patrolled it. Essentially, this involved conferences with the chief of police and precinct captains who served the black districts.[80] The results of these conferences were generally positive, and law enforcement officials showed greater sensitivity to "Negro" concerns. However, league officials recognized that the situation was more complex and began working with other city agencies, too. During his first year in office, William Evans served as assistant secretary of the city courts committee and secretary of the special committee appointed to deal with the problems of black prisoners. This committee, which was concerned with the causes of crime and delinquency, proposed that these malignancies could be alleviated substantially by hiring black policemen to patrol those districts in which blacks resided and by employing at least two African American probation officers. The proposals were "taken under advisement."[81]

Early in 1929, the Urban League initiated complaints about the flagrant vice conditions on the near East Side, especially in the area near Memorial Center, Technical High School, and along Michigan, William, and Clinton streets. Along with the Children's Aid Society, it prepared a report documenting the situation. Later the league commissioned the National Hygiene Association of New York to conduct a professional study and assumed some of the financial costs. The report implicated two city court justices, several lawyers, and police and health officials. Armed with this information, the reformers were able to close down many smoke shops and brothels, or to drive them underground. The vice then extended to downtown hotels and into better neighborhoods, but never was as open as before. This group of activists, all prominent citizens, became known as the Committee of Sixteen; however, their existence never was announced publicly.[82]

Urban League officials were well aware that their primary function was to serve Buffalo's black community, and the community constantly reminded the league of its responsibility. Often the league distributed questionnaires seeking advice about those areas in which it should push more strenuously or in which it ought to be involved. A 1931 survey of its clients concluded that the Urban League should establish a program to work with women who were detained for trial in the city jails. Members of the community also reiterated the conclusion reached by the special committee on black prisoners three years earlier—a black probation officer ought to be added to the staff of the municipal courts.[83] These suggestions received the same noncommittal response from the municipal government that the earlier ones had. Members of the Urban League staff, however, conducted a highly successful counseling program for the ex-offenders who were paroled through league intervention. The city's attempt to cope with its economic problems, however, took precedence over all other issues, and African Americans simply lacked the political clout to force the issue.

The Urban League carried on a number of successful family and welfare projects. Its Big Brother program was established in 1928 to provide positive male role models for black adolescents who had infringed upon the law. In addition to the publication of educational pamphlets, Big Brothers initiated a recreational program consisting of basketball and other athletic activities for these youngsters. The overriding concern of Big Brothers was to prevent crime among the youth, and most activities focused upon this objective.[84] As the economic plight of the city worsened, however, the program was severely curtailed, and in 1931, the black community campaigned for its restoration.

Broken cultural and family ties, the result of displacement from their communities, were social realities for many of the black youths who migrated to Buffalo after World War I. In an attempt to help the young maintain these ties and minimize the effects of anomie, the Urban League compiled information designed especially for the newcomers. A current list of individuals who were licensed to perform marriage ceremonies was made available to them. The league also provided services for individuals seeking information about relatives in Buffalo or about nonresident relatives, both of which were particular concerns of the migrants. There had been a demand for these services ever since the league opened its doors in June 1927. Such programs helped the league earn widespread respect and support within the black community. League officials were especially concerned about the large numbers of single black males who migrated to Buffalo. In order to lay the foundation for a smooth transition from the old setting to the new one, recreational programs were established for these young adults. Moreover, they were informed of the other community projects which could help them secure housing, employment, and social service benefits.[85]

On numerous occasions black parents availed themselves of the league's consultation service, which dispensed information on such educational matters as local schools, scholarships, and opportunities for employment.[86] Under the direction of the league's Visiting Teacher Service, one of its most successful groups, the Parent Education Group was organized.[87] Parents of children who were enrolled in Public Schools 32 and 75 formed the core of this group. Their meetings were devoted to discussions of problems of children in school and how parents could best cooperate with the school administration in alleviating some of these problems. This project won the support of the extension department of the Buffalo Public Schools and the Department of Adult Education at the University of Buffalo.

The league continued to manifest its interest in the welfare of students in still other ways. The Visiting Teacher Service had been established in 1929 as a result of community pressure.[88] It focused upon helping delinquent students adjust to the regimen of the public schools. During her first few weeks on the job, Beatrice Taylor, the visiting teacher, interviewed 31 youngsters and was assigned 23 cases, students who exhibited deficiencies in scholarship or discipline. Taylor's report suggested that poverty was a key factor in their behavior. General knowledge of the problems of black children was essential to the Visiting Teacher Service's popularity, for most agencies failed to provide assistance to black parents of socially and educationally maladjusted children. With the exception of the Father Baker Home for delinquent boys in Lackawanna, black youths were relegated to penal institutions.[89]

The visiting teacher program succeeded in uncovering several other factors in home environments which directly affected the performance of children in school. Children from many homes lacked adequate food and clothing. As the Depression strengthened its grasp on the community, the number of black youngsters who remained home from school because of these deficiencies was alarming.[90] The Urban League was able to help solve the dilemma of a few by securing clothing from a special fund established by the Council of Social Agencies. Three black social workers dispensed the clothing to over 300 children. At its May 1931 meeting, the league's Board of Directors sent a petition requesting

East Side Classroom. Courtesy of the Buffalo and Erie County
Historical Society.

the Council of Social Agencies to join in establishing another fund to
make clothing available to youngsters at the start of the school year,
for it surmised that the need would be even greater then.

The Urban League was also instrumental in the distribution of food
baskets to those poor families who were ineligible for other forms of
assistance.[91] The Social Services Bureau increased payments to welfare
recipients, at the league's insistence. During the holiday season, the
league established a toy fund and gave scores of Christmas parties for
community youngsters.[92] Throughout the Depression era, the league
continued to augment its social welfare program. These projects won
increased visibility for the league and the unequivocal support of the
African American populace, which was pleased by the organization's
commitment to that community.

The Urban League conducted an extensive educational program for
blacks. Its staff organized a sorority and fraternity for youngsters of various
ages, the main purpose of which was to encourage scholastic achievement

and to improve social behavior.[93] The league's affiliate Memorial Center offered classes in crafts, sewing, cooking, drawing, dancing, gymnastics, drama, singing, poetry, and other structured activities for girls.[94] Mothers' groups could study home nursing, dressmaking, and music appreciation. Girl Scout troops and YWCA groups also met at Memorial Center, thereby broadening the range of its clientele's experiences.[95]

The league's services to Buffalo's black community were designed to be all-encompassing, yet there was just so much that the league could accomplish with its skeleton crew and inadequate budget. Its greatest deficiency occurred in the area of housing, for it lacked a housing program altogether. Black people increasingly were confined to the near East Side of Buffalo.[96] As a result, blacks often paid exorbitant fees for substandard housing. The Buffalo Municipal Housing Administration reported that 57 percent of family heads who resided in census tract fourteen were African Americans. This tract was defined by Broadway and Jefferson on the north, Madison on the east, Eagle on the south, and Main Street on the west. A look at housing in that tract will illustrate general housing conditions for blacks in Buffalo.[97] The housing was described as the "most unfortunate housing in Buffalo." Only 10 to 20 percent of the family units in this tract were occupied by the owner. The median age of the buildings was over thirty years and more than 25 percent of family units lacked sanitation facilities, compared to 17.5 percent of the total population of Buffalo.

Despite their limited resources, William Evans and his staff monitored developments in public housing. The new Kenfield public housing development, which was constructed far from the nucleus of the black community, had been opened in 1933, but only whites were admitted.

TABLE 3

HOUSING STATUS OF FAMILIES IN BUFFALO, NEW YORK, 1933

| | Percentage of Families | | |
	Owner	Tenant	Unknown
All Families	42.6	55.9	1.5
White	43.5	55.1	1.4
Native parentage	39.7	58.8	1.5
Foreign or mixed parentage	44.4	54.3	1.3
Foreign born	50.0	48.7	1.2
African Americans	6.6	89.1	4.3
Other Races	3.9	85.8	10.2

Source: Report Number 73, Public Housing Administration, H-6700-6706, R.G. 196, National Archives.

Reverend Ralph B. Hindman of the Urban League expressed concern over the fact that blacks were being discriminated against in Kenfield and felt that such a policy would set a bad precedent. Charles Diebold, Jr., financier and member of the Buffalo Advisory Committee on Housing, contended that the best way to help "colored people" would be to eliminate some of the blighted areas by constructing a housing project in "their own" community. However, Diebold recommended that the housing committee pass a resolution prohibiting discrimination in assigning individuals to municipal housing units. Evans concurred with this proposal. The league, however, was unable to launch a major thrust into the area of housing until World War II and more prosperous times.[98]

One of the National Urban League's chief goals was to help foster racial harmony. Each of the branches conducted programs designed to achieve interracial accord, and certainly the Buffalo Urban League had ample opportunities to test its own programs. Race relations in Buffalo had been fairly fluid until the large-scale migration of blacks into the city following the First World War. Blacks in Buffalo had been spared the violent response to the increased black presence that some urban centers experienced between 1917 and 1921.[99] A substantial number of Buffalonians were proud of this fact and wanted to avoid such conflicts in the future. The Urban League acted as a laboratory in which concerned individuals could develop and implement social policies that would prevent increased intergroup hostilities.

After the black population had become "visible," the press depicted it as primarily a criminal element. Such reporting bred hostility in both the black and white community. In January 1928, the league began one of its major projects to ameliorate race relations, a study of the prevalent stereotype of African Americans disseminated by the news media. When the league disclosed its findings, local newspaper editors agreed to encourage their staffs to write unbiased accounts.[100]

The following year, Dr. Nathaniel Cantor, a professor at the University of Buffalo, conducted a discussion group on personal and group attitudes regarding race and nationality. Sessions were held twice a month and averaged an attendance of forty.[101] The Women's Auxiliary of the league sponsored "inter-racial teas" to allow for an exchange of ideas. Often these social hours followed cultural events, such as the production of "Porgy and Bess" by a touring company in 1929.[102] League officials annually addressed scores of community groups on such topics as the plight of African Americans and the goals and achievements of the National Urban League. In some cases, these lectures afforded an opportunity for potential supporters to secure firsthand knowledge of the conditions under which African Americans lived in Buffalo.[103] Executive Secretary William Evans conducted seminars on African Americans in the sociology departments of the Buffalo State Teachers College and the University of Buffalo.[104] In 1931, Evans reported that the Interracial Committee of the Buffalo Council of Churches was cooperating with the league in its attempt to improve race relations in Buffalo. Dr. Niles Carpenter, a white sociologist at the University of Buffalo and author of *Nationality, Color and Economic Opportunity in the City of Buffalo,* chaired this committee.

Through the Interracial Committee the league was able to extend its program to most of the "well known" Protestant churches and many women's luncheon and study clubs. League officials presided at group discussions in the academic community concerning educational and social problems of blacks in America. These sessions were "exceedingly helpful" because they focused upon the need for teachers to be educated in order to approach race problems satisfactorily. Moreover, Evans conducted class sessions at the local colleges and distributed bibliographies and other materials for the eleven students at the University of Buffalo who were preparing theses on African Americans. He continued this policy throughout the decade.[105]

The Urban League also engaged in more direct approaches to improving race relations for blacks. It joined the local chapter of the National Association for the Advancement of Colored People, the YWCA, the Buffalo Federation of Women's Clubs, and the Buffalo Presbytery in submitting a petition protesting its discriminatory practices toward blacks to the Martin Restaurant Company of the New York Central Railroad, which had refused to serve poet Countee Cullen when he arrived in Buffalo for a league-sponsored poetry reading.[106] The petition ended discrimination not only in the company's New York Central Restaurant, but in all the others it operated as well.[107] This committee also sent a letter of protest to the Food Crafts Shop, Inc. because the Buffalo company had refused to honor its contract to cater in its demonstrating rooms the Lit-Mus Club—a federated black women's club which pursued the study of music, art, and literature—because "it could not serve a club of colored women." The Buffalo Urban League also found itself involved in the settlement of the issue of separate camping facilities for black Girl Scouts.

Tension over police behavior was prevalent in Buffalo's black community in 1931. These feelings were exacerbated further when the chief of the vice squad, armed with requests from white owners of night clubs and other recreational facilities, vowed "to break up race mixing." His modus operandi was designed to stymie black businesses in the area. When the league investigated, the chief of police assured Evans that his officers would not intervene in such matters.[108] Although the league's other efforts to ameliorate race relations proved to be less successful, it continued to make its presence in this field felt in the Buffalo community.

During the thirteen years between 1927 and 1940, Buffalo's black community grew tremendously, largely the result of the southern migrants who settled in the East Side community. Concentrated mainly in ward 5, with large populations in wards 6, 8, and 12, it consequently experienced increased visibility. Concerned black and white leaders, desiring to alleviate the problems of unemployment, inadequate housing, poor healthcare delivery services, and the deteriorating race relations which plagued a disproportionate number of newcomers, created a local branch of the National Urban League. While the Urban League initiated a number of programs which addressed the many social concerns of black Buffalonians, its success in handling most of them was marginal, especially in those areas (such as employment) where whites were threatened directly. However, with the establishment of the league, Buffalo blacks, for the first time, had an agency working exclusively to improve their social conditions. Knowledge of the league's functions as a catalyst for change, and the respect it maintained in Buffalo, earned it the enthusiastic support of African Americans and place it among the most influential agencies in building the East Side community.

Civil Rights, Politics, and Community

It should not be necessary to struggle forever against popular prejudice. . . .

MARY BURNETT TALBERT, 1915

You can't beat nobody down so low till you can rob 'em of they will.

ZORA NEALE HURSTON[1]

The blacks living in Buffalo at the turn of the century were imbued with Republican party politics, like those in black communities all over the country. They had a long history of involvement with the party. At the same time they justifiably had a suspicion of the Democrats because of their conservative racial policies. Black residents in nineteenth-century Buffalo had assailed the Democratic party for what it interpreted as a false attack upon its level of political sophistication. William Talbert, long-time supporter, was president of the city's Colored Republican Party by the eve of the new century.[2] Frank Garrett, a local newspaper editor, explained that the Republican party had won the loyalty of blacks because "it was the party of Lincoln, the Great Emancipator."[3]

But with the advent of new and larger populations of blacks migrating into the city, the *Buffalo American* saw the possibility of blacks playing a major role in local and national politics. In an editorial the paper suggested that African Americans' approach to endorsing candidates indicated that they were much better informed than Garrett's comments suggest. The editor observed:

Every thinking Negro will turn solidly to the support of Harding and Coolidge not because of Abraham Lincoln, but because of [their] declaration concerning the proper treatment . . . of the submerged tenth of the American population.

. . . Lest there be those who may be misquoted and led astray, we begin now to awaken them to their senses and create in them the broad outlook on life and their full duty to the Race of which they are a part, and the nation whose security is only assured in the hands of the G. O. P.[4]

However, the blacks' loyalty to particular political parties, more often than not, was based upon the stances that the party took on issues that they considered important and crucial to the implementation of their self-determinationist agenda. For example, in 1922, when the anti-lynching bill that Congressman Leonidas Dyer wrote was reported out of committee, support for the ratification fell short. Mary Burnett Talbert, NACW president *emerita* and national director of the NAACP's anti-lynching campaign, urged women to use their newly won right to vote to oust from Congress those individuals who had opposed the bill. The *Buffalo American* reported that all of the Buffalo representatives endorsed the legislation and won reelection, including a Democrat.

William Talbert had received some national visibility at the turn of the century because of his involvement in the Colored Republican Party and because he was an organizer of the Niagara Movement that met in Buffalo in 1905. This brought him to the attention of Booker T. Washington, who suggested to one of his agents that they might solicit Talbert's aid as an informant at the proceedings. Washington had noted the cordial professional relations between their wives, both of whom were officers in the National Association of Colored Women.[5] Washington also had stayed at the Talbert home when he traveled to Buffalo.

These incidents offer insight into the political activities of Buffalo's black community. They indicate that black Buffalonians were cognizant of the major political issues and were in dialogue with major black political figures; simultaneously, they also were players. By the 1920s African Americans in the city had a clearly defined political agenda for the development of their community. They sought better housing, education, jobs, and improved race relations. Achieving these goals was a part of their self-determinationist agenda. The owners of the *Buffalo American,* migrants themselves, best articulated their concerns through editorials. The benefits Buffalo blacks had negotiated with the major political parties in Buffalo were marginal; as their numbers increased they hoped that they would be able to alter this turn of events. At the same time they recognized that they would have to devise other mechanisms to achieve their political goals.

Blacks in Buffalo during the world war and progressive eras created organizations designed to address specific issues their community faced. These political entities evolved during one of the most tumultuous periods of social and economic change in the United States and represented one phase in the political maturation of the African American populace.[6] Their successes, indeed their very existence, partially can be attributed to the migrants who wended their way to the "Queen City" of the Great Lakes, in search of economic opportunities and political power so that they could exercise control over their lives and community. The NAACP was one of these organizations.

Black Buffalonians organized the NAACP to further help it in shaping their modern, urban community. The Buffalo chapter reveals the persistent struggle of a small body of energetic and dedicated blacks and their white allies to create a world in which the legal, political, and civil rights of African Americans would be safeguarded and in which blacks could enjoy equality of opportunity. Although it often suffered because of its small numbers and paucity of funds, and although its victories were limited, the association nevertheless made significant contributions to the black community. First, it provided a sympathetic body to which the aggrieved who happened to be black and, in many instances, economically disadvantaged could take their problems. Secondly, the NAACP served as a "watchdog agency" for assuring that African Americans' right of access to public accommodations on a nondiscriminatory basis was guaranteed. Thirdly, its organizational structure was flexible and its leaders astute enough to shift policies when it was expedient to do so. The change in the kinds of cases it emphasized after the migration of blacks to Buffalo in the 1920s and 1930s is indicative of a change in the membership of the organization. Finally, NAACP-sponsored educational programs helped to foster black pride, and through its emphasis on self-help, it reinforced blacks' efforts to create a strong sense of community and to determine the shape that community would take.

The National Association for the Advancement of Colored People was founded in 1909 in New York, the response of a group of blacks and white liberals to the Springfield Riot of the summer of 1908.[7] The conditions of African Americans had deteriorated rapidly following the Compromise of 1877 that made Rutherford B. Hayes president and left southern politicians to protect their constitutional rights.[8] By 1908, blacks in most southern states had been denied the right to vote. The occupations in which southern blacks engaged had also been restricted severely and Jim Crow reigned in all aspects of their lives. Terrorism was rampant.

These were primarily southern phenomena and, although northern public opinion occasionally deplored them, for the most part northerners simply ignored the racism in their own backyard. Blacks in the North experienced restrictions similar to those faced by southern blacks, but

NAACP Amenia Conference, held at the Troutbeck estate of
Joel Spingarn in upstate New York, 1916. Mary Burnett
Talbert is seated second row center. Courtesy of the NAACP
Collection, Library of Congress.

little sentiment was aroused concerning their plight. William Monroe
Trotter, Ida Wells Barnett, W. E. B. DuBois, and other African Americans
through their writings, lectures, and other activities tried to win support
for improving the conditions of blacks in the United States, but with
limited success.

When racial violence broke out in Springfield, Illinois, the home of
Abraham Lincoln, northern racism could no longer be ignored. This
incident served as a catalyst, bringing together socialists and neo-abo-
litionists, the descendants of the antebellum abolitionists. Included in
this group were Oswald Garrison Villard, Mary White Ovington, Henry
Moskovitz, and William English Walling. Walling wrote a pamphlet entitled "The Race War in the North," an attack on racism and violence
which inspired a number of whites to sympathize with the plight of
blacks. Walling envisioned a national organization composed of "fair

minded whites and intelligent blacks to help right the wrongs of the Negro." He and Mary White Ovington met to lay the groundwork for the organization. They later invited members of the Liberal Club of New York to participate and such well-known African American spokespersons as Ida Wells Barnett, W. E. B. DuBois, and Francis J. Grimke.[9]

The NAACP was the first major black improvement association with national ties to locate a branch in Buffalo. This organization was also founded prior to the mass migration of blacks into Buffalo following the First World War. It was established in 1910, shortly after the founding of the national organization and, in contrast to the major goals of the other local affiliates of national black advancement organizations in Buffalo, the NAACP concentrated on improving the lives of blacks by initiating a comprehensive program of nonviolent agitation, well-publicized protest, propaganda, and legal maneuvers. The NAACP was also unique because it depended solely upon its members and its fund-raising drives for the financial support it needed to implement its programs. Consequently, as a result of limited black employment opportunities and wages, it constantly experienced financial difficulties.

Organizational activities of the Buffalo NAACP began in the fall of 1910 when the Phyllis Wheatley Club, an affiliate of the National Association of Colored Women's Club (NACW), headed by social activist Mary Burnett Talbert, hosted a meeting with the Reverend J. Edward Nash of the Michigan Avenue Baptist Church, John Sayles (secretary to Mayor Louis Furhmann of Buffalo) and other "interested" persons from the city, and W. E. B. DuBois and Fanny Garrison Villard of the national association.[10] By the beginning of 1911, a structured program was well under way and Chairman Oswald Garrison Villard informed the members of the Board of Directors that the Buffalo association was planning monthly meetings to be held in the black churches of the city. Villard noted further that, in addition to carrying out the work of the association, the local NAACP should implement its own regular program designed to increase the membership.[11] Since the Board of Directors of the National Association approved the constitution of the Buffalo chapter and officially accepted it as an NAACP affiliate at its January 15, 1915 meeting, little is known about the local association or the programs it initiated until after the outbreak of World War I.[12]

The NAACP functioned through an organizational structure that consisted of the Executive Committee and the Women's Auxiliary. Later, the Junior Chapter comprised another major component of the Buffalo NAACP. The Executive Committee governed the organization and made certain that its policies were in compliance with those of the national office. An integrated group of men and women comprised this body. The first president of the local association was John Brent, the black architect. He was succeeded by Rudolph Lane, a bookkeeper. After

Lane's term expired, a series of attorneys—C. M. Maloney, Julian J. Evans, and Robert A. Burrell—held the presidency; their terms spanned the 1920s through the early 1940s. Throughout this twenty-year period, with the exception of only four individuals—Mrs. C. J. Jones, social activist; Amelia Anderson; Dr. M. A. Allen, and J. Elwood Smith, mortician—no one who was selected as president of the organization lacked a law degree. All of the presidents during this period also were African Americans and were deeply committed to their community. The individuals who filled the other executive positions in the association from 1917 to 1940 were also professionals. No one field was dominant. Some officers were businessmen, such as Marshall Brown, Cornelius Ford, and Dr. Charles Patrick, a pharmacist. Social worker Amelia Anderson and educator Clara Payne were very active in the association, as were clergymen, such as E. J. Echols and Murray Howland.

In contrast to the national association, one outstanding feature about the local NAACP officers was that from the very beginning most of them were African Americans. Whites seldom were elected. Bliss Yonkers, a principal in Buffalo Public School 32, was the only white who ascended to the position of vice president of the NAACP, serving two terms from 1939 to 1940.[13] The preponderance of African American officeholders reflected the wishes of the predominantly black membership.[14]

The Executive Committee was more racially balanced. Most committee members were college-educated professionals, and many had been active or would become active in other black social uplift organizations, such as the Michigan Avenue YMCA and the National Urban League. Prior to the 1920s, the Executive Board of the NAACP had consisted of only seven individuals, including three whites, attorney Frank C. Ferguson, Jr., Dr. Jacob Goldberg, and Reverend Phillip Frick.[15] However, a marked shift in the composition of the Executive Board accompanied the rapid increase in the black population of Buffalo. The board was enlarged to nine in 1922 and thirteen in 1925. With the possible exception of one individual, the entire Executive Board of 1922 was black. From that time until 1937, the white presence on the board was minimal.

The black ministers of Buffalo were among the staunchest supporters of the association; most of the NAACP meetings were held at the local black churches. The Reverends Sidney O. B. Johnson of Lloyd Memorial Congregational Church, Elijah J. Echols of Shiloh Baptist Church, J. Edward Nash of the Michigan Avenue Baptist Church, and Henry Durham of St. Luke's AME Zion served on the Executive Board from about 1922 and remained on the committee at various times throughout the Depression and post-Depression eras.[16] Physicians Ivorite Scruggs, Marion Allen, John Walters, and H. H. Lewis, and attorneys Frank C. Ferguson, Joseph Cohen, and Robert Burrell were members of the Executive Board of the local NAACP. A number of social workers and educators were also members during these years, including Mary Burnett Talbert, Amelia Anderson, Clara Payne, Ruth Davies, and Elizabeth Talbert.

In addition to its Executive Committee, which conducted the day-to-day operations of the organization, the NAACP established other components to help facilitate the dissemination of information about its goals and tactics. The first unit, the Junior Chapter of the NAACP, was established in 1922. This group was designed to prepare the youth for active participation in the NAACP. Members sponsored social activities, fund-raising projects, and educational programs. In fact, it sponsored, in cooperation with the Michigan Avenue YMCA, annual youth conferences.

The other unit, the Women's Auxiliary, was established in 1929.[17] Antoinette Ford, social activist and wife of Cornelius Ford of the packing house firm, was elected president of the auxiliary. Robert Bagnall congratulated her on her election and explained, "The Women's Auxiliary in our branches have generally proven to be the most valuable. In many cases, they have become the dominant factor in keeping the branches alive and as a result of their activities, many dormant branches have been revived."[18] The Buffalo auxiliary set up three committees to implement its projects. The Committee on Education was focused upon the cultural progress of blacks; often it sponsored plays, lectures, and teas to raise funds for the association. During the first month that it was in operation, the auxiliary added $400 to the NAACP coffers.[19] The Fund-raising Committee also sponsored baby contests and beauty pageants. These projects attracted scores of participants, and as an added feature the winners' photographs appeared in the *Crisis*. The Entertainment Committee hosted NAACP-sponsored activities.

Antoinette Ford founded the Douglass Club of black women and was treasurer of another social circle, the Dames, devoted to cards and entertainment.[20] Like Ford, many of the other members of the Women's Auxiliary were active participants in other social uplift organizations in the black community of Buffalo. Mrs. T. J. Holcombe, Michigan Avenue YMCA; Elizabeth Talbert, the Friendship Home for African American Girls; Mrs. E. E. Nelson, the Buffalo Cooperative Economic Society; Otis Davenport Jackson, the Michigan Avenue YMCA and Urban League board member; Ruth Scruggs, federated women's clubs; and Frances Nash of the Michigan Avenue Baptist Church had a wide range of experiences, including women's clubs. All of them brought to committee assignments a wealth of skills in public relations and fund-raising.

Although women had participated in the NAACP at all levels, the auxiliary and the youth division allowed for broader involvement on the part of females and a vehicle for youths to address some of their special needs simultaneously while they were imbued with NAACP ideology. The Executive Committee, the Women's Auxiliary, and the Junior

NAACP facilitated the implementation of NAACP programs and were instrumental in bringing into the association diverse individuals from the community.

The association symbolized, in many respects, the reasons why thousands of black people had trekked from the South to the North after World War I: the quest for economic improvement, political rights, and human dignity. In the South, membership in the NAACP meant that an individual was virtually declared a criminal or troublemaker; he might even become a victim of the lynch mob.[21] In the urban areas of the North, no such restraints were placed upon blacks; African Americans responded favorably to the efforts of the association, because membership for many was in itself a radical act and a way to decry American racism. Moreover, all African Americans, regardless of their class background, were subjected to racial indignities. Therefore, NAACP membership was their attempt to coalesce around the issue of race and thus, through their combined efforts, eradicate those inimical consequences of racism.

After the peak years of migration, membership in the local chapter of the NAACP began to reflect the diverse elements of the community. Initially, the Buffalo chapter successfully conducted its membership drives and met the quotas the national office had levied upon it. Nevertheless, the branch remained small. The national office had envisioned the establishment of local chapters composed of a biracial board of directors and membership, but in Buffalo, blacks in overwhelming numbers joined the organization, while few whites were members.[22] In 1926, blacks comprised the majority of the membership, and their proportion increased steadily over the next two decades.

The great interest that black members manifested in the association was indicative of the poor conditions many blacks in the North experienced and of their desire to be involved in the alleviation of those group or racial hardships. In Buffalo, social class was not significant in determining NAACP membership; race became the crucial element. In 1926, the first year for which extensive membership lists are available, the vast majority of the Buffalo chapter's members worked in service occupations or as skilled and unskilled laborers, with white-collar and professional workers composing the rest of the membership.[23] The composition of the membership remained fairly consistent throughout the 1920s.

The Depression years weighed heavily upon the Buffalo NAACP, and its membership fell off drastically.[24] Amelia Anderson, secretary of the local branch, requested that the national association decrease Buffalo's quota. William Pickens replied that the expenses the organization incurred continued to increase despite the economic hardship; therefore, he suggested that Buffalo should simply work harder to achieve its goal. The decline in membership was indicative of the NAACP's dependency upon laborers, many of whom were newcomers, for membership.[25] When times were hard, few African Americans could afford the luxury of NAACP membership.

The NAACP, like the other social uplift organizations in Buffalo, employed a multifaceted approach to improving life for African Americans. Their program consisted of legal action, cultural and educational projects, and moral persuasion. Publicity was crucial for the success of all of the association's programs, and the local branch established a committee under Ruth Davies the sole purpose of which was to handle public relations activities. Later on, the Women's Auxiliary became the branch's biggest booster.

The national office exerted a tremendous influence on its branches. The national Board of Directors controlled the admission of new branches through its right to approve their constitutions. It also devised a dues schedule which allocated to its own coffers a minimum of 50 percent of the membership fees collected by the local branches. Policy decisions were handed down to the branches from the national headquarters. Thus the actions which the branches took or those cases in which it became involved were monitored, if not determined, outside of the local community.[26]

Despite such close scrutiny, the local branch often was able to exercise a modicum of freedom in selecting those cases it wished to pursue. The Buffalo chapter was fortunate to have Mary Burnett Talbert on the national Board of Directors of the NAACP.[27] Talbert was a well-respected Buffalonian and had received national acclaim for her advocacy work on behalf of disfranchised Americans. One of her most coveted awards was the Spingarn Medal, the highest honor which the NAACP bestowed upon individuals. Second, the nature of the cases which the Buffalo NAACP handled reflected the interest of the membership as much as it did the demands of the national office.

Even before 1920, Buffalo NAACP members shared the national's concerns over the adverse depiction of blacks in films and other media. The 1915 production of D. W. Griffith's very successful moving picture *Birth of a Nation* prompted the NAACP to launch a campaign to have films which incited racial antagonism censured. White audiences flocked to the theaters not only because of *Birth of a Nation*'s racial message but also because of its innovative cinematic techniques.[28] As early as April 1915, John Brent, president of the Buffalo NAACP, wrote May Childs Nerney of the national office to solicit her assistance in helping the branch devise a scheme for handling the film's showing in Buffalo. He informed her that the branch could take action under a section of the city ordinance governing the showing of films which stipulated that "no person, firm[s] or corporation shall conduct or keep any moving picture show in the city, in such manner as to unduly disturb the peace and quiet of the neighborhood." Brent advised that NAACP attorneys Frank Ferguson and William W. Saperston of Buffalo were prepared to take action. The *Buffalo Evening News* supported the NAACP protest of the film.[29] Although *Birth of a Nation* had not been advertised in the Buffalo area, another film, *The Nigger,* by Edward Sheldon, was being shown.[30] The national NAACP advised that Buffalo should take no action, since the film depicted whites as responsible for the conditions which plague black Americans. Moreover, Nerney observed that "crimes as are committed by colored people [in the movie] are shown in every case to be [the result of] drink and not race."[31]

In 1920, the NAACP, under President Rudolph Lane, launched a protest against the local newspapers' policy of sensationalism when writing about blacks, especially about those who had been accused of committing crimes. Their efforts met with limited success. However, M. Clark, general manager of the *Buffalo Times,* responded in a letter to President Rudolph Lane:

> . . . while there was absolutely no intention whatever to do the colored race any injury or cast any reflection upon them, I am inclined to think upon investigation that the headlines used by all Buffalo papers were really more conspicuous than the occasion called for.[32]

Clark tried to impress upon Lane that

> no paper in Buffalo has been more consistently considerate and courteous to the colored race than the *Buffalo Times* . . . . Instructions have been given to the editorial room to see that no undue exaggeration or even publicity be given to any occurrence in the future which might in shape or manner be detrimental to your cause.[33]

The local NAACP continued its protest to the editors of local newspapers whenever their coverage appeared to be biased and the NAACP considered it detrimental to blacks. In 1922 Mary Talbert and Robert Bagnall, director of the branches of the NAACP, personally led a delegation to express NAACP concern about the appearance of an advertisement in a morning paper which sought to recruit members for the Ku Klux Klan. The editor assured the activists that the notice had gone through the "normal" channels but that he would give "specific" orders that in the future no such advertisement would appear in his paper.[34]

This form of protest against racism, Buffalo-style, was one of the more successful approaches that the NAACP utilized. It was essential that the NAACP achieve these victories, limited though they may have been, for they lent respectability to the organization. Moreover, amidst resurgent Klan activity in western New York, the increased restrictions placed on blacks' freedom of movement, and the perpetual rumors of riots, it was essential that the NAACP assist in easing tensions so that Buffalo could avert the racial conflicts experienced by other northern communities.[35]

Continued migration of African Americans in the 1920s increased the black population to the point where their presence could no longer be ignored. The concerns of the local NAACP after 1920 reflected the changing status of the enlarged black community. Many of the issues pursued by the local NAACP concerned discrimination in public accommodations. Local blacks vehemently protested the fact that they were not permitted to sit in the downstairs section of theaters in both Buffalo and nearby Lackawanna, despite the fact that they could purchase orchestra seats.[36] James Weldon Johnson advised Marshall Brown, secretary of the Buffalo NAACP, that they could take no action, for the NAACP would bring suit only if it had a clear case of discrimination. He argued that Buffalo blacks had not been ejected from the orchestra seats, but had merely been ushered to the balcony when they produced their tickets. Johnson suggested that instead of complying with the requests of the ushers, the blacks should insist upon their rights. Then, if they were removed forcefully, the whole situation would be placed in a different light and the NAACP would have cause for legal action.[37]

Local NAACP officials also were concerned about the conditions of black youths who attended the city public schools. The increased enrollment of black students in the public school system led to attempts on the part of some faculty members to segregate them, especially those who attended schools with small numbers of black children. In 1922, for example, the NAACP investigated an incident involving the use of a school's swimming pool by its lone black student.[38] Most Buffalo schools lacked swimming facilities at the time, and students who attended schools that did not have pools were transferred to those schools which had them for their swimming lessons. When an African American girl arrived with her class, the instructor gave her a note informing her mother that she should attend one of the downtown schools which had a large "colored attendance." The association visited the instructor, who contended that she "only suggested that the girl would feel more at home at a downtown school" but had permitted her to use the school's facilities. Unfortunately, the student's mother did not cooperate with the NAACP investigation because she feared repercussions. NAACP evidence revealed that this discriminatory action received no official sanction, and in view of this situation, it later dropped the charges. There were no further complaints about discrimination in special classes in the public schools after this incident.[39]

For a number of years the Buffalo NAACP, Reverend J. Edward Nash of the Michigan Avenue Baptist Church, and William L. Evans of the

Urban League made several unsuccessful attempts to secure the admission of black women into the nursing training program at the city hospital. Finally, in the fall of 1936, a committee representing the NAACP discussed the hospital's admissions policy with the superintendent, Dr. Charles Goodale. Goodale informed them that the Board of Directors of the hospital had passed a resolution which "liberalized" its admission policy. The superintendent now had the authority to make final decisions regarding a candidate's application and "resolved that the Training School of the Buffalo City Hospital be made available to all suitable applicants at least eighteen years of age and equipped with the necessary educational background who, in the opinion of the Superintendent, are desirable applicants." Moreover, the board also declared that "women's general fitness, educational background, adaptability, character, reputation, personality, physique, and health shall be the chief criteria for admission to the Nurse's Training School of the Buffalo City Hospital and that race, color, and creed of applicants are minor considerations."[40]

At the time this resolution was adopted, two black women had applications for admission to the training program in nursing. One of them, Eva Bateman, passed all entrance examinations with "flying colors" and was accepted into the training class; she continued to perform at the top of her class.[41] This marked the end of a long campaign for the local NAACP and the beginning of opportunity for a few black women who, because of their race, had been confined to a narrow range of job opportunities.

In the summer of 1920, two black youngsters, Harold Robinson and William Jackson, entered the Broadway Home Made Candy Parlor and ordered ice cream. The waitress informed the youths that she had been forbidden to serve "colored people." The youths' parents referred this incident to the association and the NAACP counselor, Clarence Maloney, advised them to file suit against George Zappas, the proprietor, under the Civil Rights Act of the State of New York. According to the statute, as amended in 1918,

> All persons within the jurisdiction of this State shall be entitled to full and equal accommodations, advantages and privileges of any place of public accommodation, resort or amusement, subject only to the conditions and limitations established by law and applicable alike to all persons. No person, being the owner, lessor, employee of any such place, shall directly or indirectly refuse, withhold from or deny to any person any of the accommodations, advantages or privileges thereof, on account of race, creed, or color.[42]

Maloney later filed suit for the plaintiffs against Zappas in the New York State Supreme Court. Neither the applicants nor the respondent in the case was successful in producing the waitress in question to testify, for she allegedly had moved out of town. The court ultimately ruled that Robinson and Jackson had been aggrieved and ordered Zappas to pay them $100, plus attorney fees. The defendant appealed the decision to the New York State Court of Appeals which affirmed the lower court's ruling—a triumph for Maloney and the local NAACP.

The Buffalo NAACP handled a wide range of cases in its attempt to assure that African Americans received justice when it was obvious that they were innocent victims of discrimination and racism, and that they receive fair trials in those instances when it seemed obvious that they might have committed a crime. Because the southern system of justice merely guaranteed that most blacks would either be "railroaded" to jail or sometimes become victims of mob violence, the association found itself involved in a number of cases involving the extradition of migrants, most of whom had resided in Buffalo for some time.

The earliest involvement of the Buffalo NAACP in such a case occurred in 1922 and received international attention. Matthew Bullock, of Norlinia, North Carolina had succeeded in fleeing to western New York after he was accused of having incited a "riot" in which "several" individuals were slain. Matthew Bullock was the son of a prominent minister in Norlinia. The Bullocks had resided for some time in the Buffalo suburb Batavia, New York, but later returned to their North Carolina hometown. Matthew frequently travelled throughout the North and the South. His travels led the local whites to suspect that he was involved in clandestine activities meant to improve the conditions of blacks. Furthermore, the Bullock family was "too" prosperous. Because of these factors, whites in Norlinia wanted to eliminate the Bullock youths who they believed threatened the racial hierarchy and Jim Crow.

They got their opportunity on January 23, 1921, when Plummer Bullock made a 15-cent purchase of fruit. Feeling that the quality of his apples was not commensurate to the price, Plummer requested a refund. According to informed sources, this incident precipitated the "riot." The proprietor asked a group of his patrons to take Plummer out and "shoot him up," but Plummer managed to elude them and returned to the family home. Sentiment against the Bullock youths mounted and a mob was organized to slay them and three other young black men. The following day, a dozen white men armed with rifles went to the Bullock home and demanded that Matthew, whom they found most offensive, accompany them. Upon learning that he was not at home, local authorities made formal charges against Plummer stemming from the incident involving the apples. A warrant for his arrest was produced and the younger Bullock was incarcerated. Despite the fact that it was illegal to make an arrest in North Carolina on Sunday, the mob acted with impunity.

Reverend Bullock was warned not to accompany his son unless he desired instant death. That night a mob of whites broke into the local jail, removed young Bullock from prison, riddled his body with bullets, and then burned him to death.[43] Matthew Bullock hoped to avoid his brother's fate by seeking asylum in Canada. He was arrested in Hamilton, Ontario, however, for illegally entering the country. Canadian officials retained him in custody upon the request of the governor of North Carolina, who wished to have him extradited in order that he might stand trial for the charges resulting from the January 1921 "riot."

On Sunday, January 22, 1922, the Buffalo branch of the NAACP sponsored a mass meeting at the Shiloh Baptist Church in an attempt to arouse public sentiment for Matthew Bullock's plight and secure critical funding for his defense. Walter White, assistant secretary of the national office, explained to the well-attended gathering the details of the Bullock case which he had recently acquired during his fact-finding trip to Canada. The audience responded enthusiastically and contributed $100 to the Bullock Defense Fund.[44] This was merely the first of three such large-scale meetings designed to raise funds to be used in the Bullock case.

The local NAACP conducted a thorough investigation into the Bullock affair. Indeed, their findings resulted in gaining the support of the national office for the former resident of the Buffalo suburb of Batavia. The Buffalo chapter not only provided legal services for Bullock but also drafted a petition to New York governor Miller requesting that Bullock not be returned to his native North Carolina, where it was almost certain he would meet the same fate as his brother. As a result of various legal maneuvers, Canadian officials agreed to release Bullock, since North Carolina refused to send witnesses.[45] A welcoming committee of the NAACP met him at the border. The Bullock incident gained international attention and it was largely through the efforts of the Buffalo association and of Walter White of the national office that Bullock was released to New York state.

This case became a cause célèbre and helped win support for the Dyer anti-lynching bill that Missouri congressman Leonidas Dyer introduced into the House to make lynching a federal offense in 1923. Mary B. Talbert had directed the highly successful anti-lynching campaign for the national NAACP. The Buffalo association conducted a vigorous campaign in its attempt to secure the passage of the Dyer bill. Their efforts resulted in getting pledges from the local representatives to Congress, including a Democrat, James Mead, to vote for the legislation. Marshall Brown noted that all the representatives who supported the bill were returned to Congress in the November 23, 1922 elections. The local chapter continued to lobby for the Dyer bill's passage, sending telegrams to members of the Judiciary Committee, to New York senators Wadsworth and Calder, and to Senator Henry Cabot Lodge. Furthermore, the chapter was successful in securing "strong" editorial support advocating passage of the bill from the local newspapers.[46]

Twelve years later, the Buffalo NAACP once again intervened in extradition procedures involving alleged crimes committed by blacks in the South, although with less success than earlier. The first case involved Steve Epps of Buffalo. The governor of Georgia contended that Epps was an alias for Georgian Henry Maxwell, who allegedly had killed the white timekeeper at the plow manufacturing company where he was employed in Rome, Georgia in December 1916. On March 6, 1934, two witnesses testified that Epps had come to Buffalo in April 1916 and had remained there until his arrest, with the exception of a brief stint spent in service with the United States Army. Other than the three or four times that he had been arrested for public intoxication, Epps had a good reputation, including membership in the Elks, a black fraternal organization. Epps testified that he had not committed the murder and had not been in Rome, the site of the tragedy. The local association became interested in this incident, and NAACP president Julian Evans and attorney Clarence Maloney prepared a defense for Epps.[47]

Motivated by its desire to assure youths fair treatment by the judicial system of the South, in the fall of 1934 the Buffalo NAACP became involved in the William Taylor extradition case. Unlike the other victims whose causes the local association undertook, William Taylor admitted his guilt in perpetrating a crime. Taylor was a seventeen-year old youth convicted of committing a burglary in Virginia. He received a three-year sentence in the Virginia State Penitentiary and began to serve time on Valentine's Day, 1934. A little over six months later, however, Taylor escaped and fled from Virginia. His actions were based partly on the inhumane conditions he had suffered while working on a chain gang. Julian Evans, NAACP attorney, asked the governor of New York to intercede in Taylor's behalf so that he would not be subjected once more to conditions which were tantamount to slavery. Charles Poletti, special counselor to the governor, assured Evans that the governor would give the request "his most careful consideration." Evans also asked Walter White to investigate the possibility of placing Taylor in a reformatory school in Virginia so that he would benefit from youth status and have an opportunity to receive some type of formal education.[48] While the success of the local NAACP in handling many of these extradition cases was limited, the organization's involvement assured support from the black migrants who were coming into the city and who sympathized with the victims of southern atrocities.

The NAACP used its publications and mass rallies to foster a collective identity among blacks. If residents were not a part of the new wave of migrants, their families either had moved from the South during the post-Reconstruction era, or they descended from runaway slaves who had wended their way to Buffalo. Each group had memories of their past. Their approach to resolving issues facing blacks may have differed, but each had a clear understanding of what it meant to be black anywhere in the United States. After all, this was also the age of "Jim Crow" and *Birth of a Nation,* and a period characterized as the "Nadir" of American history by black historian Rayford Logan.[49]

The local NAACP handled several unusual cases in its efforts to assure justice for African Americans. During the summer of 1922, Morris Deitch, a middle-aged white businessman, found his way into the home of an eight-year-old black girl who resided on Hickory Street in the heart of the black community and criminally assaulted her. The girl was hospitalized for several weeks as a result of injuries she sustained. The black community became incensed over this indignity and demanded that the perpetrator of this heinous crime be punished. Petitions demanding justice were circulated throughout the community.[50] However, fearing the outbreak of racial violence, the local NAACP halted the distribution of petitions and assured the community that it had "[complete] confidence in the police and the courts of Buffalo" and advised blacks to "allow the law to take its course." The district attorney's office assured the legal committee of the local association that the case would receive its careful attention. The child's parents, recent migrants from the South, were reluctant to aid the prosecutor until NAACP officials convinced them that it was their responsibility to help prevent such an attack on other children.

After being identified as her assailant, Deitch was arrested and held for trial. The jury found him guilty as accused, and Justice Hinckley of the state supreme court sentenced him to serve from six to twenty years in prison. This decision was considered a significant victory for the NAACP, which capitalized on its success. The *Branch Bulletin* and other NAACP publications carried the story throughout the nation with such sensational headlines as "Buffalo Branch Convicts White Rapist."[51]

On occasion, the Buffalo chapter of the NAACP aligned itself with other community organizations to fight discrimination. We have already seen evidence of this collaboration when the Buffalo chapters of the NAACP and the Urban League succeeded in having restaurants at the train stations throughout New York integrated. In the 1930s the local NAACP joined forces with leftist movements such as the International Labor Defense. Before exploring the nature of this relationship, however, it is necessary that we understand the role the Communists played in the black community and how receptive blacks were to this movement. Attempts by the Communist party to gain widespread support among black workers in the 1920s were futile in most instances, for a number of reasons. First, the Communists failed to appreciate the significance of the black church as a vehicle for organizing blacks and proceeded to attack this well-respected institution. Secondly, blacks who suffered the consequences of racism were loath to have the additional stigma of radicalism attached to them. Finally, the Communist party failed to devise a platform which incorporated the unique concerns of black people.

Cognizant of its shortcomings in recruiting blacks, the Communist party in 1923 decided to strengthen the International Labor Defense, one of several such organizations established by the party to provide legal assistance for radicals and minorities; the party instructed the ILD to fight directly for the civil and legal rights of blacks by using the courts and by applying "mass pressure." The ILD also was a vehicle to oppose the NAACP, which held an unchallenged position speaking for blacks and which lacked ties to the trade union movement and vehemently opposed Communism. *New Masses,* a Party organ, attacked the NAACP and simultaneously clarified the position of the ILD:

> . . . the I. L. D. composed chiefly of workers, understands that there are two classes, and that the courts belong to the ruling class. The NAACP, under the dominance of white and Negro bourgeois reformers, attempts to deny the conflict of class interests. The I. L. D., based on class struggle, knows that mass pressure upon the courts fundamentally affects the employers' position on wages, hours, [and] living conditions. The NAACP is an instrument to conceal these truths.[52]

If the ILD opposed the NAACP, it was just as adamant in its objection to the National Urban League. These feelings of antipathy were intensified because of the controversial antilabor stance which the National Urban League had taken during a number of large industrial strikes following World War I.[53] William Evans, while industrial secretary of the Chicago Urban League, had been involved in a number of antilabor practices when he advocated the use of blacks as strikebreakers.[54] Evans argued:

> There is no reason to conclude that the Negro is by choice a strike-breaker any more than other men, but the fact is that in most instances where he has risen above the ranks of a common laborer, the strike has furnished the medium thru [sic] which his advancement is accomplished. To our notion, the policy of white unionists is more to blame than all else.[55]

Despite the obvious deteriorating status of black laborers, his attitude did not ingratiate him in the eyes of the ILD.

In the fall of 1931, the local NAACP met with the International Labor Defense to devise a scheme for handling a due-process case involving Sam Palmer.[56] Palmer was a black laborer employed by Ben Behringer, a contractor in the Buffalo suburb of Cheektowaga. Reportedly, he worked approximately five hours a day and was to have been compensated for his services at the rate of 30 cents per hour. During his first week, Palmer claimed he received $2.70 in wages, and the following week he was paid $5.00. At this juncture he quit the job, despite the fact that his employer still owed him money.[57] He secured an attorney from the Legal Aid Society to help him recover his back wages. When this effort failed, Palmer went to his former employer himself. Behringer attacked Palmer with a pick, and a scuffle ensued. Palmer left to find a policeman. When he returned, however, Behringer had already secured one and Palmer was arrested for assault. While handcuffed to the policeman who was taking him into custody, Palmer was beaten by his former employer. He was hauled before Justice Jacob Pawlak of Cheektowaga and charged with third-degree assault. Fortunately for Palmer, the ensuing events were recorded by a reporter who was assigned to cover the court proceedings for the *Buffalo Times.*

At his arraignment, Palmer requested that he be allowed legal counsel. Judge Pawlak denied his request. A conference between Pawlak and an attorney representing the plaintiff resulted in new charges being leveled against Palmer. He was then charged with the serious crime of felonious assault and was rearrested and placed in prison to await grand jury action.

William Evans of the Urban League brought Palmer's case to the attention of the association, which retained the services of Attorney Clarence Maloney to defend Palmer. The Palmer incident was widely publicized by newspapers throughout the state because his was a case of blatant denial of constitutional rights and obvious racial discrimination. A *Buffalo Times* editorial entitled "Justice in Cheektowaga" reminded its readers of the First Amendment to the United Stated Constitution and asked, "Why wasn't Palmer allowed to obtain a lawyer in this case?" It further informed them that the allegations by both the plaintiff and defendant were unsubstantiated and that the race of the defendant does not invalidate his story. It concluded:

> If Palmer had been rich and influential, instead of poor and friend-
> less, would his case have been handled with the same haste?
> We should be glad to have Pawlak's explanation.[58]

The International Labor Defense League pursued the Palmer case because of its policy of defending workers against discrimination. The combined efforts of the association and the league ultimately resulted in Palmer's exoneration.

The NAACP teamed up once more with the ILD in its defense of Alphonso Davis of Niagara Falls. Davis beat "four or five Polish citizens" during a riot which occurred in the Falls some time in August 1934.

The whites were infuriated and secured a Polish woman who falsely accused Davis of criminally assaulting her. The police arrested Davis and incarcerated him in the county jail in Lockport, New York where he was beaten and placed under heavy bail.[59]

The ILD protested this incident by sponsoring a demonstration in the Polish community. The demonstration heightened hostilities; more violence ensued and another black man was arrested. In fact, it was the ILD activities which gained the attention of the national NAACP. The ILD accused the NAACP of impeding justice by withholding judgment. It served as the conscience of the NAACP during the 1930s, and this was merely one of many attacks on the association of which the most devastating occurred over the Scottsboro case.[60] Walter White requested that Julian Evans, president of the Buffalo chapter, investigate. Evans depended heavily upon the report of officials of the Niagara Falls Community Center, which served blacks, for information. However, J. M. Pollard, secretary of the center, had retained counsel for the defendant and did not grant Evans an interview or inform him of the progress of the trial. Unable to find anything other than "hearsay" testimony about the case, the local NAACP absolved itself of responsibility for the outcome of the trial.[61]

The NAACP and the ILD once again united forces in the defense of Homer Gill, of Buffalo, who had been accused of murdering his employer during a burglary attempt. Although Gill admitted that he was at the shop when the shooting occurred, he maintained his innocence. Witnesses reported that they had seen "three Italians" rushing from the butcher shop following the incident. ILD committee members provided legal counsel for Gill, and attorneys explored a number of defense strategies in his case. Searching for legal strategies, Stephen Perkins, a local NAACP attorney, wrote to the ILD headquarters in New York in an attempt to secure a brief which the ILD presented in the Gill case or the decision in the Scottsboro case.[62] Perkins suggested a possible line of defense by using a recent court decision handed down by a Clarksdale, Mississippi judge who argued that the entire jury system of the state of Mississippi would have to be revised when he quashed indictments against two blacks who had been accused of murder.

The ILD highly publicized the case of Homer Gill; individuals representing a number of groups bombarded the national NAACP with inquiries. Ruth Davies, NAACP board member, and Pattie Ellis of the YWCA both inquired of Walter White what the NAACP's response was to the case.[63] Ellis wrote that it was essential that the YWCA be informed. Julian Evans, attorney for the NAACP, informed White of the facts in the case and notified him that he and Perkins were defending Gill.[64] Charles Houston, special counsel of the NAACP, advised his fraternity brother that Buffalo should not go into the case unless in Evans' own legal opinion Gill was innocent or risked getting an unfair trial because of his race.[65] Walter White had sent a similar reply to Ruth Davies the previous day. White cautioned her to handle association funds with care and to avoid their being used for political purposes.[66]

The local association made its opinions known on a number of issues which adversely affected the lives of African Americans during the post–World War I era. Stories regarding the devastating effect the system of peonage had on rural blacks were circulated throughout the country, especially the urban areas of the North, where migrants from the South lent a sympathetic ear. In protest of the living and working conditions of the southern black agricultural workers, the Buffalo NAACP in the spring of 1921 adopted the following petition condemning the system and demanding that the laws which prohibited it be enforced:

> Now be it resolved, that we, citizens of these United States assembled in a meeting in Buffalo, New York, do hereby . . . pray that a wide and searching investigation of peonage throughout the South be made by the Department of Justice, to the end that the facts be widely known, and that the Constitutional provision and the laws against peonage be hereafter enforced.[67]

The NAACP had become interested in the problems of black laborers as early as 1910, but the labor unions had thwarted its efforts. By 1919, an entire day of the annual conference which met in Cleveland was devoted to labor and labor problems.[68]

The Scottsboro case highlighted the political repression that African Americans experienced nationwide and at the same time the disparities that the working class faced in Buffalo. Labor organizer and Erie County Communist Party chair Sam Abbott, of Chippewa Street, reported that blacks were compelled to speak publicly at the intersection of William and Hickory Streets only, except during the election campaigns, when a few politicians circulated throughout the Fifth Ward. Police arrested Abbott for speaking publicly in support of the Scottsboro boys because he did not have a permit, although one was not required for speakers outside of the black districts. The judge sentenced him to ten days in prison.[69] Henry Wright, a member of the John Brown branch of the Communist party, also deplored the restrictions placed on blacks' right of assembly, noting that the police permitted them to speak in "dark, isolated areas and at William and Bennett Streets." Police also arrested Wright for violating their code when he publicly advocated the rights of the Scottsboro boys.[70]

The NAACP litigated on behalf of the Scottsboro defendants, and the Scottsboro defense then inspired a number of disparate groups in Buffalo to combine their resources to assure that the American system of justice worked for African Americans.[71] The Buffalo association actively participated, with a committee composed of the Socialist party, the Communist party, the YWCA, the American Civil Liberties Union, the Building Trades Council, the Women's International League for Peace and Freedom, and the National Negro Congress to raise money for the legal expenses of the Scottsboro boys.[72] A number of individuals—such as Amelia Anderson, Mrs. Lucy Bethel, and Pattie Ellis—who regularly supported human rights causes represented the above organizations.

A planning committee met in January 1936 at St. Luke's AME Zion Church to lay the foundation for a mass meeting for the early spring. The organizers planned to invite Angelo Herndon, avowed Communist and labor organizer and himself a notorious figure, to address the assembly. The Scottsboro Defense Committee conducted most of its organizational activities in the black districts of Buffalo, where it met with widespread support.[73] Julian Evans, president of the local NAACP, and Amelia Anderson, who had served the association in various capacities for some twenty years, helped to engineer projects which were compatible with NAACP ideology. The Buffalo NAACP continued its policy of working with other concerned groups who were interested in protecting the rights of African Americans, regardless of their political persuasion.

Like other sacred and secular organizations which were established in Buffalo's black community, the NAACP also had its educational component. Instruction in the association was conducted primarily through mass meetings designed to increase membership as well as to proselytize. Besides its regularly scheduled mass meetings, the association held special meetings to commemorate the birthdays of Abraham Lincoln and Frederick Douglass (the eminent abolitionist, ambassador, and spokesman for black Americans and women), and Emancipation Day. After 1921, the local association combined all of these with a general celebration of Emancipation Day. These commemorations fostered black community solidarity, for they highlighted the struggles and victories of African people in the United States. On such occasions renowned speakers, most of whom were black, addressed the African American community of Buffalo. Their presence alone indicated the achievements of blacks, often despite great odds. Frequently, as was the case with national NAACP officials, they scheduled separate meetings with selected groups of whites.[74] The "mass" meetings, however, were open to anyone who desired to attend, and the audience was usually interracial. Buffalonians flocked to the churches where they were held.

Most of the lectures that the local association presented to the blacks in Buffalo were nationalist in tone. The speakers made it quite clear that blacks were not seeking integration into American society, but merely equal opportunity and their rights as United States citizens. The lectures served several purposes, most of which revolved around the important questions of economic uplift and moral development. But they often went far beyond this. First, these meetings provided a forum through which the black community could be educated about the goals and tactics of the NAACP. Second, the lecturers attempted to keep local blacks abreast of the conditions of blacks throughout the diaspora. Third, blacks were inculcated with a self-help philosophy which not only encouraged economic uplift, but included a religious fervor emphasizing the need for black Buffalonians to lead morally impeccable lives. Indeed, many of the speakers were clergymen. All of these aspirations were consistent with contemporary African American thought.[75]

The churches in the Buffalo African American community maintained the independent stance that they always had enjoyed and were staunch supporters of the NAACP. They offered their buildings for NAACP meetings and several ministers served on the NAACP Board of Directors. Many of the NAACP guest lecturers were ministers themselves who also were connected to the Buffalo clergy through their church council networks. They provided a large amount of publicity for the NAACP and contributed much to the success of its educational programs. On special occasions, all of the clergy prepared special sermons for NAACP Sunday.[76] The ministers made it appear self-evident that NAACP membership was a part of their parishioners' civic duty and certainly a responsibility of every "race" man and woman. On these occasions, congregations were reminded of the accomplishments of the NAACP both nationwide and locally.

The local association launched its fund-raising drives and concluded its victory celebrations with mass meetings. Usually a national officer came to Buffalo to commend the local association for its "fine" accomplishments and to urge the necessity for increased membership in the organization. Robert Bagnall, clergyman and director of the branches for the NAACP, was a frequent visitor to the "City of Good Neighbors." In the spring of 1921, he discussed with an audience at Shiloh Baptist Church the needs, aims, and accomplishments of the national association, and placed special emphasis upon the organization's anti-lynching campaign.[77] Mary Burnett Talbert, board member and vice president of the NAACP, had attended the 1916 Amenia Conference at Joel Spingarn's Troutbeck estate, and she directed its national anti-lynching campaign in 1922.[78] The following year, Bagnall again addressed a mass meeting at Shiloh. After detailing his fact-finding mission to "Carolina," Georgia, Alabama, and Louisiana, Bagnall contended that "Negroes are determined to have their share in the educational, economic and political life of the South." He concluded that "the Negro is an American citizen and as such he is here to stay and fight out his own fight, solve his own problems, work out his own destiny."[79]

In March 1921, William Pickens, field secretary of the NAACP, addressed a large audience at Shiloh Baptist Church. In his speech, he related to his listeners the conditions African Americans confronted throughout the nation. He concentrated on southern peonage and the deplorable conditions of black prisoners in Leavenworth (Kansas) and Arkansas. Pickens observed how black soldiers were discriminated against in the South. "Colored" soldiers had been placed at the front of the battle lines in the recent war to make the world safe for democracy, yet they were compelled to ride on the rear of the bus at home. Apparently referring to the fact that northern whites, who were not accustomed to Jim Crow laws, found no difficulty in capitulating to the southern way of life when they confronted it, Pickens noted that "the weakest man in this country is the northern white man in the South." He dared not conclude his presentation without offering advice to his predominantly black audience. He moralized, "The Negro must think and then act."[80]

In a speech before an NAACP audience the following month, H. C. Price, "a neighbor and friend of the NAACP" and a black attorney from Virginia who provided legal services for the local association and who would become involved in the Matthew Bullock case, continued in this vein:

> Negroes today realize [that] life is not only for the present but for the future, that life is for service. All these things have awakened the Negroes to thought and action and the result is clear minds, vigorous bodies and sincere hearts.[81]

He reminded black Buffalonians that they had a moral responsibility to help alleviate the plight of African Americans in the South.[82]

The association invited Missouri congressman Leonidas Dyer, author of the anti-lynching bill, to Buffalo to launch its annual membership drive in June 1925. After discussing the accomplishments of the NAACP, Dyer criticized Buffalonians for their failure to support the civil rights organization and lamented that they [blacks] did not take advantage of the great number of opportunities which were available. He argued:

> What great opportunities you have here of helping the Negroes in the South who are denied the very opportunities which you are privileged to enjoy. God only knows your greatest fault is you're not proud of your race. You won't stand together. There are actually some colored people in this country who really believe that they are inferior to whites.[83]

It was extraordinary that a white speaker would take such license with his predominantly black audience. Yet Dyer's approach did not differ from that of a number of the black orators who spoke at NAACP functions. And, after all, Dyer had gained the respect of black Americans because of his congressional record on lynching. If Dyer had treaded on tenuous ground, he certainly gained enthusiastic support when he concluded his remarks by pointing out that "there is no democracy in this country. A democracy means a federal anti-lynching bill."[84]

Dr. Ivorite Scruggs also addressed the audience and referred to the ruthless attack on black soldiers in Alabama as "another kind of lynching." Such attacks seek "to rob the race of its manhood. We must also fight that kind of lynching."[85] In the spring of 1926, Dr. R. L. Bradby, Baptist preacher and president of the Detroit NAACP, came to Buffalo to apprise the local association of the issues involved in the Ossian Sweet case.[86] He told the large gathering at the Lloyd Memorial Congregational Church, "I believe the time has come when the Negro must fight for his rights. And any Negro who does not rise and help to fight in a crisis like this is a traitor to his race."[87]

In April 1928, James Welden Johnson, before an audience of 500 at Shiloh Baptist Church, discussed the activities of the national association. Syracuse University graduate and NAACP President Amelia Anderson launched the association's annual membership drive by informing Buffalonians of the advantages of membership in the NAACP and the obligations of the Buffalo chapter to support the national office. She argued:

> We must play [our part] so well that we will be a valuable asset to the National Office in becoming so strong, so powerful, so active and so effective that no government north or south, no party, in fact no individual will dare to commit any indignity against any member of the race without realizing that he will be defended by every legitimate and constitutional means.

Anderson continued:

> . . . newly gained members for the Buffalo Branch . . . means the awakening on the part of the Colored people to the need of organization; it means the awakening to a sense of citizenship denied, and the responsibility and obligation in bringing to themselves, to the children, and in fact, to America, herself, the realization of a fuller blessing on the part of the Colored people in the participation of the nation's political, economic and community life.[88]

James Weldon Johnson—attorney, former ambassador, author, and field secretary of the NAACP—followed Anderson on the platform. He reminded blacks that "we want power" and that it was necessary for African Americans to decide what their needs and desires are. He contended that the motto for blacks in surmounting any obstacle should be that of the French revolutionary who urged "to dare, to dare again and always

Amelia G. Anderson,
NAACP president. Anderson
Family Archives. Courtesy of
Ora Anderson Curry.

to dare." But he cautioned that success could only be achieved through power, not physical force. Johnson did not rule out force, however; he maintained that physical force for blacks became criminal if it failed. In conclusion, Johnson told his audience: "God is ever willing . . . to help any people who are interested enough to help themselves." He emphasized unity and the need for members of the race to prepare themselves for the "furtherance of this great cause."[89] These were messages that black audiences nationwide heard from NAACP officials, messages that united them around key issues.

The self-help philosophy emphasized by the association, and its concentration on the shared experiences of blacks throughout the world, was made even more explicit through the NAACP-sponsored Emancipation Day celebrations. This annual event first had been sponsored by the Ministers' Council. However, upon the suggestion of Reverend Sidney O. B. Johnson, the council voted to relegate this activity to the NAACP.[90] At the time Reverend Johnson had only been in Buffalo for about six months, but he had become an important force within the black community.[91] The Board of Directors of the NAACP, a number of whom were local black clergymen, endorsed the Johnson proposal.

In 1922 the board devised an elaborate program for the event, which was held at the Bethel AME Church. Mrs. C. J. Jones, assistant secretary, read the Emancipation Proclamation. Amelia Anderson, Dr. Charles Patrick (vice president), and the Reverends J. Edward Nash and E. J. Echols spoke of the slave experience and the achievements which African Americans had made in education, science, the arts, and other areas. But the highlight of the evening was a spirited address by Fred R. Moore, editor of the *New York Age*. In his speech, which traced the progress of the black race since Emancipation, Moore attacked those blacks "who, instead of trying to further the work and progress of the Race, were striving by their indifference to minimize the influence of the Church, the uplifting work of those engaged in social service for the uplift of their people, as well as feeling themselves above the supporting of business enterprises promoted by the group."[92] His concentration on self-help and uplift continued to unfold, thus:

> The Negro who refuses to give support to a real Race enterprise and thus help in the cooperative spirit which, in so many places, the Race is evidencing, is a traitor to his Race, not fit to be damned and unworthy of a place in hell.[93]

Thus, the editor contended that the failure to mobilize politically was the enemy of blacks. Therefore African Americans, to a greater or lesser degree, were to blame for the vice, poor housing conditions, the nature of business enterprises, and other problems which he noticed in the Buffalo and other African American communities.

Moore's presentation emphasized not only economic but moral development as well. He made a scathing attack upon those men "who were only interested in seducing young women" or who were "low and dirty enough to go into the homes of Race men and seek to cripple them by adulterous relationships with their wives." He noted that such men were a menace to the race and should be "hounded out of any community where their devilish actions were known."[94]

Dr. W. N. DeBerry, of Springfield, Massachusetts, speaking at the 1924 Emancipation Day celebration at Shiloh Baptist Church, if somewhat less graphic than Moore, still brought the same message to black Buffalo. He maintained that a people can only be as strong as their institutions. DeBerry further noted:

> It may not be amiss to call attention to what . . . is one of the most alarming tendencies of our age. It is the utter carelessness with which

growing numbers of people are disposed to treat the marriage crown. . . . No nation nor people could have moral or social health so long as the home, the very citadel of the social systems, is thus allowed to degenerate. . . .[95]

DeBerry again echoed Moore and the other black spokesmen when he acknowledged that "racial efficiency" would only come when African Americans exhibited racial solidarity: ". . . this means a realization of the fact that in community interests and destiny we are one regardless of our numerous physical, social, mental and moral differences, as classes or individuals. . . . We should therefore be united as a people in the effort to overcome the obstacles, the wrongs and the injustice with which as a people we are afflicted." Reverend DeBerry concluded his remarks by reciting a poem by the famous lyric poet Paul Laurence Dunbar which expressed DeBerry's message to the race, entitled "Keep a Pluggin' Away."[96]

A crowd of over 300 turned out to hear Dr. W. E. B. DuBois, editor of the *Crisis*, address the Emancipation Day celebration of 1925. To emphasize the commonality of their experience, DuBois discussed his recent tour of the black nations of the world. He also raised questions germane to the social, political, and economic development of blacks throughout the world. The Emancipation Day celebrations remained one of the more successful projects which the association undertook through the next decade. These events continually attracted large audiences, and the speakers whom the NAACP engaged constantly attempted to inculcate blacks with the need for greater "self-help" in order to alleviate their plight. The NAACP's emphasis on an African American collective identity was yet another dimension in its attempt to build a viable community.

From 1915 to 1940 the Buffalo NAACP attempted to alleviate many of the indignities suffered by African Americans. In particular, the NAACP fought against Jim Crow when it manifested itself in theaters, restaurants, and other public accommodations. By the 1920s, the Buffalo NAACP's interest in discrimination in this area waned somewhat because the national association had won a number of precedent-setting cases, based upon the New York State Civil Rights Act, and because recent African American arrivals from the South were especially concerned about the judicial process and fair treatment for blacks through the legal system. The NAACP shifted its priorities and began to adjudicate cases involving the extradition of blacks who allegedly had committed crimes in the South. This change in emphasis was essential if the organization was to retain the membership of the working class blacks who contributed the largest sum of money to the local association, and who were migrants from the South. Occasionally, the Buffalo

NAACP joined forces with leftist groups such as the International Labor Defense and moderate organizations like the National Urban League, in an attempt "to safeguard the political and civil rights of Afro-Americans." The organization, thereby, provided blacks with an arena in which to develop the sophisticated political skills they would need to penetrate the Democratic party machine. The association, always cognizant of the need to proselytize, continuously sponsored mass meetings where eminent national and local personalities emphasized the need for self-help and racial solidarity among black Buffalonians. This multifaceted approach fostered black pride and was instrumental in helping blacks to develop and maintain a strong sense of community.

The NAACP's integrationist model was not the only approach that Buffalo African Americans considered to create a modern community and to effect changes in their lives. Some residents had become imbued with the philosophy of the charismatic Jamaican social critic Marcus Garvey, who had arrived in New York in 1916 and had taken much of the African American urban population by storm. Garveyism's appeal lay in the fact that the post-migration experience for many blacks had been disappointing, for its promise of new and lucrative employment options remained largely unfulfilled. Likewise, residential segregation became the norm in most areas and racial hostilities, including violence against blacks, increased. His appeals to self-help and racial solidarity struck a cord with newcomers, too.

Marcus Garvey came into this environment and made racial appeals to urbanites. His self-determinationist ideology that called for the development of business enterprises, cultural purity, and even the establishment of an independent black nation found willing adherents among this segment of the population. In short, Garvey told a people that had been assaulted in so many areas of their lives that they were somebody and that their destiny lay in their hands.[97] Subsequently, the Garvey movement enjoyed the largest membership of any contemporary organization of blacks in the country. But these people were rational and did not offer Garvey an uncritical mass of support. They took those tenets from Garvey's program that they considered pragmatic and began to proselytize among their people.[98]

Local #79, a group of representatives from diverse class backgrounds, organized an affiliate of the Universal Negro Improvement Association and African Communities League (UNIA and ACL) in Buffalo in 1920. Dr. Theodore Kakaza (a physician from South Africa), President Cornelius McKnight (a window washer), Alfred Boykin (a grocer), and *Buffalo American* publisher Arthur Lewis were instrumental in founding this organization. Other key organizers included Richard and Lillian Willis, who later left Buffalo to work for the national organization, and many veterans of the war.

Immediately upon its founding in the summer of 1920, Local #79 invited Garvey to address a meeting of supporters in Buffalo. Garvey declined the invitation because of a previous commitment and sent Reverend James Eason, chaplin general of the UNIA and the ACL, in his stead. Dr. Eason explained the philosophy that undergirded the organization but made a less than stellar impression upon the audience, according to a *Buffalo American* editorial.[99] But when Garvey finally arrived in Buffalo in August, he was met by an enthusiastic crowd of several hundred African Americans. Garvey mesmerized the audience as he told them of the advantages of self-help and self-determination in charting their future and as he spoke of the prospects for the UNIA's business enterprises.

On October 14, 1920 Garvey returned to Buffalo amidst pageantry and splendor and once more addressed a crowd of several hundred blacks at the Technical High School. Garvey appealed to blacks across lines of gender and class because his message was couched in the traditional African American ideology of self-help and racial solidarity. But Buffalonians did not blindly follow him. Arthur Lewis, vice president and chair of the advisory board of #79 and ACL, and Secretary Lillian Willis explained: "Our affiliation with the UNIA was brought about after a thorough understanding of its principles and ideals that sought the universal co-operation of negroes everywhere; [and] in every line of endeavor, that it denounce radicalism . . ."[100]

Garvey addressed Buffalo audiences on two other occasions in October, attracting over 1,000 people. The *Buffalo American* noted that the three meetings were the "greatest meetings ever held in our city."[101] The editor suggested that curiosity had propelled people from their homes, but observed that "by Sunday afternoon (October 17) interest replaced curiosity."[102] The *Buffalo American* predicted that the UNIA would succeed because of its recognition that both the leadership and the rank and file must be integrated. Furthermore, it contended, "the idea to build for ourselves everything; to prepare for another day; to stimulate all movements among our Race for progress; to become an independent, self-sustaining people is the doctrine of the age."[103] In other words, Garveyism was in the mainstream of contemporary black political thought. But as ambitious and as meritorious as the programs of the UNIA seemed, the *Buffalo American* cautioned that "[we] not let any doctrine cause [us] to denounce the Stars and Stripes and this the only home of which we know."[104]

Although support for the UNIA in Buffalo was widespread, some prominent African Americans expressed doubt and suspicion about the movement. Buffalo black clergy were prominent among this group of doubters. In September 1920, Reverend E. Daniels of the St. Philip's Episcopal Church denounced Garveyism because of its failure to "take measures that would bring peace between both races."[105] Reverend Elijah J. Echols of the First Shiloh Baptist Church was the most vociferous in his criticism of Garvey. Like Daniels, he objected to what he perceived to be Garvey's racist appeals. Echols distrusted Garvey, his organization, and his business enterprises, especially the Black Star Shipping Line.[106] But in a letter to Garvey, Echols explained that as a "chosen leader" of a segment of the black population, his constituents often sought counsel from him regarding the UNIA and he wished to be better informed to respond to them. Echols raised several questions about Garvey's personal life, business endeavors, and motives. He asked him to identify ten of the leading black educators who had endorsed his ideology and to explain why the first UNIA conference had met in New York instead of Africa or the West Indies. Echols requested a "brief and immediate response." This was the beginning of a long-running feud between the two men that frequently occurred through the pages of the *Buffalo American*.[107]

Buffalo clergy and the local affiliate #79 also took offense at the attack on the Reverend J. Edward Nash, respected pastor of the Michigan Avenue Baptist Church, that appeared in the UNIA publication *Negro World*. In fact, the charges against Nash seemed so blatant that both Lewis and Willis issued a formal apology in the *Buffalo American* and asked that the local unit be dissociated from the article. Some Buffalo clergymen also were appalled because Garvey had planned to sell shares of stock in the Black Star Line in their churches and in violation of the Sabbath. Echols refused to permit the sales to occur in his church altogether and shortly thereafter local #79 found a new temporary site for its meetings at the Lloyd Memorial Congregational Church of Reverend Sidney O. B. Johnson.

Historian Ralph Watkins suggested that opposition to Garvey occurred, in part, because the Buffalo clergy comprised a theocracy that tenaciously guarded its power.[108] Like their counterparts nationwide, these clergy also exerted disproportionate influence within their communities. But other sectors of the population also provided effective and powerful leadership, such as the black press, the professional and business classes, and the administrators of some social organizations. In fact, during this period some contended that Mary Burnett Talbert—president of the National Association of Colored Women, NAACP board member, and a reformer of national and international prominence—was not only the undisputed leader of the black community, but the most well-known Buffalonian.

Nevertheless, in the post–World War I Buffalo climate, churches in the black communities frequently provided the only meeting places for large audiences and the ministers were guardians of their space. Consequently, during this era the clergy collectively formed a formidable

force whose blueprints for shaping a modern community were sometimes shortsighted and subordinate to their desire for control.[109] Their
views obviously varied according to their circumstances. Frequently these
same players also were in the vanguard of progressive reform movements
or became the biggest boosters of such initiatives.

Opposition from the clergy notwithstanding, Local #79 continued
to enjoy widespread support in Buffalo and the surrounding areas.[110]
The local unit organized a band and a choir and performed at local
events; one of the highlights of the Erie County fair was the performance
of the UNIA band.[111] These units provided the opportunity to train
African American youths in music techniques. Resplendent in their col-
orful uniforms, these youngsters also were given an experience that
helped to build their self-esteem, and such performances presented
positive images of blacks to the western New York community.

Drill teams were also a part of the local UNIA program. These units
taught self-discipline and acted as honor guards for visiting dignitaries.
W. L. Buchanan, the FBI agent who had infiltrated the Garvey organization, reported that the drill team, consisting of black men and women,
flanked Garvey and field organizer Henrietta Vinton Davis during their
February 19, 1921 visit to Buffalo. He also noted that there were thirty
women dressed in white who represented the African Black Cross.[112]
In this regard, Garveyism functioned much like benevolent organizations in black communities across the nation.

The local Garvey unit also offered African Americans a forum in
which to discuss and to debate national and local politics and their
racial implications. President Boykin, in his address to this same body,
expressed his views that the recent Washington disarmament talks were
not called to promote peace per se. Boykin contended that the peace
conference was called "for the sole purpose of disarming Japan, as the
white nations realized that they were unsafe as long as the colored, or
yellow races were as strong as Japan; and the white races also realized
that another war among themselves would give the colored races, including yellow, the upper hand in the universe."[113] Such discussions
reinforced in members' minds the idea that an international organization like UNIA was essential for blacks to protect their best interests.
Ironically, they did not discuss the possibility of forging ties with other
people of color either in the United States or abroad.

Local #79 was a means of forging coalitions in Buffalo, and it was
a training ground on which individuals could rise through the ranks
of the UNIA. Frank C. Perkins, a well-known Socialist and the first to
be elected to the Buffalo Common Council in 1922, supported #79's
programs. When Gabriel M. Johnson, the mayor of Monrovia, Liberia,
was the guest of the UNIA, at the public gathering Perkins welcomed
him to Buffalo.[114]

Several people from Africa and other regions of the diaspora wended their way to Buffalo and adopted Garveyism. Percival L. Burrows, a "self-made man," had immigrated to the United States from his native Barbados in 1904.[115] Burrows rose through the ranks after he joined Buffalo's Local #79 in 1920. He published *The Voice of Buffalo,* a small newspaper which became the official organ of the chapter and offered Buffalonians an alternative to the "disproportionately negative" articles that appeared in the *Buffalo American.* The Buffalo unit elected Burrows as their official delegate to the 1921 convention. Garvey and his administrators were so impressed that they appointed him high commissioner for the islands of Trinidad, Tobago, St. Vincent, and Grenada, as well as for Venezuela and Brazil. He helped the UNIA establish 21 new divisions in the region and in 1923 Garvey appointed him to be the first assistant secretary-general of the UNIA parent body.[116] Lillian Willis served as branch secretary. In November, 1920, Willis joined Garvey and Dr. William H. Ferris, literary editor of the *Negro World,* as keynote speakers at a meeting in New York City. Soon thereafter she and her husband became national organizers for the UNIA.[117]

Dr. Theodore Kakaza had left South Africa to become a doctor. He began his training in medicine at the famed Mehary Medical School in Nashville and completed his course of study at the University of Toronto Medical School.[118] Then he moved to Buffalo to establish his general medical practice and became an active member of local #79, serving as president. In December 1923, Kakaza wrote Congressman Clarence MacGregor to request that he initiate an investigation of the charges against Garvey for allegedly using the mail to defraud. He also sought Garvey's release from prison pending the results of the investigation.[119]

The Universal Negro Improvement Association allowed women to have access to leadership positions. In fact, one of its most effective organizers was Henrietta Vinton Davis, who frequently travelled with Garvey or substituted for him at important functions. Women in Buffalo were key players in the local unit, as well. Women organized the Black Cross Nurses within guidelines from the parent organization, and they worked with children's groups. Local #79 women joined the drill teams, practicing with men, and participating in ceremonies alongside them. However, #79 had a parallel administrative structure, with women serving in positions with titles similar to those that men held. In February 1922, for example, Alfred A. Boykin was president, while Mrs. Beatrice Washington was "lady president." The unit sent Washington as delegate to the 1922 UNIA convention.[120]

The Garvey movement offered Buffalonians another approach to creating a community. Just as important, however, was its emphasis on the dignity, intelligence, and worth of African Americans. African American soldiers, returning from Europe, saw Garveyism as an opportunity to achieve the respect and dignity that had eluded them in post–world war America. Industrial workers also seized upon its tenets to maintain their self-worth in the hostile and often alien environment of the workplace. The local unit also developed programs for all sectors of the black population and even won the support and respect of many upper-middle-class people. This trend suggested an awareness that the entire population must play a role in creating their modern community.

The economic and social circumstances of their community affected black women and their perceptions of the world. The informal networks that characterized much of their nineteenth-century efforts remained important, but the increasing population compelled them to give way to new formal, structured groups designed to improve their status and that of their community. African American women in Buffalo had keen notions of the meaning of community and they were deeply involved in the creation of their twentieth-century Buffalo. These women persistently had struggled to improve the lives of their people.

Outspoken critic Mary Burnett Talbert expressed the belief that undergirded much of their thought when she told an assembly of delegates to the NACW in 1916 that "no Negro woman can afford to be an indifferent spectator of the social, moral, religious, economic, and uplift problems that are agitated around [her]."[121] This spirit had governed their activities in the nineteenth century and had given them ample experiences necessary for devising new mechanisms and approaches to deal with contemporary concerns of blacks. Their network of kin and friendship still allowed black women of Buffalo to work within their tradition of self-help and mutuality and facilitated action on their part. This tradition and the ethos of the Progressive Era informed their decisions.

The Phyllis Wheatley Club was one of Buffalo black women's most significant organizations and suggests how they approached many of the contemporary issues that surfaced at the turn of the century. Its activities personified black women's reform in the Progressive Era and their notion of community. Although a volunteer organization, professionalism characterized the Phyllis Wheatley Club. Members included Oberlin College graduate Mary Burnett Talbert and Mrs. Charles H. Banks, an alumna of Hampton Institute in Virginia. Susan Evans had attended college in Chicago and had worked at a settlement house there prior to moving to Buffalo.

Club women were well aware of the creeping racism that seemed to permeate the country on the eve of the twentieth century, and they believed that black women had to take a stance against it. Early on, the Phyllis Wheatley Club protested the exclusionary racial policies of the Board of Directors of the Pan American Exposition, held in Buffalo in 1901, which highlighted the technical innovations that made Buffalo one of the most advanced cities in the hemisphere.[122] The board's decision to exclude an African American exhibit set back the exhibition's policy a generation, for all recent expos had included blacks. At an interracial forum of 200 that the club sponsored at the Michigan Avenue Baptist Church, Mary Talbert cogently argued for the inclusion of blacks. Pragmatist that she was, Talbert also spoke of the financial success of previous exhibits on African peoples, noting how important such exhibits had been in helping to break down negative racial stereotypes.

Black politicians like James A. Ross and white reformers like Mrs. A. B. Wilson pledged their support to try to persuade the intransigent board to repeal its previous decision. The assembled group adopted unanimous resolutions to support this position and the appointment of a black commissioner.[123] The Phyllis Wheatley Club's challenge to the power structure proved to be a pyrrhic victory, however, for the commissioners failed to appoint a black to their board. Although they approved "The Old Plantation," an exhibition on blacks, it focused on slavery and minstrelsy and depicted blacks in negative stereotypes. The official Pan American exhibition catalogue used the derogatory language prevalent at the time in reference to blacks. The live scenes bore such titles as "Three Cullud Gemmen" and "Pickaninnies at Craps." This was hardly what the Phyllis Wheatley Club had envisioned. The opulence that the gothic and neoclassic architecture represented and the well-dressed upper-class visitors stood in stark contrast to the African American slave cabins and the Africans in the parade on the Midway. Although these images reflected little in reality, they highlighted the disparities in the experiences of blacks and whites.[124]

The Phyllis Wheatley Club's fight against racism was to be a protracted one, with limited victories. It and the community continued to be plagued by the negative images of blacks that the press depicted.[125] The club envisioned the formation of key alliances to succeed in its efforts toward change. It had been instrumental in organizing the NAACP in 1910, and it enjoyed widespread support from blacks and whites.

Several black women's clubs joined the struggle to mitigate the harmful effects of racism. They believed that education was a viable means to change people's attitudes and behavior. Therefore, they specifically targeted public schools and libraries for their crusade. The Phyllis Wheatley Club donated the literary works of Phyllis Wheatley and other leading black writers to the public library in 1901.[126] Organized to "improve [its] community and to provide sociability [sic] among members," the Lit-Mus Club also provided avenues for Buffalonians to learn about black life and culture. It introduced "Negro History Week" to Buffalo, and annually, beginning in 1928, it made arrangements for the public library to set up special exhibits during its observance.[127]

Black women's organizations also invited prominent speakers, such as educators Charlotte Hawkins Brown, Nannie Helen Burroughs, and Mary Church Terrell, historian J. A. Rogers, and poet Countee Cullen to discuss contemporary issues that confronted black Buffalonians.[128] The presence of these eminent intellectuals boosted morale among blacks and acted as a catalyst in gaining some white support for black causes in the city. They also helped to keep blacks in Buffalo informed of political ideologies and struggles that were being waged throughout their communities across the country.

Buffalo black women understood well the importance of political action to help effect social change, and they had long participated in organizations established to shape public policy. Earlier they had been involved in abolitionism, the ratification movement for support of the Fifteenth Amendment to the Constitution, and the school integration movement in the city. Black women organized suffrage groups, participated in suffrage demonstrations, and pursued what political scientist Martin Kilson referred to as "mature" political action. They lobbied legislators and tried to influence the vote of black and white men in Buffalo. These women could draw upon their affiliation with the NACW, the Western New York Council of Women, and the Buffalo Federation of Women's Clubs for support. Buffalo club women perceived the NAACP, with its branches across the nation, as an effective tool for addressing the critical issues that the Buffalo community experienced. Such a network, dedicated to the eradication of racism and human rights violations, meant that communities with small black populations, like Buffalo, could draw on that network to avoid isolation and political suicide.

Women's participation in the new world order ushered in after the war and the ratification of the Nineteenth Amendment was key to effecting change in the lives of black folk. The *Buffalo American* reported the following assessment of women's role in the process:

> . . . our women are not liabilities but assets in this fight. [The struggle] cannot be won without us, and it is a sacred duty as well as a privilege [that] we exercise our right of franchise in such a way as to bring renown upon the Race. . . .
>
> We want to train an army of women to battle for economic, political, and social justice. We are hoping that the underlying principles of true womanhood will so abound that there will be nothing at fault, but all to praise. Under this appeal [we] admonish all women to be mindful of their importance at the polls. Your vote measures with the vote of any and every American citizen.[129]

The NACW proposed the establishment of schools of citizenship for newly enfranchised black women. Georgia Nugent, chair of the NACW Executive Committee, told delegates at the 1920 convention held at

Tuskegee, "The ballot without intelligence back of it is a menace instead of a blessing and I like to think that women are accepting their recently granted citizenship with a sense of reverent responsibility."[130] In the 1920s, black women in Buffalo founded the Negro Women's Civic and Research Club to address just such challenges. It met frequently at its headquarters on Clinton Street, in the heart of the growing black community. Organized to study "thoroughly vital points pertaining to our government and the Negro race," the club hoped to guide and teach "self-independence" as it pursued equality of opportunities for African Americans. At its inaugural meeting, Mrs. John Campbell, president, discussed the "real significance" of being a true American. Mrs. Edith Payne facilitated an open forum entitled "The Value of the Vote." Members conducted seminars on the speeches of local and national political figures, and blacks' struggles for self-determination.[131]

The denial of justice to African Americans was always a pressing issue for black women and in the 1930s they joined forces with other local and national groups in support of the defense of the Scottsboro Boys.[132] Women's participation in such forums provided them with the requisite skills to assume roles in politics. After the ratification of the Nineteenth Amendment, Buffalo black women began to organize Republican clubs. Support for Marcus Garvey's Universal Negro Improvement Association remained strong among women, too. By the middle of the 1930s, their participation in politics had evolved to a new stage of political maturation. At that time they founded Democratic women's clubs and held office in mixed-gender political groups.[133]

World war and the migration and depression years were particularly difficult for black women and provided an impetus for action predicated upon consciousness of their identity as black women. The protection of black women, especially the young who came to the city in search of economic opportunities, was a major concern for black women's organizations. Club women knew that these women were vulnerable to exploitation, and tales of the slavelike conditions under which some young black women domestics lived in the North were rampant. The Douglass Club, a group of progressive black women, uncovered such a case in Buffalo and used their political savvy to redress this grievance. A young black woman who had been brought to Buffalo as a child had been forced to work for a white attorney's family for eighteen years without any financial compensation. This family also denied her access to education beyond elementary school, and they prevented her from attending church and communicating with people outside of their family. The Douglass Club, with the aid of prominent black businessman Cornelius Ford, rescued the young woman from this fate and found her a new home and a job that paid wages.[134]

Black women in Buffalo carried out their reform activities in a variety of independent clubs and auxiliary units. The establishment of black women's auxiliaries was the result of both the marginalization that women frequently experienced in mixed-gender groups, as well as their desire to maintain vehicles through which to exercise a ritual of solidarity. These forums, like black women's independent clubs, provided a laboratory in which women could pursue social engineering policies. It also offered them a nurturing environment in which to acquire leadership training.

The women's auxiliaries of the National Urban League and the NAACP illustrated ways in which women carried out what they perceived to be their mandates in these secular organizations. Women's church organizations offer another illustration and an opportunity to observe the ways in which women acquired the necessary skills for political involvement and self-empowerment. The key was that these organizations allowed them the opportunity to work in an environment that promoted their subordinate culture and simultaneously enhanced their stature within the parent organization.

The Women's Mite Missionary Society (WMMS) of the Bethel African Methodist Episcopal Church was one of these groups and brought women from diverse backgrounds together.[135] WMMS activities reflected a distinct woman's culture characterized by benevolence, mutuality, and nurturance. Their activities also taught them that they could effect change by pooling their collective resources. The WMMS frequently combined with local and state women's missionary societies to promote their political views, supporting reform movements and educational programs in Buffalo as well as in Haiti, Africa, and other parts of the African diaspora.

Buffalo black women, regardless of the vehicles they used, articulated community concerns, galvanized their collective power, and seized the opportunity to provide leadership in their communities. They focused upon community uplift through education, benevolence, self-improvement, and the amelioration of race relations. Their successes resulted from an ability to mobilize resources such as their collective organizational and management skills, and their effective fund-raising techniques.[136] Moreover, they utilized their knowledge of African Americans' historical experiences and their national network of women as weapons to effect social change. They worked with black men and gained their respect and that of the white community. Their organized activities indicate continued awareness of their community's greatest social concerns and a firm commitment to reform. It was just such beliefs and activities that helped to further shape and strengthen the modern African American community of Buffalo.

Conclusion

Think only of the best, work for the best, expect the best.
Learn from history's mistakes and press on to greater
achievements.

ADAPTED FROM "THE OPTIMIST'S CREED," BY
ADA L. WILLIAMS[1]

The lives of African Americans in Buffalo from 1900 to 1940 reveal much about race, class, and gender in the development of urban communities. These workers had begun their journeys to the North in Mississippi, Alabama, South Carolina, Georgia, Virginia, and other southern states. Many had gained work experience in the steel factories in Virginia, Pennsylvania, and Illinois before following kin and friends, and their own dreams, to Buffalo. Others came directly from agricultural regions and brought their only bargaining tool—their labor. But it was they who decided where they would locate and in what factories they would work. Laborers had established a network among themselves and sought better working conditions and pay.

In most industries blacks worked close by with one another since they were restricted to a limited range of job options. The environment of the workplace often reinforced their bonds of mutuality. Simultaneously, their work assignments sometimes served to drive a wedge between them and white workers, many of whom believed that union membership was beyond the grasp of black workers, whom they perceived as competitors rather than members of the brotherhood of laborers. Just as blacks left the South to seek jobs in Buffalo, so did whites, and they also carried with them their attitudes regarding racial hierarchies. However, their views on race were shared by most whites by the end of World War I. Employers also conducted their own campaigns to undermine union organizing activities, arguing that African Americans would be blacklisted in the closed shops. They sometimes targeted the spouses of black workers to dissuade them from participating in union activities.

Black migrant workers transformed the landscape by their mere presence. It was they who opened up factory jobs for their group. Increasingly, they were able to move into Buffalo's growth industries—iron and steel, brass and alloyed products, meat packing, and cars and transportation. But for the most part they could not penetrate beyond the lowest entry-level positions because white workers, labor unions, and employers relegated them to a subordinate station in the labor market. For black women the occupational structure was even more restricted; they were limited primarily to domestic jobs in families and institutions. Only a handful of black women worked in clerical positions. When they found employment in factories, it was usually also in the service sector. However, both genders increased their earning power and the greater control that they were able to exercise over their lives, in contrast to their southern experiences, must have justified the move for them.

The creation of the black industrial work force in Buffalo made concrete the vast divisions that existed between black and white workers, while the increasing black population heightened racial discord just as it had in Chicago, Milwaukee, Detroit, New York, and other urban areas where blacks settled during the Great Migration. Buffalo, however, did not experience the race riots that the other cities did. Their economic and social disparities led blacks to draw upon their friendship and kin networks and their sense of mutuality to create new organizations to redress their grievances. They contributed precious time and monies to develop and support these social, political, and economic organizations.

Black organizations in twentieth-century Buffalo were confronted with a dual problem: improving the social and economic conditions of blacks in their community and ameliorating the conditions which confronted them in the larger community. As a result, blacks had to devise new methods for solving their problems. Most black organizations employed a philosophy predicated upon self-help and racial solidarity in devising schemes and implementing their social programs because their members were pragmatists. This self-help philosophy seemed to be the most appropriate means of challenging the status to which blacks had been relegated.

Some may contend that the programs which black organizations promoted were conservative and detrimental to blacks because they often did not challenge the status quo, but such assertions are irresponsible. These organizations must be evaluated within the context of their time and their ability to function in their contemporary settings. The case of black employment and how such groups as the Urban League or the Michigan Avenue YMCA handled it is a primary example which sheds some light on this issue. Black parents, like all parents, wanted their children not only to survive, but to thrive and to achieve heights from which they had been excluded. This meant that the younger generation must have access to education and to secure, steady jobs. Buffalo blacks, like those nationwide, were restricted to the lowest paying and the least remunerative positions, usually service jobs. Furthermore, the propaganda campaign being waged by the Buffalo white news media through their depiction of blacks as brutes or criminals had to be countered by an educational philosophy which had its genesis within the black community. Thus, through self-help—i.e., self-reliance—blacks were best able to ward off the debilitating psychological effects of racism and to launch a campaign for human dignity and equality, as well as for social, economic, and political improvement.

Migration also made more visible class differences in the African American community. The differences between the old Buffalo elite and the migrants were extensive. The migrants found the elite to be indifferent or "bourgeois," while the elite often were offended by "southern culture"—"clannishness," dress, and speech patterns. The old guard argued that the restrictions on their freedom that seemed to accompany the arrival of these newcomers were the result of southern "boorish" ways. The old guard seemed to be oblivious to the rising membership in the Ku Klux Klan in their own backyard and throughout the North; in fact, Buffalo had one of the largest increases in Klan membership in the 1920s.[2] They also seemed to ignore the violence against blacks that, ironically, increased following World War I.

But this is only part of the story. It is also important to note that these "old" Buffalonians had a long protest tradition. Indeed, while southerners became dominant in the NAACP, the old guard had founded the organization that was to become the most important civil rights organization in the century. Their legacy of protest could benefit southerners, too, but this old elite group soon was superseded by a largely professional and business class with deep roots in the South.

Racial solidarity frequently became the basis for the mediation of such differences. Blacks crossed class and regional lines to ward off the effects of racism. While each class undoubtedly had different interests, the social distances between them may not have been as great as may have appeared, because of a number of factors. There was some residential stratification along class lines, but black professionals and workers tended to live close together in their neighborhoods. These same workers comprised the clientele for black attorneys, physicians, pharmacists, social workers, ministers, and entertainers. Increasingly, black professionals provided more of the services that black working-class people needed.

Historian V. P. Franklin noted that education was one of those core values to which blacks subscribed.[3] As "race" men and women the migrants had great respect for African Americans who had acquired an education. They held in especially high regard those who used their education for the benefit of the community. The letters of migrants that the National Urban League collected during the Great Migration are replete with examples of the genuine bonds of friendship and respect that these migrants held for the professionals from their hometowns. Most of the black professionals in Buffalo had come from the South also, and knew the oppressive regimes under which black workers had lived. Some black workers were members of the Prince Hall Order of Masons, the Order of the Eastern Stars, and other benevolent societies, and such memberships gave them high status within their communities and public recognition that they subscribed to middle-class values; the professional and business elite also joined these same groups.

The present study suggests that despite upheavals arising from in-migration and an increase in both racial prejudice and diverse social problems (such as inadequate housing, health, and recreational facilities, and tenuous economic circumstances), the black migrant population brought with it from the South the seeds with which to establish viable communities in the North. This conclusion recognizes and acknowledges that African Americans were agents in the process of relocating and transforming their lives, as well as the urban landscape.

No one will deny the existence of social ills in poor urban communities, nor that these problems manifested themselves more frequently with the increase of the population of urban centers like Buffalo. But by focusing on these "problems," investigators have failed to grasp an understanding of the dreams and aspirations of black people and how African Americans cope amidst adversity. Hence Ralph Ellison's *Invisible Man* is invisible because others refuse to see him, and black poet Nikki Giovanni is compelled to write:

> and I really hope that no [person
> who is insensitive to cultural
> diversity] ever has cause to write
> about me
> because they never understand Black
> love
>   is Black wealth and they'll
> probably talk about my hard
> childhood and
>   never understand that
> all the while I was quite happy.[4]

The life preparation black youths received emphasized the difficult days which would invariably arrive, and African American folklore is replete with examples of the weak overcoming the powerful, despite insurmountable obstacles. It is with this resolve that blacks migrated to northern urban centers like Buffalo at the turn of the twentieth century and successfully carved out a niche for themselves.

APPENDIX I: FIGURES

1A. AGE DISTRIBUTION OF BUFFALO POPULATION
BY RACE AND SEX, 1920

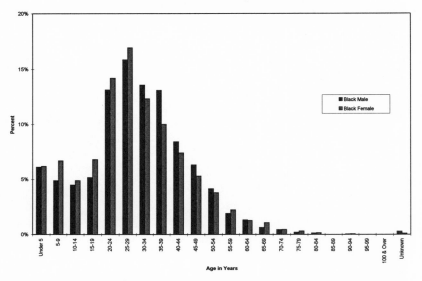

Source: 14th Census of the United States taken in the Year 1920, Volume II;
General Report and Analytical Tables.

1B. AGE DISTRIBUTION OF BUFFALO POPULATION
BY RACE AND SEX, 1920

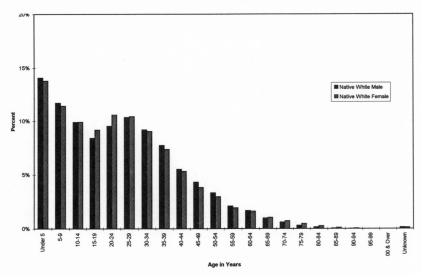

Source: 14th Census of the United States taken in the Year 1920, Volume II;
General Report and Analytical Tables.

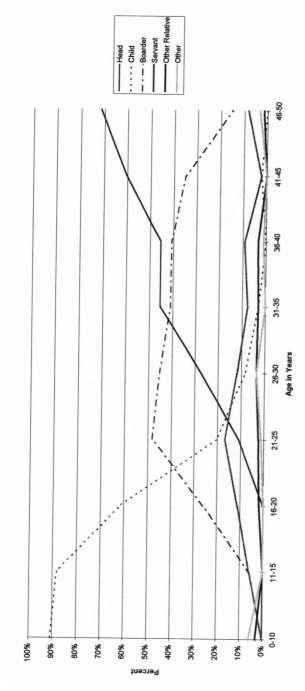

2. HOUSEHOLD STATUS OF BLACK MALES, 1905

Source: Compiled from data taken from the New York State Manuscript Census Schedule for 1905.

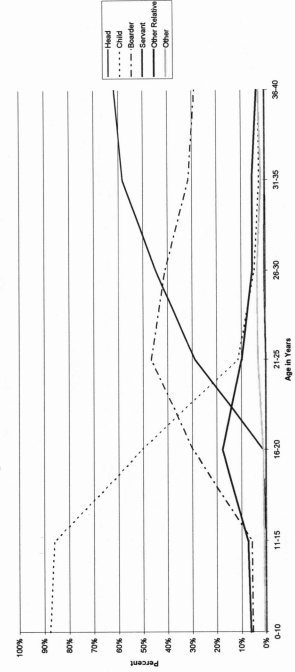

Figure 3. Black Male Household Status, 1925

Source: Compiled from data taken from the New York State Manuscript Census Schedule for 1925.

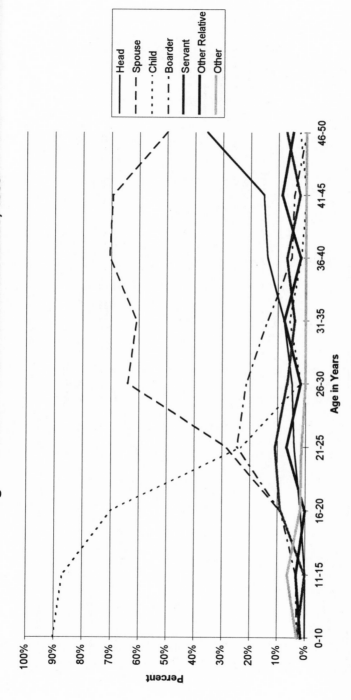

Figure 4. Black Female Household Status, 1905

Source: Compiled from data taken from the New York State Manuscript Census Schedule for 1905.

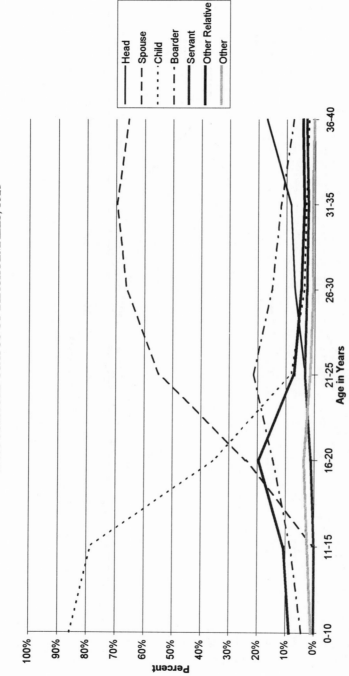

5. HOUSEHOLD STATUS OF BLACK FEMALES, 1925

Source: Compiled from data taken from the New York State Manuscript Census Schedule for 1925.

6. MEDIAN SALARY AND WEEKLY EXPERIENCE—HIGH SCHOOL AND GRAMMAR SCHOOL

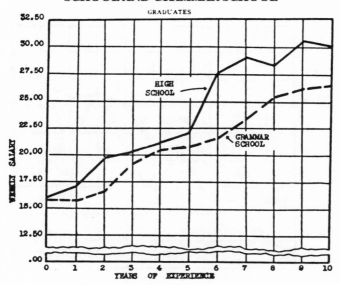

7. MEDIAN SALARY AND WEEKLY EXPERIENCE —PROTESTANT, CATHOLIC, AND JEWISH WOMEN

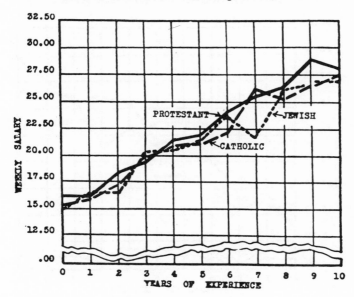

Source: Niles Carpenter, Nationality, Color, Occupation, and Income, *Buffalo: University of Buffalo, 1927.*

8. MEDIAN SALARY AND WEEKLY EXPERIENCE—AMERICAN AND "OLD IMMIGRATION" GROUPS

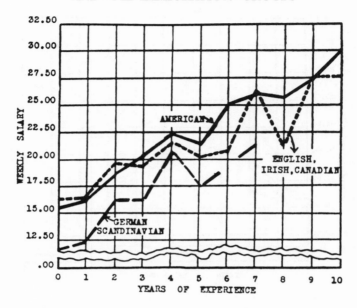

9. MEDIAN SALARY AND WEEKLY EXPERIENCE—AMERICAN AND "NEW IMMIGRATION" GROUPS

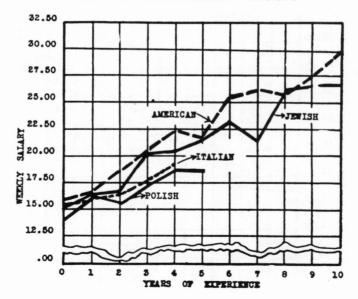

Source: Carpenter, Nationality, Color, Occupation, and Income.

10. MEDIAN SALARY AND WEEKLY EXPERIENCE—AMERICAN AND "OLD IMMIGRATION" GROUPS
(high school graduates only)

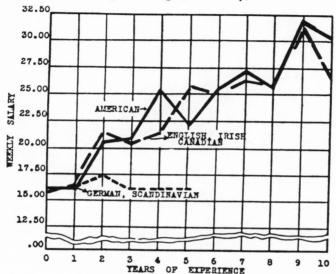

11. MEDIAN SALARY AND WEEKLY EXPERIENCE—AMERICAN AND "NEW IMMIGRATION" GROUPS
(high school graduates only)

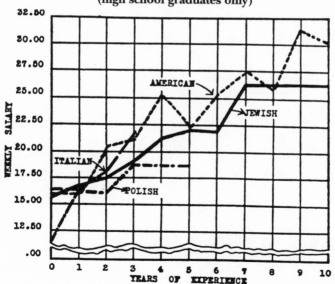

Source: Carpenter, Nationality, Color, Occupation, and Income.

APPENDIX II: MAPS

1. BLACK POPULATION IN THE CITY OF BUFFALO, 1905

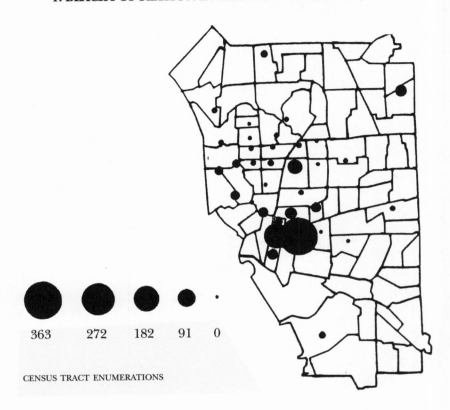

363   272   182   91   0

CENSUS TRACT ENUMERATIONS

Source: Generated from New York State Manuscript Census Schedules for Buffalo, 1905, University at Buffalo, SUNY Archives.

2. BLACK POPULATION IN THE CITY OF BUFFALO, 1915

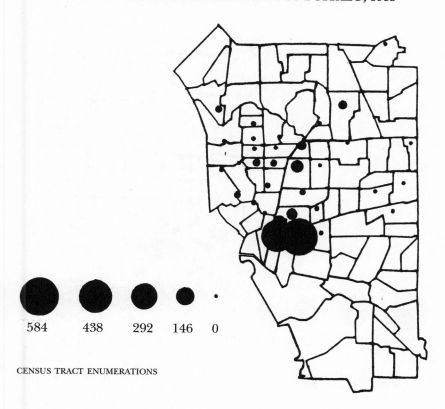

584   438   292   146   0

CENSUS TRACT ENUMERATIONS

Source: Generated from New York State Manuscript Census Schedules for Buffalo, 1915, University at Buffalo, SUNY Archives.

3. BLACK POPULATION IN THE CITY OF BUFFALO, 1925

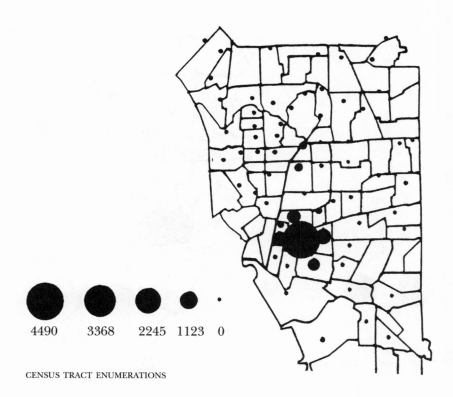

4490   3368   2245 1123   0

CENSUS TRACT ENUMERATIONS

Source: Generated from New York State Manuscript Census Schedules for Buffalo, 1925, University at Buffalo, SUNY Archives.

4. ETHNIC SETTLEMENTS IN BUFFALO AT THE TURN OF THE TWENTIETH CENTURY

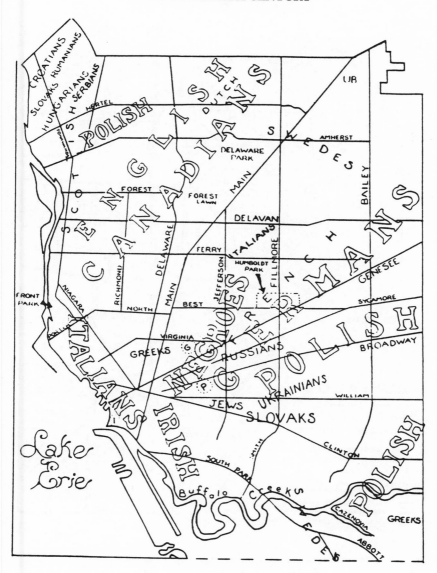

Source: S. Gredel, Pioneers of Buffalo *(Buffalo, 1966), p. 41. Reprinted here courtesy of the Buffalo Common Council.*

5. BUFFALO TRACTS, WARDS, COUNCILMANIC DISTRICTS

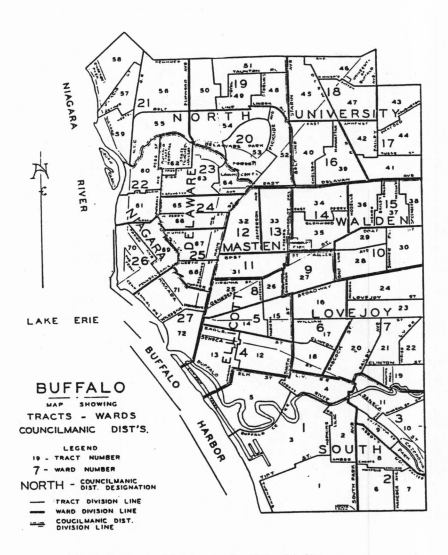

Source: R.G. 196 Public Housing Administration files, National Archives; reprinted here courtesy of the Buffalo Common Council.

APPENDIX III: METHOD OF COMPUTERIZATION AND OCCUPATION CODES

DATA DESCRIPTION: BUFFALO BLACKS, 1925[*]

I. Method of Computerization

The technique for the computerization of the dataset was an adaptation of that used for the Buffalo, Pittsburgh, and Allegheny materials already completed. Briefly, we used a modified fixed-field system without coding; i.e., textual variables were not assigned codes at the keypunching stage but done later by machine. The 1925 set was punched directly from the microfilm into this fixed-field system. Once the entire dataset had been punched, a series of programs were run to edit, encode, and aggregate the data to produce the finished product. The first program was checked for obvious keypunching errors like alpha punches in numeric fields, or vice versa. Once the data had been cleaned in this manner, the next step was to substitute numeric codes for the textual variables, since numbers are easier for the computer to manipulate. Street name, race, sex, citizenship, and occupation were all originally keypunched with alphabetic codes. Street and occupation were punched exactly as they appeared on the film, while the other alpha variables were assigned a single letter to denote the proper value. A program was then written to go through the data and find all of the unique codes for these alpha variables. Once they had been found, a numeric code was assigned to each unique alpha value or combination of letters. This part of the coding process was done by hand. After all codes had been assigned, still another program was run to substitute the actual numeric codes for the alpha text on the records. Only name was left as an alpha variable. The final step in the process was to go through and aggregate on household units. Each household was isolated and descriptive material such as sex of the head, the age of the head, the number of people in the

---

[*]This procedure was used in the computerization of the 1905 and 1915 manuscript census, too.

household, and number of adults was added to each person's record in that household.

Once this stage was reached, the data were felt to be ready for analysis. A number of sorts were performed and the data printed to provide the capacity to sight-check the material. (In addition, some researchers find it quite useful to work with material in this form.) The data were alphabetized by name and also sorted by ward, election district, assembly district, and block number. For the computer-assisted aspect of the analysis, a card check of the transformed records was generated.

II. Household and Household Head Determination

One of the major programming problems was the determination of households and their heads. The easiest thing to do for household determination seemed to be to define a household as all of the persons living at the same address. This was especially practical in the Buffalo data, since different living quarters at the same address were generally so noted by the use of references like "R" for rear and "Upper" for second floor. In a select number of cases, apartment numbers were given, although there did not seem to be a large number of people in the sample living in big apartment houses or tenements.

Household heads were a much bigger problem. The census did report the information on relationships to head, but it was not unusual to find more than one person in any given household designated as a head. In addition, unlike the data in the Federal census, the household head did not always appear on the first line of each household. In many cases, the order in which people appeared in the manuscript census schedule was almost random and seemed to have little to do with family relationships. Consequently, the assumption was made that the designation "head" was often used to denote a husband of another person in the household. This made exact determination of the head a virtual impossibility.

The solution finally arrived at was to assume that the first person designated as a head would be called the household head. Any other "heads" in the household would continue to be called such, but for the determination of sex, race, occupation, et cetera of the head, the first person would be used.

One additional problem in this connection stemmed from the fact that not every household we punched in had a head. This was no doubt a result of one of two conditions. First of all, we were punching only blacks, and if there was a white household with a large number of whites but only one or two blacks, only the blacks were punched. If, on the other hand, there was a predominantly black household with a few whites, the whites were punched. This procedure could easily result in a number of households entering the sample without a head being punched. Secondly, some of the dwellings were no doubt special institutions like hospitals, prisons, and hotels. These dwellings we would not expect to have a head, per se.

While this procedure was not altogether satisfactory, it seemed the only workable one. Whenever such a household was encountered, it was flagged. In the end, out of 1,787 total households, 215, or about 12 percent, were so noted.

III. Explanation of the Variables

All of the manuscript's variables were included in the data. In addition, as previously noted, a number were computed. The complete list and a brief explanation of each is provided below:

Year—since there would eventually be three years, it was noted.

Ward—ward of the city.

Election District—provided on the manuscript.

Assembly District—provided on the manuscript.

Page Number—the page number of the manuscript was noted.

Line Number—the line number of the manuscript. The combination of ward, page, and line number provides a unique identification number for each record. In addition, it makes it easy to find any person on the original film.

Street Code—a number was assigned in place of the street name for each unique street.

Street Number—street address.

Last Name—limited to eight characters.

First Name—limited to six characters.

Household Relationship—as given in the manuscript, but coded numerically.

Race—ditto.

Sex—ditto.

Age—ditto.

Nativity—while the majority of the persons were native born, those who were not were coded by country of birth.

Years in U.S.—for nonnative born only.

Citizenship—if a person was a citizen, this was noted.

Occupation—coded in the same nine-digit code used for the Pittsburgh and Allegheny materials.

Number of Persons in Household—computed after household was determined.

Number of Children—anyone under eighteen was considered a child; the total number was noted for each household.

Number of Adults—eighteen years or older was considered an adult; the total number was noted for each household.

Sex of Household Head—based on determination of who the head was. If, as noted above, no head could be determined, this variable was coded "9."

Occupation of Head—based on determination of household head and coded like the individual's occupation.

Age of Head—based on determination of household head.

Race of Head—ditto.

Number of Boarders in Household—based on relationship to head as given, this variable was computed for every household.

Number of Relatives in Household—this included all relatives who were not designated as either a son or daughter or spouse.

Number of Domestics in Household—again, based on the relationship to head variable.

Note: In cases where the household head could not be determined, all variables based on the head were coded "o" with the exception of sex, as noted above.

Occupation Codes Used in the Buffalo Study Follow the Schema Detailed Below:

The codes used for the encoding of the Pittsburgh and Allegheny manuscript census for 1860 were originally devised by Laurence Glasco for the computerization of the 1855 New York State Census for Buffalo, New York. The basic intent of the code is to define each occupation in two ways: by the industry in which an individual works and by the amount of skill required to perform the job. The industry and level-of-skill categories are largely based on those outlined in Duncan and Blau's *American Occupational Structure,* and were changed little from the original Buffalo data for the encoding of the Pittsburgh materials.

The actual computer code for occupation is a telescopic one. Briefly, what this means is that a series of small codes (two digits in this case) are combined to form a single large one. Each of these small codes had a meaning of its own as well as within the larger code.

More specifically, the total code contains nine digits, which can be broken up into a series of fields, each having a different meaning. The 1860 code is primarily composed of three fields, one describing the industry, one giving the type of industry, and one describing skill level for the job. These three fields combine to form the nine-digit occupational code.*

---

*This discussion could be confusing for those using the code in the SPSS Save Files. When those files were created, the occupation codes were broken down into a number of different variables. This problem is further detailed under the heading "Use with SPSS Save Files."

I. Industry Codes

The first six digits of the code are a classification by industry. This comes as close as possible to a functional code. These first six digits are then divided up into three groups of two, each describing a different area within an industry. Thus, for example, within the general industry classification of Transportation, digits 3–4 and 5–6 are used to distinguish between streetcar driver and railroad engineer.

DIGITS 1–2

Each occupation is, first of all, classified into one of 35 industry groups. These industry groups are then used as the first two digits in the occupational code. The 35 codes are:

Code	Industry Group
00	At home
01	Banking
02	Finance
03	Insurance
04	Land
05	Private service business
06	Public service
07	Other service
08	Clerical
09	Sales
10	Communications-utilities
11	Transportation
12	Maritime
13	Transportation equipment
14	Construction
15	Mining
16	Petroleum
17	Rubber
18	Tobacco
19	Food-beverages
20	Clothing
21	Wood and wood products
22	Printing-publishing
23	Leather
24	Stone, clay, glass
25	Chemicals
26	Jewelry
27	Metals
28	Metal products
29	Electrical products
30	Misc. nonmanufacturing

31	Misc. manufacturing
32	Agricultural
33	Professional
34	Semi-professional

The best classification, then, is by the first two digits. Thus, for example, the code for the occupation of tailor would begin with 20, clerk with 08.

DIGITS 3-6

The next four digits are used to further define occupational groups and individual occupations within those groups. The full nine-digit code for woodturner is 210301113, and that for cabinetmaker is 210403113. Both use the same industry code of 21 (for wood and wood products). The second two digits of the code are used to further differentiate among areas within the general industry groupings. Likewise, the third two digits can be used to distinguish less important differences. The code for cabinetmaker, as we saw, was 210403113, while the code for chairmaker is 210409113. Unfortunately, the assignment of codes within the general industry groups was not made in any systematic or hierarchical fashion, so that while subcategories have great meaning within these industry groups, the structure of all groups is not identical. Indeed, it may be that such a structure is not only difficult but impossible to establish.

II. Level of Skill (Digits 7-8)

The seventh and eighth digits of the code represent an attempt to describe the skill content of the occupation. Each occupation encountered was classified in one of 25 level-of-skill categories. Those 25 are as follows:

Code	Industry Group
Laborers:	
01	Farm laborer
02	Tenant, cropper
03	Misc. unskilled laborer
04	Laborer in manufacturing or construction
Semi-skilled:	
05	Operative-service
06	Operative-misc.
07	Operative manufacturing or construction
08	Foreman, supervisor—semi-skilled
Skilled:	
09	Craft apprentice
10	Craft in construction
11	Misc. crafts

| 12 | Manufacturing crafts |
| 13 | Master craftsman |

Nonmanual:

14	Nonmanual low (messengers, office boys)
15	Misc. nonmanual
16	Clerks
17	Nonmanual owners
18	Nonmanual sales
19	Manager-official

Professionals:

| 20 | Professional–salaried |
| 21 | Professional–self-employed |

Others:

96	Student
97	Retired
98	Undetermined ("works in")
99	Not employed

Uses of this code should take note of the implied hierarchy of the level of skill categories. While even a cursory examination shows rather clearly that there is some ranking implied as we move from code 01 through code 21, that ranking is not absolute nor it is meant to be. The groupings of laborer, semi-skilled, craft, nonmanual, and professional are perhaps a fairer approximation of skill rankings, but the order of categories within those groups is purely random. Therefore, while in some cases (such as apprentice and master) a lower code represents a lower skill value, no such assumption can be made, for example, between construction crafts and miscellaneous crafts.

Looking back at our earlier example, cabinetmaker, we can get a better idea of how the code works. Assume two occupations appear: one is "cabinetmaker" and the other is "app to cabinetmaker." Both of these would receive the same six-digit industry code, and level of skill would be used to differentiate between the craftsman and the apprentice. Thus, the code for cabinetmaker would be 210403113; the code for "app to cabinetmaker" 210403093.

III. Type of Industry (digit 9)

Finally, each industry was further classified by its type and this code put in the last, or ninth digit of the 1860 code. Those industry codes were as follows:

Code	Type of Industry
01	Primary agriculture
02	Primary extractive

03	Secondary miscellaneous
04	Secondary industrial
05	Tertiary miscellaneous
06	Tertiary service
07	Tertiary transportation
08	Tertiary sales, finance
09	Not determined

IV. Use with SPSS Save Files

Subsets of the Pittsburgh and Allegheny data have been saved as SPSS save files. When these files were created, the occupation code was broken down into a number of variables. Basically, the nine-digit code exists in those files in three separate variables: OCC, LOS, and Type.

The first of these variables, OCC, is the first six digits of the total occupational code. This is the industry classification. If a user ran a codebook on variable OCC, the output would display only the first six digits of the occupational code. Thus, while the full code for cabinet-maker is 210403113, a codebook on OCC would show all cabinetmakers as having code 210403.

LOS is another variable, and it consists of the two-digit level-of-skill code described above (digits 7–8 of the total nine-digit code). A code-book performed on this variable will show only the distribution of skills in the labor force and show nothing by way of specific occupations.

Like OCC and LOS, the ninth digit of the code is also a separate variable and is called TYPE. It has values ranging from 1 to 9 and gives only a general classification of type of industry.

In addition to these three variables, each person's record will also have three variables, OCC1, OCC2, and OCC3. These three variables are the three fields of the industry code, so that OCC1 is the first two digits (1–2), OCC2 the second two (3–4), and OCC3 the third two (5–6). OCC1 is a particularly valuable variable since it shows reasonably specific industry distributions.

From time to time users may find it necessary or desirable to display the entire code for an occupation via a codebook run. In such a case, the three variables OCC, LOS, and TYPE can be combined mathematically to recreate the original nine-digit code. This is done with SPSS via the "compute" statement:

$$\text{COMPUTE OCC9} = (\text{OCC} * 1000) + (\text{LOS} * 10) + \text{TYPE}$$

Where OCC9 is the full nine-digit occupation code, such an operation will also require that the user supply a new "PRINT FORMATS" specification of (0) and new "VALUE LABELS" as well.

NOTES

PREFACE

1. Toni Morrison, *Sula* (New York, 1973), 90.

2. Oscar Handlin, *Boston's Immigrants* (Cambridge, 1951) and *The Uprooted* (New York, 1951); Gilbert Osofsky, *Harlem: The Making of a Ghetto* (New York, 1963); Allan Spear, *Black Chicago* (Chicago, 1967); David Katzman, *Before the Ghetto* (Urbana, 1973); Kenneth Kusmer, *A Ghetto Takes Shape* (Urbana, 1976).

3. For a comprehensive analysis of the historiography of African American migration to urban communities, see Joe William Trotter, "African Americans in the City: The Industrial Era, 1900-1950"; and Kenneth Kusmer, "African Americans in the City since World War II: From the Industrial to the Post-Industrial Era," in the *Journal of Urban History* 21, no. 4 (May, 1995), 438-504.

4. George Edmund Hayes, "Conditions among Negroes in the Cities," *The Annals* XLIX (September, 1913), 110.

5. *Buffalo Courier Express,* July 20, 1975, 19.

6. John Blassingame, "Before the Ghetto: The Making of the Black Community in Savannah, Georgia, 1865-1880," in *The Journal of Social History* VI (Summer, 1973), 463.

7. Recent monographs that address the internal dynamics of urban African American communities and the development of the industrial working class during the critical migration period at the turn of the century include the following: James Borchert, *Alley Life in Washington* (Urbana, 1991); Allen Ballard, *One More Day's Journey* (New York, 1984); Joe William Trotter, *Black Milwaukee* (Urbana, 1985); Peter Gottlieb, *Making Their Own Way: Southern Blacks' Migration to Pittsburgh 1916-1930* (Urbana, 1987); James R. Grossman, *Land of Hope: Chicago, Black Southerners, and the Great Migration* (Chicago, 1989); Richard Thomas, *Life Is What We Make It* (Bloomington, 1990); Earl Lewis, *In Their Own Interest* (Berkeley, 1990); Albert Brussard, *Black San Francisco: The Struggle for Racial Equality in the West, 1900-1954* (Lawrence, 1993); Quintard Taylor, *The Forging of a Black Community: Seattle Central District, 1870 through the Civil Rights Era* (Seattle, 1994). Also, see Joe William Trotter, ed., *The Great Migration in Historical Perspective: New Dimensions of Race, Class, and Gender* (Bloomington, 1991).

8. Richard Thomas, *Life Is What We Make It,* p. xii.

9. Stephan Thernstrom, "Reflections on the New Urban History," in Alexander Callow, Jr., *American Urban History* (New York, 1973), 672-682, discusses the benefits that can accrue to scholars who wish to write "grassroots" history

or "history from the bottom up." Also see Robin Kelley, "We Are Not What We Seem: Re-thinking Black Working-Class Opposition in the Jim Crow South," in the *Journal of American History* 80 (June, 1993), 75-112.

INTRODUCTION

1. Figures compiled from the New York State manuscript census schedules in Archives, University at Buffalo, SUNY.

2. Figures taken from the New York State manuscript census for the years 1905, 1915, and 1925.

3. Interview, B. Lee, long-time resident of Buffalo, in Chevy Chase, Maryland, April 1970. Also see *Crisis* XVI (March, 1918), 249.

4. The Public Housing Administration, RG 196, Folder H 6700-6706 in National Archives; see especially *Buffalo Real Property Inventory*.

5. Transcript of the Hearings of the New York State Temporary Commission on the Condition of the Colored Urban Population (TCCUCP), December 7, 1937, 744-745 (Archives, New York State Library, Albany, N.Y.).

6. Ibid.

7. For a discussion of the Ku Klux Klan in Buffalo, see Kenneth Jackson, *The Ku Klux Klan in the City: 1915-1930* (New York, 1967).

8. See, e.g., W. E. B. DuBois, *The Philadelphia Negro* (New York, 1899), revised 1967; St. Clair Drake and Horace Cayton, *Black Metropolis*, two volumes (New York, 1945), revised 1970; Kenneth Kusmer, *A Ghetto Takes Shape* (Urbana, 1976).

9. Johnson, 15-16.

10. Ibid. Although the New York State manuscript census figures are not available for machine readable analysis for whites in Buffalo, these results are consistent for African Americans.

11. The year 1915 witnessed a shortage of men in this age category.

12. New York State TCCUCP, 744.

1. THE EARLY YEARS

1. Zora Neale Hurston, *Their Eyes Were Watching God* (New York, 1937), 9.

2. The growth and development of Buffalo is discussed in the following works: Robert Holder, *Beginnings of Buffalo Industry* (Buffalo, 1928); Lloyd Graham, *Buffalo Metropolis of the Niagara Frontier* (Buffalo, 1967); Robert Bingham, *Cradle of the Queen City* (Buffalo, 1931).

3. Bingham, 456.

4. Ibid., 489.

5. Stephen Gredel, *Pioneers of Buffalo* (Buffalo, 1966), 16.

6. Ibid., 25, 26.

7. Ibid., 31.

8. Holder, 2.

9. Ibid., 6.

10. Ibid., 16.

11. Gredel, 34.

12. Laurence Glasco and Herbert Gutman in "The Negro Family, Household Structure and Occupational Structure, 1855-1925," Yale Conference on 19th-

Century Cities, November, 1968, discuss this phenomenon in great detail (unpublished manuscript in possession of author).

13. Charles Johnson, "The Negro in Buffalo," Buffalo, New York, State University at Buffalo Archives, 1923, 74-76.

14. Gredel, 34.

15. Records, St. Philip's Episcopal Church, in the collection of the Afro-American Historical Association of the Niagara Frontier, in the North Jefferson Branch of the Buffalo and Erie County Library.

16. E. Franklin Frazier, *The Negro Church in America;* Wilmore Gayraud, *Black Religion and Black Radicalism: An Examination of the Black Experience in Religion* (Garden City, N.Y., 1972); Cornell West, *Race Matters* (Boston, 1993); Albert B. Cleage, Jr., *Black Christian Nationalism* (New York, 1972); Benjamin E. Mays, *The Negro's God* (New York, 1968).

17. Dorothy Porter, "The Organized Educational Activities of Negro Literary Societies, 1828-1846," in August Meier and Elliott Rudwick, *The Making of Black America,* Vol. I (New York, 1969), 277.

18. Desmond Hamlin, "Early Black American Poetry" (unpublished manuscript in author's possession).

19. *Buffalo City Directory,* 1838.

20. Ibid., 1848.

21. For biographical information on William Wells Brown, see *Narrative of William Wells Brown,* 2d edition, Boston, 1848. For information regarding his abolitionist activities in Buffalo, refer to William Farrison, "William Wells Brown in Buffalo," in *The Journal of Negro History* 39 (October, 1954), 298-314.

22. Farrison, 298; Thomas J. Davis, "A Historical Overview of Black Buffalo: Work, Community and Protest," in Henry Louis Taylor, Jr., ed., *African Americans and the Rise of Buffalo's Post-Industrial City, 1940 to Present* (Buffalo, 1990), 10.

23. Farrison, 301-303.

24. Ibid., 303.

25. John H. Hopkins, D.D., "Slavery: Its Religious Sanction, Its Political Dangers, and the Best Mode of Doing It Away," January 10 and 13, 1851 (Buffalo, 1851), 14-16, in the Moorland Spingarn Research Center at Howard University.

26. Farrison, 312-313.

27. Proceedings, *National Negro Convention of Colored Citizens, Buffalo,* New York, 1843, 3-6, 10, Schomburg Research Center, New York Public Library.

28. Ibid., 10.

29. Mary Burnett Talbert, "History of the Michigan Street Baptist Church, 1836-1908," a speech delivered at the reopening of the church, December 27, 1908, in Buffalo Baptist Association papers, Buffalo and Erie County Historical Society.

30. Proceedings, 4-7; *Buffalo Evening News,* April 3, 1973, B-3.

31. Hamlin, nd., np.; Richard Barksdale and Kenneth Kinnamon, *Black Writers of America* (New York, 1972), 222-223. Joan R. Sherman, "James Monroe Whitfield, Poet and Emigrationist: A Voice of Protest and Despair," in *The Journal of Negro History* 57 (April, 1972), 169-176.

32. Ibid., Richard Barksdale and Kenneth Kinnamon, *Black Writers of America* 222-223.

33. Sherman, 169.

34. Ibid., 173–174.

35. Ibid., 174–175.

36. Farrison, 310–311.

37. Peyton Harris was one of the most prominent black landowners in Buffalo, with parcels valued at $12,000 in the mid-nineteenth century. The Harris-Talbert family also possessed large real estate holdings on nearby Grand Island. Deeds to Harris and Talbert property transactions in Talbert family papers, in possession of author. Also see Thomas J. Davis, p. 15.

38. See Herbert Gutman and Laurence Glasco, "The Buffalo Negro Study: Household Structure and Occupational Structure, 1855–1925" (unpublished manuscript in possession of author).

39. Glasco and Gutman, "The Buffalo Negro Study."

40. *Buffalo Express,* November 26, 1867.

41. This finding is similar to Herbert Gutman's postbellum southern blacks in *The Black Family in Slavery and Freedom* (New York, 1976); *Buffalo Evening News,* April 7, 1973, B-3.

42. Laurence A. Glasco, "Ethnicity and Social Structure: Irish, Germans, and Native-born of Buffalo, New York, 1850–1860," Ph.D. dissertation, SUNY at Buffalo, 1973.

43. Phyllis F. Field, *The Politics of Race in New York: The Struggle for Black Suffrage in the Civil War Era* (Ithaca, 1982), 31–32; Leon F. Litwack, *North of Slavery: The Negro in the Free States, 1790–1860* (Chicago, 1961). Also, see Thomas J. Davis, "A Historical Overview of Black Buffalo: Work, Community and Protest," in Henry Louis Taylor, Jr., ed., *African Americans and the Rise of Buffalo's Post-Industrial City, 1940 to Present,* 13–43.

44. The New York State Manuscript Census Schedules for Buffalo, New York, 1855.

45. *Buffalo Evening News,* April 7, 1973, B-3.

46. *Buffalo Express,* August 31, 1867, 4.

47. Harris as quoted by Thomas J. Davis in *African Americans and the Rise of Buffalo's Post-Industrial City, 1940 to Present,* vol. 2, Henry Louis Tylor, ed. (Buffalo, 1990), p. 14. Monroe Fordham, *A History of Bethel AME Church: Buffalo New York, 1831–1977;* Arthur O. White, "School Segregation and Its Critics in a Northern City: A Case Study, Buffalo, New York, 1837–1880," 20–21, unpublished manuscript in possession of author, later published as "The Black Movement Against Jim Crow Education in Buffalo, New York, 1800–1900," *Phylon* XXX, No. 4 (Winter, 1969), pp. 375–393.

48. *Buffalo Express,* October 25, 1879, 6.

49. Ibid.

50. *Buffalo Courier,* January 25, 1897, 2.

51. *Buffalo Courier,* April 4, 1897, 6.

52. Clipping, February 25, 1880, "Secretary's Minute Book, 1875–1915," of the Medical Alumni Association of the University of Buffalo (University Archives #19/3/154).

53. *Buffalo Courier,* January 4, 1897, 4.

54. *A History of the Club Movement Among the Colored Women of the United States of America,* 1902, as contained in the minutes of the conventions of the National

Federation of Afro-American women held in Boston, July 29-31, 1895 and of the National League of Colored Women held in Washington, D.C., July 20-22, 1896, in the Moorland Spingarn Research Center at Howard University.

55. The second biennial convention of the NACW was held in Buffalo in 1901. Black women discussed the following topics: "Kindergartens," "Elevating the Standards of the Home," "Child Study," "Schools of Domestic Science," "The Cause of Temperance," "Woman's Domain," "The Convict Lease System," "Needs of Our Organization," "Women as a Factor in the Solution of the Race Problems," "Day Nurseries," and "Nurse Training for Colored Women." Elizabeth Lindsay Davis, *Lifting as They Climb* (Washington, D.C., 1933), 48.

56. *Buffalo Courier,* March 3, 1901, 5; *Buffalo Courier,* March 11, 1902, 5.

57. *The Buffalo Illustrated,* March 6, 1906; ethnic groups—blacks in Buffalo and Erie County Historical Society.

58. Laurence A. Glasco, "Ethnicity and Social Structure: Irish, Germans, and Native Born of Buffalo, New York, 1850-1860," (diss., State University of New York at Buffalo, 1973).

59. Charles Johnson, "The Negro in Buffalo," 7, unpublished manuscript, State University of New York at Buffalo Archives, Buffalo, New York; Virginia Yans McLaughlan, *Family and Community* (Ithaca, 1978).

60. United States Census, 1900.

61. These figures were compiled from data taken from the New York State manuscript census for 1905.

62. Ibid. The U. S. decennial figures for the population of Buffalo are reported in the Table below:

Population of Buffalo, By Color, 1880-1920

	Total	White	African American	Indian, Japanese Chinese, etc.
1880	155,134	154,268	857	9
1890	255,664	254,495	1118	51
1900	352,387	350,586	1698	103
1910	423,715	421,809	1773	133
1920	506,775	502,042	4511	222

63. Charles S. Johnson, "The Negro in Buffalo," *The National Urban League,* unpublished manuscript in the archives at the University at Buffalo, 75. For another perspective on the ways in which blacks benefitted from paternalistic relations with whites, see Kathryn Grover, *Make a Way Somehow: African-American Life in a Northern Community, 1790-1965,* 245-249.

64. Ibid.; also, see Noel Ignatiev, *How the Irish Became White* (New York, 1996). Map 4 indicates that African Americans and Germans resided in the same neighborhoods.

65. Niles Carpenter, *Nationality, Color, and Economic Opportunity in the City of Buffalo* (University of Buffalo, 1927, rpt., 1970), 156.

66. Johnson, 76.

67. For a biographical sketch of Mary Talbert and the Burnett family, see Lillian S. Williams, "Mary Morris Burnett Talbert," in Darlene Clark Hine, et al., *Black Women in America: An Historical Encyclopedia* (Bloomington, 1994), 1137-1139. Also see Lillian S. Williams, "Mary Morris Talbert," in Jessie Carney Smith, ed., *Notable Black American Women* (Detroit, 1992), 1095-1100.

68. Lillian S. Williams, "Marriage Patterns in St. Philip's Episcopal Church in Buffalo, 1875-1925" (unpublished manuscript). Many of the old families worshipped at St. Philip's. It is one of only two high Episcopal churches in Buffalo today.

69. Johnson, 83.

70. Johnson, 77.

71. Niles Carpenter, *Nationality, Color, and Economic Opportunity in the City of Buffalo* (Buffalo, 1927), 159; Charles Johnson, "The Negro in Buffalo" (Buffalo, 1923), 56-57.

72. Quoted in Jim Watts and Allen Davis, *Generations* (New York, 1974), 44. See also Kenneth Kusmer, *A Ghetto Takes Shape* (Urbana, 1973).

73. Interviews, Joseph Brown, April, 1970.

74. Interview, Bruce Lee, in Chevy Chase, Maryland, April 1970; May 1996; October 1993. Also, see *Crisis* XVI (March, 1918), 249.

75. Johnson; William Evans, transcript, New York State Temporary Commission on the Urban Colored Population. Mary Burnett Talbert to Mary White Ovington, December 16, 1920, C76, NAACP Papers, Manuscript Collection, Library of Congress.

76. Buffalo Federation of Churches, *Foreign Speaking and Negro Sections of Buffalo* (Buffalo, 1923).

2. GROWING UP BLACK

Statistics for this chapter were compiled from data taken from the New York State manuscript census schedules for Buffalo for 1905, 1915, and 1925, University at Buffalo, SUNY Archives.

1. Elizabeth Talbert testimony, New York State Temporary Commission on the Condition of the Urban Colored Population (TCCUCP); Derrick Byrd testimony TCCUCP, December 7, 1937, 841-842. Elizabeth Brown Talbert was the second wife of William Talbert. Mary Burnett Talbert died in 1923.

2. Elizabeth Brown Talbert, testimony, TCCUCP, December 7, 1937.

3. The Talbert family was one of the fortunate ones that had discovered gold during the nineteenth-century rush in California and subsequently invested in real estate, from California and Oregon to New York. Talbert papers in Buffalo and Erie County Historical Society and in author's possession; interview, Conrad Talbert, September 18, 1974; *The Courier,* January 22, 1930. Also, see typescript of Mary Burnett Talbert's "Michigan Avenue Baptist Church History," in Buffalo Baptist Association papers, Buffalo and Erie County Historical Society.

4. *Charter and Ordinances of the City of Buffalo as Revised in 1881* (Buffalo, 1881), 190-195.

5. Diary, Will Talbert, January 1-June 8, 1881, in Talbert Family papers in Buffalo and Erie County Historical Society.

6. Ibid.

7. Ibid.

8. Ibid. Many of these individuals were able to read, but could not write.

9. Ibid., diary of Will Talbert, January 1–June 8, 1881. While the data are not nearly as rich for the twentieth century, life changed little for black youths until after the World War I migration of southern blacks into the community.

10. Figures 2-5, depicting household status, are located in Appendix I.

11. Here we examine the life cycles of blacks in Buffalo in 1905 and 1925 to ascertain what affect the migration had on them. In this context David L. Featherman contends that the social scientist is seeking "the causal bases of age stratification within the social system that lead to some level of age-graded events for a collectivity at a particular historical moment and to broad similarities in individual life courses or psychological biographies during that period," quoted in John Modell, *Into One's Own: From Youth to Adulthood in the United States, 1920–1975* (Berkeley, 1989), p. 17. Although the life process by definition involves perpetual change, "stability," when applied to life cycles, implies healthy, "normal" patterns. Stability is measured in terms of that which is expected. For example, in twentieth-century America, children usually live with their parents. The child who lives in a household headed by someone other than his parents is unusual; furthermore, those children who are boarders or live-in servants are also a rarity. However, examining the life cycles for any given year will not permit one to make predictions about the future, because each stage in one's cycle is affected by one's social and economic environment. Unfortunately, machine-readable census data are not available to permit a comparison of the cycles of black and white youths in Buffalo. For a discussion of national demographic trends of black and white youths, see Modell, *Into One's Own,* especially chapters 1 and 2.

12. Michael Katz, *The People of Hamilton* (Cambridge, 1975), 266. Many of these boarders, of course, were migrants.

13. W. E. B. DuBois, *The Philadelphia Negro* (New York, 1899, revised 1967), 194.

14. Katz, 304. See also John Modell and Tamara Hareven, "Urbanization and the Malleable Household: An Examination of Boarding and Lodging in American Families," in Michael Gordon, *The American Family in Social-Historical Perspective* (New York, 1978). John Modell, *Into One's Own,* especially chapter 3.

15. "Head of household" is the classification listed in the census; few blacks in Buffalo lived alone.

16. The census for 1905 made no distinction between those women who did housework at home and those who worked out.

17. DuBois, 69.

18. Interview, Bruce Lee, April, 1970. Charles Johnson made similar observations of the African community in "The Negro in Buffalo."

19. DuBois, *The Philadelphia Negro;* see also E. Franklin Frazier, *The Negro Family in the United States* (Chicago, 1939).

20. Fewer females than males among the 11–15-year-olds lived in households in which their parents were heads. Also, slightly more females in this age group than males worked in 1905.

21. St. Philip's Episcopal Church, marriage records, 1876–1925, in Church Archives in Buffalo.

22. Fertility rate equals the number of children 0-15 years over the number of females 16-45 years, times 100.

23. Herbert Gutman and Laurence A. Glasco, "The Negro Family, Household Structure and Occupational Structure, 1855-1925," paper prepared for the Yale Conference on Nineteenth-Century Cities, November 1968.

24. DuBois, 168; Jessie Rodrique, "The Black Community and The Birth Control Movement," in Ellen DuBois and Vicki Ruiz, *Unequal Sisters* (New Brunswick, 1990), 333-344.

25. Ibid., 165; Charles Johnson, "The Buffalo Negro Study," 1923, unpublished manuscript, State University of New York at Buffalo Archives.

26. Buffalo Federation of Churches, "Foreign-Speaking and Negro Sections of Buffalo" (Buffalo, 1923), 27.

27. Laurence A. Glasco, "Ethnicity and Social Structure: Irish, Germans and Native Born of Buffalo, New York, 1850-1860," unpublished dissertation, State University of New York at Buffalo, 1973, 224; Katz, 289.

28. Glasco, ibid.

29. Virginia Yans-McLaughlan, "Patterns of Work and Family Organization: Buffalo's Italians," in Herbert Gutman and Gregory Kealey, *Many Pasts* (Englewood, 1973), 201.

30. Gutman and Glasco, "The Buffalo Negro Study."

31. DuBois, *Darkwater* (New York, 1920, reprinted 1969), 172.

32. Grace Halsall also discusses the problems which confronted black female servants in *Soul Sister* (Greenwich, 1970). For a discussion of the experiences of migrant women in domestic service during the Great Migration, see Elizabeth Clark-Lewis *Living In, Living Out* (Washington, D.C., 1994).

33. Herbert Gutman, *The Black Family in Slavery and Freedom* (New York, 1976), 168. Women's attitudes about work and the kinds of jobs that they desired are, of course, the other story that must be explored.

34. Elizabeth Pleck, "A Mother's Wages," in Michael Gordon, *The American Family in Social-Historical Perspective* (New York, 1978), 495.

35. Ibid.

36. Ibid. Mary White Ovington notes this same phenomenon among black women in New York. See *Half a Man* (New York, 1911, reprinted 1969), 58.

37. These figures are biased upward slightly because they include children who are listed as relatives or boarders. But few black children, in either 1905 or 1925, fell into either category, as indicated above.

3. TO HELP SEE ONE ANOTHER THROUGH

1. Lucille Clifton, *Generations in good woman: poems and a memoir 1969-1980* (Brockport, N.Y., 1987), 275.

2. Niles Carpenter, *Nationality, Color, and Economic Opportunity in the City of Buffalo* (Westport, Conn., 1970), 176-178.

3. Gutman, *The Black Family in Slavery and Freedom* (New York, 1976); Janheinz Jahn, in *Muntu* (New York, 1958), discusses the nature of African culture.

4. Carol Stack, *All Our Kin* (New York, 1974).

5. Patricia Guthrie, *Catching Sense: African American Communities on a South Carolina Sea Island* (Westport, Conn., 1996), especially 31-39.

6. Guthrie, ibid., chapter 6, "Household Composition"; see, especially, 58-62.

7. See, for example, Spear, *Black Chicago* (Chicago, 1967); David Katzman, *Before the Ghetto* (Urbana, 1973).

8. Gutman, 454.

9. Statistics were compiled from data from the New York State manuscript census schedules for 1905, 1915, and 1925 (University at Buffalo, SUNY Archives).

10. Gutman and Glasco, 9, 12.

11. See, e.g., Moynihan, "Employment, Income, and the Ordeal of the Black Family" (Washington, D.C., 1965).

12. It is impossible to determine the head of household for those who were boarders or servants and who were listed alone, or those who had "other" household classifications. Patricia McDonald, in her study of Baltimore women, discovered that a substantial number of black women who worked as live-in servants had families in other parts of the city ("Baltimore Women, 1870-1900," unpublished Ph.D. dissertation, University of Maryland, 1976). The Buffalo data did not lend itself to such an analysis. Unknown household heads comprised 16 percent of all household listings.

13. One in five of those households headed by males had one boarder. Thirty-five households (7.2 percent) had two boarders, and sixteen (3.7 percent) had three. Only 24 male-headed households had four or more boarders; they comprised a mere 5.7 percent.

14. See, e.g., W. E. B. DuBois, *The Philadelphia Negro* (New York, 1967, originally published in 1897).

15. It was impossible to determine the head of household for unmarried individuals who lived alone or who maintained other types of households. This difficulty will be explained further under kin-related households.

16. Interview, Bessie Williams, February 26, 1976.

17. Males tended to migrate as singles; men who had families sent for them after they were established. See, e.g., DuBois, *The Philadelphia Negro,* and Frazier, *The Negro Family in the United States.*

18. The "pathology thesis" would assume that these women "bred like rabbits."

19. Unfortunately, it is impossible for us to determine how these people were related to the household head.

20. *Buffalo Forum,* January-February, 1928, computed from Table II—Birth, Deaths, Under One Year of Age, and Infant Mortality Rates of Babies of Negro Mothers, by Wards of Buffalo and Non-Residents, for the Year 1926, and for the Five Years of the Infant Mortality Study, 1922-1926. During this period 1,070 white babies were born out of wedlock; data are not available to allow for a comparison of illegitimacy rates by race.

21. Case studies for this section were taken from the manuscript censuses for 1905, 1915, and 1925.

22. It is quite plausible that the brothers facilitated their securing jobs on the railroad. Families containing both lodgers and relatives were even more rare than extended families. Although there were too few to reach any conclusions, single males (two) and single females (two) most frequently admitted both into their homes.

23. Gutman, *The Black Family in Slavery and Freedom,* xxiii-xx, 450-456.

24. Ibid.

25. Stack, 104.

26. Guthrie, 42–44.

27. This behavioral pattern implies that there was some linkage of black migrants with relatives who were in the city prior to World War I. Unfortunately, because of the nature of the census data, it is impossible to link relatives from year to year.

28. Stack, 90, 92.

29. James P. Comer, M.D., *Maggie's American Dream* (New York, 1988), xiii, 32, 36, 49–50. Also, see James Borchert, *Alley Life in Washington* (Urbana, 1981).

30. Ibid., 51. James Borchert also discusses the importance of rituals attendant to birth and death, as well as church homecomings, in maintaining an African American southern culture among the migrants. See *Alley Life in Washington* (Urbana, 1981), especially chapter 6.

31. Pauli Murray, *Pauli Murray: The Autobiography of a Black Activist, Feminist, Lawyer, Priest, and Poet* (Knoxville, 1987), x, 3. See also V. P. Franklin, *Black Self-Determination* (Brooklyn, 1992).

32. Ibid., 28.

33. Interview, Welford R. Wilson, former Buffalo resident, Los Angeles, California, October 14, 1978. Mr. Wilson noted that in the 1920s Buffalo blacks boarded friends, but never strangers. He further observed that these friends did not pay for housing accommodations but occasionally provided favors for the families with whom they resided.

34. Charles Johnson, "The Negro in Buffalo" (New York, 1923), unpublished manuscript, State University of New York at Buffalo Archives, 103.

35. Ibid., 102.

36. Guthrie, 57–58.

37. Stack, 24.

38. None of the families cited here were present in Buffalo in either 1905 or 1915, hence, more than likely, they were a part of the post–World War I migration.

39. Gutman, *The Black Family in Slavery and Freedom*; Allen Ballard, *One More Day's Journey*.

40. See, for example, John Bodnar, *Lives of Their Own: Blacks, Italians and Poles in Pittsburgh, 1900–1960* (Urbana, 1982); Virginia Yans-McLaughlan, *Family and Community* (Ithaca, 1978). Niles Carpenter, "Color, Nationality and Economic Opportunity" (Buffalo, 1923).

41. Michael Katz, *People of Hamilton* (Cambridge, 1975), 37.

42. Johnson, 55.

43. Ibid.

44. Interview, Bessie Williams, February 26, 1976.

45. Johnson, 93. Johnson noted that this was true even for those whom professionals recruited.

46. Letters of black migrants, Urban League Papers, Series VI, Container 86, Manuscript Collection, Library of Congress, Washington, D.C.

47. Ibid.

48. Ibid.

49. Lucille Clifton, *Good woman: poems and a memoir 1969-1980* (Brockport, N.Y., 1987), 270.

50. Okon Uya, *The African Diaspora and the Black Experience in New World Slavery* (New Rochelle, 1992).

51. Connie Porter, *All-Bright Court* (Boston, 1991), 4-6.

52. Johnson, 106.

53. Ibid.

54. Lucille Clifton, *Generations* (New York, 1976), 27.

55. A number of writers have addressed the nature of relationships between black mothers and their children. See, e.g., Robert Hill, *The Strengths of Black Families* (New York, 1972), and Patricia Bell Scott, et al., eds., *Double Stitch: Black Women Write about Mothers and Daughters* (Boston, 1991).

4. WORK

1. Unless otherwise indicated, statistics for this chapter were compiled from data taken from the 1905, 1915, and 1925 manuscript census schedules for New York State.

2. New York State Temporary Commission on the Condition of the Urban Colored Population, December 7, 1937, B-69, 808.

3. Joe William Trotter, Jr., in *Black Milwaukee,* discusses these same phenomena in a city whose black population is about the same size as that of Buffalo.

4. Charles Johnson, "The Buffalo Negro Study," 8.

5. Niles Carpenter, "Nationality, Color, and Economic Opportunity" (Buffalo, 1927), 105.

6. Etta Hein to Hon. James M. Mead, April 6, 1934, R.G. 280, 176-822, National Archives, Washington, D.C. See also Sterling Spero and Abram Harris, *The Black Worker* (New York, 1931; revised 1969); Elliott Rudwick, *Race Riot at East St. Louis* (New York, 1972); William Tuttle, *Race Riot* (New York, 1970); Philip Foner and Ronald Lewis, eds., *Black Workers: A Documentary History from Colonial Times to the Present* (Philadelphia, 1989).

7. Hein asked Congressman Mead to keep the contents of her letter confidential and to correspond with her anonymously because of her position at the YWCA. Ibid.

8. For more detailed information on job discrimination, refer to chapter 6, below.

9. New York State Temporary Commission on the Conditions of the Urban Colored Population (TCCUCP), p. 932, New York State Archives, Albany.

10. See, for example, Rayford Logan, *The Betrayal of the Negro* (New York, 1965); C. Vann Woodward, *The Strange Career of Jim Crow,* 2d ed. (New York, 1966).

11. See, for example, Kenneth Kusmer, *A Ghetto Takes Shape* (Urbana, 1976), 67-90; Albert Broussard, *Black San Francisco,* 38-58; Richard Thomas, *Life for Us Is What We Make It,* 2-48; Quintard Taylor, *The Forging of a Black Community,* 49-78.

12. Comparing these figures with Italian males in Buffalo in 1905, one finds that 9 percent of the Italians (381) were retailers.

13. Data on Italians taken from a table prepared by Virginia Yans-

McLaughlan for Herbert Gutman and Laurence Glasco, "The Buffalo Negro Study" (unpublished paper in possession of author).

14. In fact, at the opening of the Kentucky Derby in 1882, thirteen of the fourteen jockeys were black. James Weldon Johnson, *Black Manhattan* (New York, 1968), 60.

15. Ibid., 62.

16. This figure is about the same for professional Italians (1.0 percent).

17. A substantial number of black males worked in positions where it was difficult to determine their level of skill. In most instances, these informants reported to the census takers that they "worked at" various places of employment. But because of the nature of some of the businesses, it is quite evident that a number of them worked in nonmanual positions. E.g., William Talbert, husband of social activist Mary Burnett Talbert, reported working in the "city treasury department." Talbert was a bookkeeper. He actually was an accountant with the title of bookkeeper because of the city practice of excluding blacks from that job classification.

18. Charles Johnson, "The Buffalo Negro Study," pp. 3-8.

19. Charles Johnson, "The Negro in Buffalo" (New York, 1923), unpublished manuscript, State University of New York at Buffalo Archives, 27.

20. Carpenter, 113-114.

21. Lloyd Plummer interview, New York State Temporary Commission on the Conditions of the Urban Colored Population, 773.

22. TCCUCP, 773.

23. Ibid.

24. R.G. 228, Final Disposition Report, File 2-BR-308, National Archives, Washington, D.C.

25. Philip S. Foner and Ronald L. Lewis, *Black Workers: A Documentary History from Colonial Times to the Present* (Philadelphia, 1989), 463-465, 479; Olin Wilson testimony, TCCUCP, 779.

26. James McDonnell, "Interview with Olin Wilson: Charter Member, Steelworkers Organizing Committee, Bethlehem Steel Corporation, Buffalo, New York," *Afro-Americans in New York Life and History* 21 (January, 1997), 90.

27. Carpenter, 109.

28. Johnson, 42.

29. Carpenter, 109.

30. Johnson, 42.

31. Ibid.

32. R.G. 183, Lawrence Oxley File, Box 1387. Johnson, 26-27.

33. R.G. 183, Memorandum to Mr. Kerwin from Karl Phillips, Commissioner of Conciliation, March 25, 1927.

34. Fred and Frederick Croxton, "Unemployment in Buffalo," in *Buffalo Forum*, in R.G. 73, File 620.1, National Archives, Washington, D.C.

35. Interview, Brown. Workers usually had to reimburse employers for transportation costs.

36. Robin Kelley, in "'We are Not What We Seem.' Rethinking Black Working-Class Opposition in the Jim Crow South," in *Journal of American History* 80 (June, 1993), 75-112, discusses black workers' agency as they sought to control their lives under exploitative conditions.

37. Johnson, 57.

38. Johnson, 59.

39. The Buffalo Foundation conducted a five-year study of the cost of living for fifty families headed by women. All were widows and received financial assistance from the Erie County Board of Child Welfare. These families were compelled to live frugally and the foundation findings are below:

Expenditures of the Nearest-to-Average Family, 1920-1924

	1920	1921	1922	1923	1924	Total
Shelter	$144.00	$156.00	$156.00	$156.00	$164.00	$776.00
Food	505.43	454.46	456.91	414.49	507.50	2,338.79
Fuel/Light	53.90	72.38	91.20	80.20	58.64	356.32
Clothing	104.87	129.83	159.80	233.00	192.72	820.22
Miscellaneous	53.74	58.18	92.86	82.10	69.80	356.68
Total	$861.94	$870.85	$956.77	$965.79	$992.66	$4,648.01

Source: *Buffalo Forum* (April, 1926), 5.

40. U.S. Civil Service Commission Application, 5 June 1940, in Joseph Brown papers, and interview, Joseph Brown, June 4, 1970.

41. James R. McDonnell, "Interview with Olin Wilson: Charter Member, Steelworkers Organizing Committee, Bethlehem Steel Corporation, Buffalo, New York," in *Afro-Americans in New York Life and History* 1 (January, 1997), 81-83.

42. Lucille Clifton, *Generations* (New York, 1976), 73.

43. *Buffalo Forum* (September, 1923), 7.

44. Derrick Byrd's testimony, New York State Temporary Commission on the Conditions of the Urban Colored Population, pp. 841-842.

45. National Urban League, Series IV, Box 28, Folder "1930-1931"; National Urban League papers, manuscript division, Library of Congress.

46. Ibid., McDonnell, 93.

47. Ibid., McDonnell interview with Wilson, 84.

48. TCCUCP, 780.

49. Johnson, 22.

50. Niles Carpenter, 115-130; 146.

51. Carpenter, 115-116.

52. Ibid., 116. Mary Talbert to Mary White Ovington, December 16, 1920, NAACP Papers, C76, Manuscript Collection, Library of Congress, Washington, D.C.

53. The Buffalo Urban League examined the special needs of African American women who faced discrimination when seeking admission to educational institutions, or nontraditional "black" jobs. See chapter 6, below.

54. See chapter 2 for a discussion of the effects of age and household status on the employment picture for black females.

55. *Buffalo Foundation Forum,* March 1923, 11.

56. Johnson, 32.

57. Carpenter, 166.

58. Ibid. Joe William Trotter contends that blacks lost their domestic jobs to immigrants in Milwaukee because the city did not have a history of a caste system that relegated them to these positions. Buffalo, on the other hand, did have a tradition of employing black service workers and yet most still preferred white workers when they could find them.

59. Carpenter, 166.

60. Johnson, 64; Foner and Lewis, 465–469.

61. Ibid.

62. Mary White Ovington, *Half a Man* (New York, 1969), 88; originally published in 1911. Also, see Philip S. Foner and Ronald L. Lewis, *Black Workers: A Documentary History from Colonial Times to the Present* (Philadelphia, 1988), 465–469.

63. Carpenter, 167.

64. V. Freda Seigworth to Arnold T. Hill of the National Urban League, August 27, 1926, Series IV, Box 28, Manuscript Division, Library of Congress.

65. Ibid., Seigworth to Hill.

66. Memorandum on Buffalo, File Buffalo, 1926–1928, 1930–1931, NUL Series IV, Box 28.

67. Ibid., Carpenter, 166.

68. Transcript of the hearings of the New York State Temporary Commission on the Condition of the Urban Colored Population (TCCUCP), 746. For further discussion, Ibid., 765–772.

69. Ibid., 765–772.

70. R.G. 3, Francis Mahoney to James Ford, February 6, 1919, Box 306, National Archives, Washington, D.C.

71. Johnson, 71.

72. *Buffalo Forum*, September 1923, 6.

73. TCCUCP, 751.

74. *Buffalo Forum*, April, 1912.

75. Ibid., 11.

76. TCCUCP, 751.

77. See Public Housing Administration RG 196, files H6700–6706.

78. *Crisis* 47 (May, 1937), 138. R.G. 196, H-6700, Memorandum, H. J. deSiboni and O. C. Winston to Robert B. Mitchell, February 16, 1935.

79. See, e.g., Trotter, *Black Milwaukee*, 80–114.

80. *Buffalo American*, March 27, 1929.

81. *Buffalo American*, April 25, 1925.

82. *Buffalo American*, July 22, 1925.

83. *Buffalo American*, September, 1921.

84. The *Buffalo American* is the only one of these newspapers that is extant. It is located in the archives of the Buffalo and Erie County Historical Society in Buffalo, New York.

85. The *Buffalo American*, February 7, 1920–May 1, 1924. Also see V. P. Franklin, "Education for Life: Adult Education Programs for African Americans in Northern Cities, 1900–1942," in Harvey Neufeldt and Leo McGee, *Education of the African American Adult: An Historical Overview* (Westport, Conn., 1990), 113–134.

86. *Buffalo American*, May 7, 1925.

87. John Bracey, et al., *Black Nationalism in America* (Indianapolis, 1970), 266.

88. *Buffalo American,* August 5, 1920.

89. *Buffalo American,* July 15, 1920.

90. *Buffalo American,* August 5, 1920. The occupations of the board members listed here are taken from the 1925 manuscript census of New York State.

91. *Buffalo American,* August 12, 1920.

92. *Buffalo American,* November 4, 1920.

93. *Buffalo American,* June 8, 1922.

94. *Buffalo American,* July 8, 1920.

95. *Buffalo American,* August 26, 1920.

96. *Buffalo American,* June 8, 1922.

97. *Crisis* 41 (January, 1923), 456.

98. Monroe Fordham, "BCES, Inc., 1928-1961: A Black Self-Help Organization," in *Niagara Frontier* (Summer, 1976), 44.

99. Ibid.

5. PHILANTHROPY AND UPLIFT

1. Buffalo Federation of Churches, *Foreign Speaking and Negro Sections of Buffalo* (Buffalo, 1923), 30.

2. Mary Talbert to Mary White Ovington, December 16, 1920, NAACP Papers, C 76, Manuscript Collection, Library of Congress, Washington, D.C.

3. See testimony by Reverend Sidney O. B. Johnson, TCCUCP, 1937, 762-767.

4. Kenneth C. Hausauer, *The Second Fifty Years* (Buffalo, 1970), 48.

5. *Men of Buffalo,* XXI, December 1922, 13.

6. Ibid., 13. See also Buffalo Federation of Churches, *Foreign Speaking and Negro Sections of Buffalo* (Buffalo, 1923).

7. Ibid., 13.

8. Ibid., 13.

9. Hausauer, 39-63.

10. *Men of Buffalo,* XXII, May 1, 1922-May 1, 1923, 5.

11. Records of the Michigan Avenue YMCA *Handbook,* 1928. These records are located in the archives of the University at Buffalo, State University of New York; they were collected and microfilmed by the Afro American Historical Society of the Niagara Frontier, and the microfilm version is in the organization's archives at the North Jefferson Branch Library, Buffalo and Erie County Library, Buffalo, New York; hereafter referred to as Records, MAYMCA.

The official history of the Buffalo YMCA lists the founding of the Michigan Avenue Y in the fall of 1922. See Hausauer, 51. Also see *Men of Buffalo,* XXII, 5. The discrepancy can be attributed to the fact that the historian of the Michigan Avenue Y wrote about it only after William Jackson had been appointed executive director.

12. Records, MAYMCA. "Recognition Week Programs," April 21-27, 1947.

13. A Church with a Strange Beginning," *Buffalo Morning Express,* May 20, 1906; *Buffalo Evening News,* May 20, 1906; *Buffalo Courier,* September 18, 1927, in archive of the Durham Memorial AME Zion Church. I am grateful to Reverend Richard C. Stewart for making these documents available to me.

14. Ibid., Abbreviated History.

15. Ibid.

16. See biographical sketches below.

17. Records, MAYMCA, "Memorabilia, 1926–1936."

18. Ibid.; *Buffalo Courier Express,* March 17, 1955.

19. Rudolph Lane, a member of the Bethel AME Church, former president of the local chapter of the NAACP, and the first chairman of the Board of Managers of the Michigan Avenue YMCA, worked as a bookkeeper for the Buffalo Optical Company (Buffalo City Directory, 1923). Justice Taylor was a contractor. The 1923 City Directory listed Ray W. Coan as an agent (railroad). It is impossible to determine the nature of his business. Charles E. Sims operated a furniture store with Edward Towne on Michigan Avenue, across the street from the future site of the Y. With the exception of Taylor, these men resided in the heart of the black community.

20. In 1906, Ford moved to Buffalo from Addison, Michigan. A native of Jonesboro, Tennessee, Ford worked his way through Warner Institute, an American missionary school in Jonesboro. One of Ford's instructors was impressed favorably with his performance and secured a job for him on his father's farm in Addison. After working for Fred H. Smith for only three years, Smith entered into a partnership dealing in livestock with him. Business demands necessitated that Ford travel to Buffalo frequently. He soon decided to remain there and to set up a livestock brokerage firm in 1906. Ford was active in the NAACP and served as treasurer of the *Buffalo American,* a black newspaper which was affiliated with the National Negro Press Association (*Buffalo Courier Express,* April 20, 1951).

21. Dr. J. Edward Nash was born in Occuquan, Virginia in 1868. His parents had been slaves and Nash was compelled to secure positions as farm laborer, dockhand, teamster, mason, and blacksmith while acquiring an elementary education. He was able to save money, and at the age that most American youths who enroll in institutions of higher education do, Nash entered Whalen Seminary, today known as Virginia Union University, where he completed the requirements for a bachelor of divinity degree (*Buffalo Evening News,* January 26, 1957.)

22. *Buffalo City Directory,* 1923.

23. Interviews: Bessie Williams, Garveyite and member of Women's Committee, Michigan Avenue YMCA, Buffalo, New York, February 26, 1976; Arthur Griffa, associate general executive, East Side Branch YMCA, Buffalo, New York, February 27, 1976; Raymond Jackson, former member, Board of Management, Michigan Avenue YMCA, June 20, 1977. *Men of Buffalo,* XXVI (December, 1927), 2.

24. Letter, Amelia G. Anderson to Robert Bagnall, June 7, 1922; letter, Walter White to Amelia G. Anderson, November 12, 1922; letter, Amelia G. Anderson to Walter White, November 9, 1922, NAACP Branch Files, G-130, Administrative Files, Box C300, Manuscript Division, Library of Congress.

25. *Buffalo Forum,* September, 1923, 7.

26. *Buffalo American,* May 3, 1923.

27. *Buffalo American,* January 15, 1925.

28. *Men of Buffalo,* XXIV, July, 1925, 3.

29. Ibid., 4. African American YMCAs in larger cities had been constructed before World War I. See Spear, *Black Chicago* (Chicago, 1967); Osofsky, *Harlem:*

The Making of a Ghetto (New York, 1966); Katzman, *Before the Ghetto* (Urbana, 1973). The black population of Buffalo before the war was too small to warrant the establishment of a separate branch of the YMCA. While there is no evidence that local African Americans were in contact with other black YMCA directors, William Jackson, secretary of the Michigan Avenue Branch, and himself a new-comer to Buffalo, was a veteran YMCA man who had served as secretary of the Center Avenue Branch YMCA in Springfield, Ohio. Undoubtedly, he had contacts among other black YMCA secretaries across the nation. Apparently, interest in YMCA work among blacks was renewed in the 1920s. A conference was held in Washington, D.C. in 1925 to discuss the purpose of the "Colored" YMCA, its present field, what new fields it should enter, and how these plans could best be implemented. *Crisis,* 31 (November, 1925), 14.

30. *Buffalo American,* December 4, 1924.

31. *Men of Buffalo* (July, 1925), 3.

32. Ibid., 4.

33. Records, MAYMCA, Memorabilia.

34. Hausauer, 63.

35. Hausauer, 64; *Men of Buffalo,* XXV (November, 1926), 5; Records, MAYMCA, Memorabilia 1926-1936.

36. William Jackson was notified of the terms of the donation in a letter; a copy of the Deed of Trust which was to remain undisclosed was included also. Whitford to Jackson, November 6, 1926, Records, MAYMCA.

37. Records, MAYMCA, Memorabilia.

38. Hausauer, 50-56; *Men of Buffalo* (December, 1922), 13.

39. Ibid.; Michigan Avenue Branch YMCA, *Twenty Years in the Service of Youth,* 1943.

40. *Buffalo American,* March 4, 1926.

41. *Twenty Years,* 7. The plans for the Michigan Branch were enlarged to comply with the request of George Mathews (Records, MAYMCA, Memorabilia 1926-1936).

42. Records, MAYMCA, Memorabilia.

43. Interview, Mrs. Bessie Williams.

44. Interview, Mrs. Bessie Williams; *Twenty Years,* 10, 12, and 21.

45. Interview, Mr. Arthur Griffa, Buffalo, New York, February 27, 1976.

46. Hausauer, 84.

47. Interview, Griffa.

48. Herman Daves was added to the staff as Boys Work Secretary in 1927. Leon J. Hall assumed the position of Physical Department Director and Boys Work Secretary. Records, MAYMCA.

49. *Buffalo American,* May 3, 1923 and December 4, 1924; *The Y's Messenger,* November, 1938.

50. Records, MAYMCA

51. Records, MAYMCA, *Handbook for 1928-1929.*

52. Each club was scheduled to use the gymnasium twice a week with the exception of the younger boys clubs which were assigned three weekly sessions. Physical director Leon Hall's report for the fiscal year May 1, 1928 through April 1, 1929 indicated that 537 senior members, 755 young men, and 1,869 boys used the gymnasium; 4,751 men and boys used the swimming pool. During

that same period, 60 persons participated in individual work programs, and 52 visitors availed themselves of the services offered by the YMCA (Records, MAYMCA.)

53. Records, MAYMCA.

54. Ibid., Memorabilia.

55. The Michigan Avenue YMCA received the National Program Award at the New York World's Fair for its Second Western New York Assembly of black youths and for its work with young people.

56. Ibid., *The Y's Messenger,* Vol. I, January, 1937.

57. MAYMCA, *Handbook,* 1928–1929.

58. Records, MAYMCA, "Program Y Activities, Fall and Winter, 1931–1932"; "Studies in the Teaching of Jesus: Finding a Religion to Live By" was scheduled for the fall of 1931. The following topics were scheduled:

October

2	What And Who Is A Christian?
9	How May One Get Acquainted With God?
16	Is The Spiritual Life Real Or Just Say-So?
23	Why Is The Gate Narrow Which Leads To Life?
30	What And Where Is God?

November

6	Does A Christian Need To Join A Church?
13	Is The Bible A Book To Live By Today?
20	What Is Sin?
27	What Has The Death Of Jesus To Do With Me?

December

4	Does Prayer Get Us Anything Or Anywhere?
11	Is The Golden Rule Workable?
18	Are Any Of Us Wholly Bad Or Wholly Good?
25	Is There Life After Death?

59. MAYMCA, *Handbook,* 1928–1929.

60. Ibid., "Artistic" seemed to refer to classical music, i.e., European music.

61. Hausauer, 16–17. Hausauer indicated that the YMCA had established a plumbing trade school, an automobile school, and an accountancy school. Moreover, it had established the Lackawanna Institute in 1912, which was an extension program designed primarily to teach English and to "extend a helping hand to the foreigner seeking Americanization" (ibid., 17–18).

62. MAYMCA, *Handbook,* 1928–1929.

63. Ibid.

64. Ibid.

65. Michigan Avenue YMCA, *The Y's Messenger,* November, 1937. Although there was no formal employment agency at the Y, Secretary Jackson was able to place individuals in jobs because of his numerous contacts within the city and because of the respect he had earned.

66. Hausauer, 117.

67. Ibid., 76.

68. Hausauer, 72–76.

69. Ibid., 84.

70. Michigan Avenue YMCA Program 1931–1932 in MAYMCA.

71. Until her death in 1923, Mary Burnett Talbert convened a group of teenage girls at her home, where they discussed social concerns as well as the problems confronting adolescent girls. Occasionally, they hosted parties and other social gatherings (*Buffalo American*, March 24, 1921).

72. Michigan Avenue YMCA, Program 1931–1932.

73. Ibid.

74. Ibid., 7.

75. Ibid., 17.

76. Chapter 6 provides a detailed account of the social and economic conditions that African Americans faced, especially in the critical decade of the 1930s.

77. The Buffalo Urban League reported that there were 173 African Americans enrolled in high school in the academic year 1928–1929; ten years later the number had nearly tripled. *Twenty Years of Service by Memorial Center and Urban League, Inc., Buffalo, New York, 1927–1947*, p. 4, Series 13, Box 6, Folder "Buffalo 1945–1953" in Urban League Papers, Manuscript Division, Library of Congress.

78. *The Y's Messenger*, April, 1939.

79. *Buffalo American*, July 8, 1920.

80. New York State Temporary Commission on the Urban Colored Population, 1937, B-69, 808.

81. *The Y's Messenger*, October, 1937.

82. MAYMCA, *Scrapbook*, Memorabilia, 1926–1936. Dr. R. S. Wilkinson, president of State College at Orangeburg, North Carolina; Dr. Channing H. Tobias, National Council, YMCA; Dr. R. R. Moton, president, Tuskegee Institute; Dr. George Washington Carver; Dr. A. L. McCrory, president, Johnson C. Smith University; Bishop L. W. Kyles, AME Zion Church; Dr. Charles H. Garvin, president, National Negro Medical Association; and Congressman Arthur Mitchell participated in the annual forums.

83. Ibid., Charles H. Houston to Walter White, May 23, 1923; July 31, 1935, NAACP Papers, Administrative File, Container C-64; folder Charles H. Houston. Also see John Hope Franklin and Alfred Moss, *From Slavery to Freedom*, 7th ed. (New York, 1994).

84. Ibid., *Scrapbook*, Michigan Avenue YMCA.

85. Ibid., Interviews, Mrs. Bessie Williams.

86. Records, MAYMCA, Memorabilia.

87. In 1927, the Urban League was incorporated as part of the Memorial Center, a settlement house within the black community, because it was felt that the two organizations performed the same kinds of functions (Urban League Papers, Series V, William Evans to Eugene Jones, February 5, 1929, Container 13, Manuscript Division, Library of Congress).

88. MAYMCA, Memorabilia, newspaper clippings, July 24, 1932.

89. Ibid.

90. Antoinette Ford to Robert Bagnall, May 13, 1932; Bagnall to Anderson, October 11, 1932; Pickens to Anderson, June 20, 1933; Pickens to Jackson,

October 18, 1933, NAACP Branch Files, Container G131, Manuscript Collection, Library of Congress.

91. Interview, Griffa; Records, MAYMCA, "Recognition Week Program," April 21-27, 1947; *The Y's Messenger,* January, 1937, 1.

92. Interview, Griffa.

93. By 1934, additional property on Cypress Street was purchased so that the Y could provide accommodations for transient couples who were visiting Buffalo. Wales Hollow, a 40-acre camp site, was purchased and equipped by the Michigan Avenue Y. Both of these purchases were gifts of the Mathews (MAYMCA, "Program Recognition Week," April 21-27, 1947).

94. Interview, Griffa.

6. NOT ALMS, BUT OPPORTUNITY

1. For further discussion, see Nancy Weiss, *National Urban League 1910-1940* (New York, 1974); John Hope Franklin and Albert Moss, *From Slavery to Freedom,* 7th ed. (New York, 1994).

2. Gwendolyn Greene, "A Study of Social Group Work as a Function of the Buffalo Urban League, Inc.," unpublished master's thesis, University of Pittsburgh, 1952, 62.

3. Charles Johnson, "The Buffalo Negro Study," 1923, unpublished manuscript, State University of New York at Buffalo Archives. The league wanted to organize in Buffalo to enhance its influence. Buffalonians were interested in establishing a branch of the league because there was no single agency in Buffalo which handled the multiplicity of social problems confronting African Americans at the time.

4. T. Arnold Hill to S. O. B. Johnson, September 20, 1926, Urban League, Series IV, Container 28; Johnson to Hill, September 25, 1926. Johnson reiterated the necessity of soliciting support from the "right people" and told Hill that he hoped "to avoid the mistakes of the past this time."

5. Greene, 63.

6. Hill's memorandum of Buffalo visit September 28-October 2, Urban League Papers, Manuscript Collection, Series IV, Container 28, Library of Congress, Washington, D.C.

7. Ibid.

8. Minutes, Organizational Committee, October 1, 1926, Urban League Papers (ULP), Manuscript Collection, Library of Congress, Series IV, Container 28.

9. Ibid.

10. Ibid.

11. Ibid.

12. Interview, Teresa Evans, secretary of the Buffalo Urban League, 1927-1964 and wife of William Evans. February, 1977; July 26, 1986.

13. Memorandum on Buffalo visit. The Reverends Washington, Echols, Palmer, Johnson, Van Buren, and Brown, along with the unidentified secretary, were present at this meeting.

14. Teresa Evans, interview.

15. Ibid.

16. "Recommendation of Organizing in Buffalo," Urban League Papers, Manuscript Collection, Library of Congress, Series IV, Container 28.

17. Ibid.

18. Press release, Urban League Papers, Library of Congress, Series IV, Container 28.

19. Minutes, Board of Directors, February 11, 1927, Urban League Papers, Series IV, Container 28.

20. Irene Graham to Arnold Hill, February 26, 1927, Urban League Papers, Series IV, Container 28. The disdain that these liberal whites held for their black peers was widespread. Other historians have observed this same phenomenon. However, in most instances, they attributed their differences to the fact that a new southern leadership whose economic status depended solely upon the black community had emerged. See, for example, Kenneth Kusmer, *A Ghetto Takes Shape*; Alan Spear, *Black Chicago*; and Joe Trotter, *Black Milwaukee*.

21. Teresa Evans, interview.

22. Evans had taught drawing and design at Louisville High School from 1910 to 1916. He was a partner in an architectural firm, 1916–1919, and was industrial secretary of the Chicago Urban League, 1919–1926 (Interview, Teresa Evans, February 26, 1977 and curriculum vita of William Evans in Teresa Evans papers).

23. First Annual Report, 1928, Buffalo Urban League, headquarters on Broadway, Buffalo. Interview, Teresa Evans; Buffalo City Directory, 1930.

24. Ibid.

25. First Annual Report, Buffalo Urban League.

26. Ibid.; Teresa Evans.

27. Greene, 20–21.

28. Ibid.

29. First Annual Report, Buffalo Urban League.

30. Report of a Committee Appointed to Review the Work of Memorial Center and Urban League, Incorporated, 1929–1930. Urban League Papers, Series V, Box 13, Manuscript Collection, Library of Congress.

31. Ibid., Report of Committee Appointed to Review the Work of Memorial Center and Urban League, Incorporated, 1929–1930, Urban League Papers, Series V, Box 13, Manuscript Collection, Library of Congress.

32. Hill Memorandum, October 12–29, 1927, Urban League Papers, Series IV, Container 28, Library of Congress.

33. Fourth Annual Report, December 15, 1931, Buffalo Urban League Headquarters, Broadway, Buffalo, New York.

34. First Annual Report, Buffalo Urban League.

35. Interview, Teresa Evans.

36. V. Freda Seigworth to Hill, August 27, 1926, Series IV, Container 28, Urban League Papers, Manuscript Collection, Library of Congress.

37. First Annual Report, Buffalo Urban League.

38. Report of the Executive Secretary, November, 1928, Series IV, Box 28, Urban League Papers, Manuscript Collection, Library of Congress.

39. Report of Memorial Center and Urban League, Inc. for July–October, 1929, Urban League Papers, Series V, Box 13, Manuscript Collection, Library of Congress.

40. *Twenty Years of Service by Memorial Center and Urban League, Inc., Buffalo, New York, 1927–1947*, p. 4. Series 13, Box 6, Folder "Buffalo, 1945–1953." Urban League Papers, Manuscript Division, Library of Congress.

41. Report, Executive Secretary, November, 1928.

42. Fourth Annual Report, Buffalo Urban League, December 15, 1931.

43. William Evans to Arnold Hill, January 14, 1928, Urban League Papers, Series IV, Container 28, Manuscript Collection, Library of Congress.

44. Second Annual Report of the Buffalo Urban League, 1929, Broadway Headquarters, Buffalo, New York.

45. Evans to Eugene Kinckle Jones, February 2, 1929, Urban League Papers, Series IV, Box 28, Manuscript Collection, Library of Congress.

46. TCCUCP Hearings, December 7, 1937, 768–772.

47. TCCUCP, 762–763.

48. Ibid., 764.

49. Evans to Jones, February 2, 1929.

50. *Twenty Years Report*, 5.

51. Evans to Hill, September 12, 1929, Urban League Papers, Series IV, Container 28, Manuscript Collection, Library of Congress.

52. Evans to Hill, February 11, 1930, Series IV, Box 28, Urban League Papers, Manuscript Collection, Library of Congress.

53. Fourth Annual Report, Buffalo Urban League, 1931.

54. Trends in Household Employment 1930–1931, Urban League Papers, Series IV, Container 5, Manuscript Collection, Library of Congress. Fourth Annual Report, 1931. Evans to John Clark, May 16, 1934, Series IV, Container 2, Urban League Papers, Manuscript Collection, Library of Congress.

55. Fourth Annual Report, 1931.

56. This program employed men to rake leaves, shovel the sidewalks, and to perform other maintenance tasks on the blocks on which they resided. See W. N. Kessel to Porter Lee, January 13, 1931, President's Emergency Committee on Employment, R.G. 73, File 620.1, National Archives, Washington, D.C.

57. Fourth Annual Report, December 15, 1931.

58. New York State TCCUCP, 747.

59. Evans, *The Twenty Year Report*.

60. The General Secretary noticed an increase in radicalism among blacks in Buffalo who joined white radical movements. Blacks had begun to organize and to demonstrate with local Communists (Fourth Annual Report, December 15, 1931).

61. Ibid.

62. PECE, R.G. 73, File 620.1, National Archives, Washington, D.C.

63. *Twenty Years* report, p. 13.

64. Second Annual Report of Buffalo Urban League, 1929.

65. See Arvarh Strickland, *Chicago Urban League* (Urbana, 1966).

66. Evans to Hill, February 11, 1930.

67. M. H. Moultrie to Frances Perkins, April 12, 1939, Lawrence A. Oxley Files on New York State, in National Archives, Record Group 174.

68. *The Twenty Years* report, 8, 12. For a discussion of the racial discrimination that black nurses experienced, see Darlene Clark Hine, *Black Women in White: Racial Conflict and Cooperation in the Nursing Profession* (Bloomington, 1989).

69. Strickland, *Chicago Urban League,* 112-113, 121. Evans to Clark, May 16, 1934.

70. Clark to Evans, May 18, 1934, Series IV, Box 2, Urban League Papers, Manuscript Collection, Library of Congress.

71. Evans to Clark, May 16, 1934; ibid.

72. Evans to Elmer Carter, September 12, 1933, Urban League Papers, Series IV, Box 21, Manuscript Collection, Library of Congress.

73. First Annual Report, Buffalo Urban League, 1928.

74. Fourth Annual Report, Buffalo Urban League, 1931.

75. Ibid.

76. Fifth Annual Report of Buffalo Urban League, 1932, Headquarters on Broadway in Buffalo, New York.

77. A group of unemployed black men were arrested as they were leaving the Big Brothers Home, which was established by black men to provide food and shelter for such newcomers; Elijah Echols of the Shiloh Baptist Church was prominent in this organization. See *Buffalo American,* March 10, 1921.

78. New York State TCCUCP, 746, 755.

79. William L. Evans, *Twenty Years of Service,* p. 10.

80. First Annual Report of Buffalo Urban League, 1928.

81. Ibid.

82. Evans, *Twenty Years,* p. 4.

83. Fourth Annual Report of Buffalo Urban League, December 15, 1931.

84. Arvarh Strickland, *Chicago Urban League,* 17; Fourth Annual Report.

85. First Annual Report, Buffalo Urban League, 1928.

86. "A Three Year Contribution," 1931.

87. Fifth Annual Report of Buffalo Urban League, 1932.

88. "A Three Year Contribution," 1931.

89. Report of Buffalo Urban League, July 10, 1929, 8. New York State officials were cognizant of this development, yet there was no attempt to alleviate the problems of delinquent black youths. The Children's Aid Society of Buffalo suggested that the Urban League expand its own services.

90. Fourth Annual Report, Buffalo Urban League, 1931.

91. Visiting Teacher Report, 1929-1931; Urban League Papers, Series V, Box 13, Manuscript Collection, Library of Congress.

92. Fourth Annual Report, Buffalo Urban League, 1931.

93. "A Three Year Contribution to Inter-Racial Understanding," 1931.

94. Cooking classes and other structured activities organized for males who were discipline problems proved highly successful in eliminating their aberrant behavior. Report of a Committee Appointed to Review the Work of Memorial Center and Urban League, Inc., 1929-1930, Series V, Box 13, Urban League Papers, Manuscript Collection, Library of Congress.

95. Ibid.

96. As early as 1919 there was concern in Buffalo about the shortage of affordable housing for laborers. Francis Mahoney to James Ford, February 6, 1919. U.S. Housing Commission, R.G. 31, National Archives. By 1933, only 21 percent of housing in the city was described as "good"; Public Housing Administration, R.G. 196, File H-6700-6706, 1933; Second Annual Report of Buffalo Urban League, 1929.

97. Public Housing Administration, R.G. 196, File H-6700, National Archives.

98. Minutes, Buffalo Advisory Committee on Housing, R.G. 196, H-6700–6703, March 31, 1937. William Evans, *Housing and Race Fear* (New York, 1946).

99. William Tuttle, *Race Riot* (New York, 1972); Arthur Waskow, *From Race Riot to Sit-In* (Garden City, N.Y., 1966); Elliot Rudwick, *Race Riot at East St. Louis* (New York, 1972).

100. Douglas Falconer to Eugene Kinckle Jones, December 10, 1930, Series V, Box 13, Urban League Papers, Manuscript Collection, Library of Congress.

101. Second Annual Report of Buffalo Urban League, 1929.

102. Ibid.

103. Annual Reports, Buffalo Urban League, 1928–1932.

104. Fifth Annual Report, Buffalo Urban League, 1932.

105. Fourth Annual Report, Buffalo Urban League, 1931.

106. *Buffalo Evening Times,* November 17, 1930, Series V, Box 13, Urban League Papers, Manuscript Collection, Library of Congress; Derrick Byrd testimony, TCCUCP, 841–842.

107. Fourth Annual Report, Buffalo Urban League, 1931.

108. Ibid.

7. CIVIL RIGHTS, POLITICS, AND COMMUNITY

1. Talbert in *The Crisis,* 10, 4 (August, 1915), 184; Zora Neale Hurston *Their Eyes Were Watching God* (New York, 1937), p. 31.

2. William Talbert, in *Who's Who of the Colored Race,* Vol. I, 1915, reprinted (Detroit, 1976), p. 258.

3. Garrett Interview, June 14, 1973; Frank Lincoln Mather, *Who's Who of the Colored Race,* Vol I, 1915 reprinted (Detroit, 1976).

4. *Buffalo American,* August 12, 1920. Existing data simply will not permit an analysis of the local candidates blacks supported and the rationale for their choices. Linda Hanaka, in "The Negro During the Depression in Buffalo," argues that by and large politicians did not make appeals to the African American population even when their numbers were much larger in the 1930s (unpublished manuscript in the Buffalo and Erie County Historical Society).

5. Louis Harlan and Raymond Smock, *The Booker T. Washington Papers* 8 (Urbana, 1979), p. 321.

6. Martin Kilson describes the evolutionary stages in the political maturation of African American communities in Martin Kilson, "The Political Status of American Negroes in the Twentieth Century," in Martin Kilson and Robert Rotberg, *The African Diaspora: Interpreting Essays* (Cambridge, 1976), 459–484.

7. Charles Kellogg, *The NAACP,* Vol. I (Baltimore, 1967).

8. Rayford Logan, *The Betrayal of the Negro* (New York, 1965); C. Vann Woodward, *The Strange Career of Jim Crow* (New York, 1966).

9. Charles Kellogg, *The NAACP,* 11–26.

10. Minutes, NAACP Board of Directors Meeting, November 29, 1910, NAACP Papers, Container A 8, Manuscript Collection, Library of Congress.

11. Ibid., March 7, 1911.

12. Ibid., January 15, 1915.

13. Election Lists 1939–1940, NAACP Branch Files, Box G 131, Manuscript Collection, Library of Congress.

14. This finding is not surprising despite the fact that most members came from the working class. Working-class members tended to purchase one-dollar memberships which made one an associate member of the organization, but did not permit one to vote. Minutes, Executive Committee Meeting, May 25, 1910, NAACP Administrative File, Container A 8, Manuscript Collection, Library of Congress.

15. NAACP Branch Files, Membership List for 1917, Box G 130, Manuscript Collection, Library of Congress.

16. Ibid., Membership Lists 1922–1940.

17. NAACP membership lists indicate that women comprised well over 50 percent between 1926–1940. Branch files G 130, 131, Manuscript Division, Library of Congress.

18. Robert Bagnall to Antoinette Ford, April 11, 1929, NAACP Branch Files, Box G 130, Manuscript Collection, Library of Congress.

19. Report for Twentieth Annual Conference, prepared by Amelia Anderson, July 2, 1929, NAACP Branch Files, Box G 130, Manuscript Collection, Library of Congress.

20. "Pen Pictures of Prominent Colored Folk," *Buffalo Morning Express,* December 7, 1919, section 4, p. 8.

21. Ida Wells Barnett, *On Lynchings* (New York, 1969; originally published 1892, 1895, 1900, respectively).

22. Membership lists in NAACP Branch files G130–131, Manuscript Division, Library of Congress.

23. Ibid., Data compiled from membership lists.

24. Ibid., membership lists, 1926–1940.

25. Amelia Anderson to William Pickens, Pickens to Anderson, Branch Files, Box G 130, Manuscript Collection, Library of Congress.

26. See Kellogg's *NAACP* for further discussion.

27. Mary Burnett Talbert was born in Oberlin, Ohio in 1866 and was graduated from Oberlin College at age nineteen. She went on to have an illustrious career as a social activist. Burnett married William H. Talbert of Buffalo in 1891 and soon thereafter moved to Buffalo, where she continued the work to which she dedicated her life. Mary Talbert was elected president of the National Association of Colored Women and served in this capacity from 1916–1920. Talbert was invited to represent the NACW at the International Council of Women held in Christiana, Norway in 1920. She also served as a nurse with the Red Cross in France during World War I, and by 1923 was a vice president of the NAACP; *Crisis* 27 (December, 1923), 77. Her last major project before her death in October 1923 was to lead the nationwide anti-lynching crusade and campaign for the passage of the Dyer Anti-Lynching Bill. *Crisis* 25 (March, 1923), 213–214. Talbert worked to bring about prison reform in the South. She had been the first Worthy Matron of Naomi Chapter Number 10, Order of the Eastern Star, in Buffalo and had conducted Sunday sessions of the Culture Congress at the Michigan Avenue Baptist Church.

For further information on Mary B. Talbert, see Lillian S. Williams, "Mary Morris Burnett Talbert," in *Black Women in America: An Historical Encyclopedia* (Bloomington, 1994), 1137–1139.

28. See Thomas Crippes, *Slow Fade to Black* (New York, 1976).

29. John Brent to May Childs Nerney, April 16, 1915, NAACP Administrative Files, Films and Plays, Box C 299.

30. *Buffalo Express*, December 19, 1915; *Buffalo Express*, December 26, 1915. The advertisement for this film read:

"The Birth of a Nation," the most marvelous picture so far shown on the screen will be at the Star shortly after the holidays. . . . This will be Buffalo's first opportunity to see [the film], although it has been shown in nearly all the larger cities.
Ibid.

31. Nerney to Brent, April 22, 1915, NAACP Administrative Files, C 299.

32. M. Clark to Rudolph Lane, December 10, 1920, Box G 130, NAACP Branch Files, Manuscript Collection, Library of Congress.

33. Ibid.

34. Marshall Brown to Robert Bagnall, December 29, 1922, NAACP Branch Files, Box G 130, Manuscript Collection, Library of Congress.

35. Robert Bagnall Report, May 29, 1922, NAACP Correspondence Files, Box C 62, Manuscript Collection, Library of Congress; Walter White to Amelia Anderson, May 13, 1932; Anderson to White, May 16, 1932; Brown to Bagnall, June 20, 1933; NAACP Branch Files, Box G 130, Manuscript Collection, Library of Congress.

36. Secretary Marshall Brown to Walter White, March 21, 1923, NAACP Branch Files, Box G 130, Manuscript Collection, Library of Congress.

37. James Weldon Johnson to Marshall Brown, March 27, 1923, Box G 130, ibid.

38. Marshall Brown to Robert W. Bagnall, December 29, 1922, Box G 130, Manuscript Collection, Library of Congress.

39. Ibid.

40. Ruth Davies to Walter White, October 1, 1936, Box G 131, NAACP Branch Files, Manuscript Collection, Library of Congress. Dr. Charles Goodale's 1937 testimony before the TCCUCP indicated that securing admission for African American women was still an uphill battle. He also reported that the hospital had problems in hiring African American professionals in general. It also had refused to hire black doctors because white women might feel "uncomfortable" when they performed their physical examinations. TCCUCP, 1014–1032.

41. Ruth Davies to Walter White, October 1, 1936, Box G 131, NAACP Branch Files, Manuscript Collection, Library of Congress.

42. Section 40 of the New York State Civil Rights Law, as amended in 1918, Box G 130, NAACP Branch Files, Manuscript Collection, Library of Congress.

43. *Buffalo American*, January 26, 1922. The incident involving the Bullocks does not appear to be unique. Ida Wells Barnett observed that most victims of the lynch mob were prosperous or outspoken blacks who challenged the southern status quo. See Ida B. Wells Barnett, *On Lynchings*.

44. Ibid.; Anderson to Ovington, January 24, 1922, Box G 130, NAACP Branch Files, Manuscript Collection, Library of Congress.

45. Bagnall to Brown, February 28, 1922, Box G 130, NAACP Branch Files, Manuscript Collection, Library of Congress.

46. The Dyer Anti-Lynching Bill was passed by the House of Representatives;

however, it was not passed by the Senate. Brown to Bagnall, December 29, 1922, NAACP Branch Files, Box G 130, Manuscript Collection, Library of Congress.

47. Julian Evans to Walter White, March 14, 1934, NAACP Branch Files, Box G 131, Manuscript Collection, Library of Congress. The outcome of the Epps case is not certain, for the national office did not handle it. Local NAACP records are not available.

48. Evans to White, October 15, 1934; Charles Poletti to Evans, October 17, 1934; Evans to White, October 26, 1934, Box G 131, NAACP Branch Files, Manuscript Collection, Library of Congress. There were three reform schools for blacks in Virginia.

49. Rayford Logan, *The Betrayal of the Negro* (New York, 1957).

50. Marshall Brown to Robert Bagnall, December 29, 1922, Box G 130, NAACP Branch Files, Manuscript Collection, Library of Congress.

51. People v. Deitch, New York Court of Appeals, December 27, 1923. Deitch appealed this decision to the appellate court, where the earlier ruling was reversed because the corroborative evidence was considered to be insufficient; after a lengthy court battle, the New York State Court of Appeals affirmed the lower court's ruling.

52. Wilson Record, *The Negro and the Communist Party* (New York, 1971), 36.

53. Wilson, 38.

54. Arvarh Strickland, *History of the Chicago Urban League* (Urbana, 1966), 73–74.

55. Ibid., 74.

56. *Buffalo Times,* November 13, 1931, NAACP Branch Files, Box G 130, Manuscript Collection, Library of Congress.

57. Ibid.

58. Ibid.

59. Julian Evans to Walter White, September 2, 1934, Box G 130, NAACP Branch Files, Manuscript Collection, Library of Congress.

60. The Scottsboro incident involved nine youths from Huntsville, Alabama who were falsely indicted for raping two disreputable white women. For further information, see Dan Carter, *Scottsboro* (New York, 1971).

61. Julian Evans to Walter White, November 26, 1934, Box G 131, NAACP Branch Files, Manuscript Collection, Library of Congress. Pollard made reference to this case before the TCCUCP in 1937. He noted: "When Negroes appear [before the court], two things happen: they are browbeaten, and made to feel uncomfortable even when they are only witnesses. Exaggerated emotion is appealed to. There was a boy on trial for rape. He was given 20 years." TCCUCP, 832.

62. Stephen Perkins to International Labor Defense, October 8, 1935, Box G 131, NAACP Branch Files, Manuscript Collection, Library of Congress.

63. Ruth Davies to Walter White, December 10, 1935; Pattie Ellis to White, November 4, 1935, Box G 131, NAACP Branch Files, Manuscript Collection, Library of Congress.

64. Evans to White, November 6, 1935, Box G 131, NAACP Branch Files, Manuscript Collection, Library of Congress.

65. Charles Houston to Evans, December 17, 1935, NAACP Branch Files, Manuscript Collection, Library of Congress.

66. White to Davies, December 16, 1935, NAACP Branch Files, Box G 131, Manuscript Collection, Library of Congress. The outcome of the Gill case, like many others in which the Buffalo NAACP became involved, is unknown. It is necessary to explore these cases to indicate the broad range of activities of the NAACP.

67. Petition, received May 27, 1921, NAACP Branch Files, Box G 130, Manuscript Collection, Library of Congress.

68. Kellogg, 271.

69. NYSTCCUCP, 938.

70. Ibid., 943.

71. Mrs. A. Kennedy to Morris Shapiro, n.d., NAACP H. Addenda, Box 6, Manuscript Collection, Library of Congress.

72. C. I. Clafin to Morris Shapiro, April 1, 1936, NAACP H. Addenda, Box 6, Manuscript Collection, Library of Congress.

73. The Scottsboro Defense Committee set aside the entire week of June 21–28 to be known throughout Buffalo as "Scottsboro Week." An outdoor meeting was scheduled on June 27 in the heart of the black community. The local police objected to the location of the rally because they feared large crowds would gather because of their sentiment in support of the Scottsboro Defense Committee and because blacks had already made verbal attacks on the police. Police officials asked the crowds to relocate to an area six blocks away. When the protestors refused to move, the police moved in and arrested them. They were placed under heavy fines and their constitutional rights were violated. A. Kennedy to Morris Shapiro, ibid.

74. *Buffalo American,* March 25, 1925.

75. See, for example, August Meier, et al., *Black Protest Thought in the Twentieth Century* (Indianapolis, 1965); Joy James, *Transcending the Talented Tenth* (New York, 1997).

76. *Buffalo American,* April 21, 1921.

77. *Buffalo American,* May 19, 1921.

78. Lillian S. Williams, "Mary Burnett Talbert," in Darlene Clark Hine, *Black Women in America: An Historical Encyclopedia* (Bloomington, 1994), 1137–1139.

79. *Buffalo American,* March 23, 1922.

80. *Buffalo American,* March 31, 1921.

81. *Buffalo American,* April 21, 1921.

82. Ibid.

83. *Buffalo American,* June 18, 1925.

84. *Buffalo American,* June 25, 1925.

85. Ibid.

86. Dr. Ossian Sweet, a black physician in Detroit, had been indicted for murder stemming from an incident involving a mob attack upon his recently purchased home, which was located in a white community. The NAACP handled Dr. Sweet's defense and conducted a nationwide campaign to raise money for legal expenditures.

87. *Buffalo American,* January 14, 1926.

88. *Buffalo American,* April 28, 1928.

89. Ibid.

90. *Buffalo American,* January 2, 1922.

91. Johnson had come to Buffalo from Meridian, Mississippi, where he had been very active in community life. Under the auspices of the Lincoln Community Center in Meridian, Mississippi, Johnson established several programs, including an employment bureau, a night school for soldiers returning from the recent war, a hospital for the wounded and destitute victims from the storms which swept through the area in 1917, a home science department for black women, and a playground for youngsters. He succeeded in winning the local Meridian Hospital's support for the establishment of a wing for tuberculosis patients. *Buffalo American,* June 9, 1921.

92. *Buffalo American,* January 4, 1923.

93. Ibid.

94. Ibid.

95. *Buffalo American,* January 3, 1924.

96. "Keep a Pluggin' Away"

> I've a humble little motto
> That is homely though its true —
> Keep a pluggin' away
> It's a thing when I've an object
> That I always try to do —
> Keep a pluggin' away
> When you've rising storms to quell,
> When opposing waters swell,
> It will never fail to tell —
> Keep a pluggin' away.

(*Buffalo American,* January 3, 1924)

97. See Robert Hill, *The Marcus Garvey Papers,* and David Cronin, *Black Moses,* for a discussion of the Garvey movement. Ralph Watkins, "The Marcus Garvey Movement in Buffalo, New York," in *Afro-Americans in New York Life and History* 1 (July, 1977), 37–47.

98. During our interview, I asked Bessie Williams about Garvey's "back to Africa movement," and she replied that "we had no intention of moving to Africa" (February, 1977).

99. *Buffalo American,* August 5, 1920.

100. *Buffalo American,* October 2, 1920.

101. Robert A. Hill, *The Marcus Garvey and UNIA Papers,* Vol. 3 (Los Angeles, 1983), 61.

102. Ibid.

103. Ibid.

104. Ibid.

105. *Buffalo American,* September 2, 1920.

106. *Buffalo American,* November 11, 1920.

107. *Buffalo American,* October 20, 1920.

108. For a discussion of this view, see Ralph Watkins, "The Marcus Garvey Movement in Buffalo, New York," in *Afro-Americans in New York Life and History* (July, 1977), 41–44.

109. Hill, of the National Urban League, reported that some black clergy

initially opposed the establishment of a branch of the Urban League in Buffalo because they feared that it would compete with the social programs that their churches offered. See chapter 6 above.

110. Local #79 established branches of UNIA in Lackawanna and Tonawanda, where the steel industry was especially important in employing migrant black workers, and in the industrial and resort center of Niagara Falls.

111. Robert A. Hill, *The Marcus Garvey and UNIA Papers*, Vol. 3 (Los Angeles, 1983), 74; interview with Bessie Williams, ibid.

112. Hill, *The Marcus Garvey and UNIA Papers*, Vol. 4 (Los Angeles, 1984), 521.

113. Ibid., 523.

114. Ibid., 46; *Buffalo Evening News*, June 27, 1933.

115. Hill, *The Marcus Garvey and UNIA Papers*, Vol. 5 (Los Angeles, 1986), 294.

116. Ibid.

117. Ibid., Vol. 3, 73.

118. Department of Graduate Records, May 13, 1948; University of Toronto Archives, Thomas Fisher Rare Book Library; *Buffalo Evening News*, July 13, 1974. Courtesy Robert A. Hill of the Marcus Garvey Historical Project at the University of California at Los Angeles.

119. Ibid.

120. The records of the local UNIA unit are not extant; unfortunately, I just discovered the existence of this parallel structure. The documents do not reveal what the responsibilities of these female offices entailed, nor is there any discussion of honorary positions. Cheryl Gilkes suggests that this structure may have been a mechanism whereby women could wield a modicum of power in traditionally male-dominated groups. See Cheryl Townsend Gilkes, "'Together and in Harness': Women's Traditions in the Sanctified Church," in *Signs* 10, 4 (Summer, 1985), 678–699.

121. *National Association Notes* 19 (October 1916), 3, Frissell Library, Tuskegee University, Tuskegee, Alabama, hereinafter cited as *National Association Notes*.

122. *National Association Notes* (January, 1901), in Mary Church Terrell Papers, Box 102-113, folder 244; Moorland-Spingarn Research Center at Howard University.

123. Ibid.

124. Ibid.; "Old Plantation Exhibit," *Official Catalogue and Guide to the Pan-American Exposition* (Buffalo, 1901); Richard H. Barry, *Snapshots on the Mid-Way of the Pan-American Exposition* (Buffalo, 1901), 125–128; 161.

125. John Brent to May Child Nerney, April 16, 1915, NAACP Administrative Files, Films and Plays, Box C299; M. Clark to John Brent, December 10, 1920, Box G 130, NAACP Branch Files, Manuscript Division, Library of Congress.

126. *Buffalo Courier*, March 3, 1901.

127. *Fiftieth Anniversary Banquet Program, Lit-Mus Club, 1922–1972*, in author's possession, hereinafter cited as *Fiftieth Anniversary*.

128. Report for Twentieth Annual Conference, 1929, NAACP Branch Files, Box G 130, Manuscript Division, Library of Congress; *Buffalo Evening Times*, November 17, 1930, National Urban League, Series V, Box 13, Manuscript Division, Library of Congress; *Fiftieth Anniversary*.

129. *Buffalo American,* August 19, 1920.

130. Minutes, Biennial Conference of the NACW, Tuskegee, July, 1920, pp. 40-41.

131. *Buffalo American,* August 12, 1920.

132. C. I. Claflin to Morris Shapiro, April 1, 1936; Mrs. A. Kennedy to Morris Shapiro, n.d., NAACP Papers, H Addenda, Box 6, Manuscript Division, Library of Congress.

133. *Buffalo American,* October 7, 1920; November 20, 1920; September 22, 1921; October 13, 1921.

134. *Buffalo American,* December 9, 1920; ibid., December 16, 1920. Also, Clark-Lewis, *Living In, Living Out.*

135. WMMS was founded as a response to James H. Johnson's essay "Women's Exalted Station" in which he argued that women's roles should be circumscribed by gender. He further contended that "the true woman" drew the line between man's constitution and her own. Johnson's views contradicted the historical relations whereby black men and women worked together to benefit their families and community. They maintained their separate unit, for it provided them with a forum for self-expression. *AME Church Review* 8 (April, 1892), 403-404. For a discussion of the origin of WMMS, see the "AME Philadelphia Conference Branch, 1874," in the Moorland-Spingarn Research Center, Howard University. See also Lewellyn Longfellow Berry, *A Century of Missions of the AME Church, 1840-1940* (New York, 1942), 101-103.

136. For a discussion of the impact of such resources on grassroots organizations and reform movements, see Aldon Morris, *Origins of the Civil Rights Movement: Organizing for Change* (New York, 1984).

CONCLUSION

1. Unpublished manuscript in possession of the author.

2. See Kenneth Jackson, *The Ku Klux Klan in the City* (New York, 1967).

3. V. P. Franklin, *Black Self-Determination* (Brooklyn, 1992).

4. Nikki Giovanni, *Selected Poems of Nikki Giovanni* (New York, 1996), p. 42.

BIBLIOGRAPHY

Ballard, Allen B. *One More Day's Journey: The Story of a Family and a People.* New York: McGraw-Hill, 1984.

Barksdale, Richard, and Kenneth Kinnamon. *Black Writers of America: A Comprehensive Anthology.* New York: Macmillan, 1972.

Barton, Josef J. "Immigration and Social Mobility in an American City, Studies of Three Ethnic Groups in Cleveland, 1890–1950." Ph.D. dissertation, University of Michigan, 1971.

———. *Peasants and Strangers: Italians, Rumanians, and Slovaks in an American City, 1890–1950.* Cambridge: Harvard University Press, 1975.

Bateman, Fred, and Foust, James. "A Matched Sample of Households Selected from the 1860 U.S. Manuscript Censuses." *Historical Methods.* Newsletter 6 (1973), 141–148.

Bell, Derrick. *Faces at the Bottom of the Well: The Permanence of Racism.* New York: Basic Books, 1992.

Bernard, Jessie. *Marriage and Family Among Negroes.* Englewood Cliffs, N.J.: Prentice-Hall, 1966.

Berry, Mary Frances. *Black Resistance, White Law.* New York: Appleton Century Crofts, 1971.

———. *Black Resistance, White Law.* New York: A. Lane-Penguin, 1994.

———. *Politics of Parenthood: Child Care, Women's Rights and the Myth of the Good Mother.* New York: Viking Press, 1993.

———. *Why ERA Failed.* Bloomington: Indiana University Press, 1986.

Bigham, Darrel E. *We Ask Only a Fair Trial: A History of the Black Community of Evansville, Indiana.* Bloomington: Indiana University Press, 1987.

Billingsley, Andrew. *Black Families in White America.* Englewood Cliffs, N.J.: Prentice-Hall, 1968.

———. *Climbing Jacob's Ladder.* New York: Simon and Schuster, 1992.

Blackwelder, Julia K. "Women in the Work Force: Atlanta, New Orleans, and San Antonio, 1930–1940." *Journal of Urban History* 4 (May, 1978), 331–358.

Blassingame, John. "Before the Ghetto: The Making of a Black Community in Savannah, Georgia, 1865–1880." *The Journal of Social History* 6 (Summer, 1973).

———. *Black New Orleans 1860–1890.* Chicago: University of Chicago Press, 1973.

Bloom, Jack M. *Class, Race, and the Civil Rights Movement.* Bloomington: Indiana University Press, 1987.

Blumin, Stuart. *The Urban Threshold.* Chicago: University of Chicago Press, 1976.

Bodnar, John. *Immigration and Industrialization: Ethnicity in an American Mill Town, 1870–1940.* Pittsburgh: University of Pittsburgh Press, 1977.
———. *Lives of Their Own: Blacks, Italians, and Poles in Pittsburgh, 1900–1960.* Urbana: University of Illinois Press, 1982.
———. *The Transplanted: A History of Immigrants in Urban America.* Bloomington: Indiana University Press, 1985.
———. *Workers' World: Kinship, Community, and Protest in an Industrial Society, 1900–1940.* Baltimore: Johns Hopkins University Press, 1985.
Bond, Horace Mann. *Negro Education in Alabama.* Washington, D.C.: The Associated Publishers, 1939.
Bontemps, Arna, and Convoy, Jack. *Anyplace But Here.* New York: Hill and Wang, 1966.
Borchert, James. *Alley Life in Washington.* Urbana: University of Illinois Press, 1981.
Bracey, John; Meier, August; and Rudwick, Elliot. *Black Nationalism in America.* Indianapolis: Bobbs-Merrill, 1970.
Broom, Leonard, and Glenn, Norvel. *The Transformation of the Negro American.* New York: Harper and Row, 1965.
Broussard, Albert. *Black San Francisco: The Struggle for Racial Equality in the West.* Lawrence: University Press of Kansas, 1993.
Buffalo City Directory. Buffalo: Polk-Clement Company, 1900–1937.
Bunche, Ralph. "A Critical Analysis of the Tactics and Programs of Minority Groups." *Journal of Negro Education* 4 (July, 1935).
Cadbury, Edward; Matheson, M. Cecile; and Shann, George. *Women's Work and Wages: A Phase of Life in an Industrial City.* Chicago: 1907.
Callow, Alexander. *American Urban History.* New York: Oxford University Press, 1969 (revised 1973).
Carpenter, Niles. "Color, Nationality, and Economic Opportunity." Buffalo: University of Buffalo, 1927. Rpt. Westport, Conn.: Negro Universities Press, 1970.
Carter, Dan T. *Scottsboro: A Tragedy of the American South.* Baton Rouge: Louisiana State University Press, 1969.
Cayton, Horace R., and Drake, St. Clair. *Black Metropolis: A Study of Negro Life in a Northern City.* Vols. I-II. New York: Harper and Row, 1945 (rev. ed. 1970).
Chudacoff, Howard P. *Mobile Americans: Residential and Social Mobility in Omaha, 1880–1920.* New York: 1972.
Clark-Lewis, Elizabeth. *Living In, Living Out.* Washington, D.C.: Smithsonian Press, 1994.
Cleage, Albert B., Jr. *Black Christian Nationalism.* New York: Morrow, 1972.
Clifton, Lucille. *Generations.* New York: Random House, 1976.
———. *Good woman: poems and a memoir 1969–1980.* Brockport, N.Y.: BOA Editions, 1987.
Comer, James P. *Maggie's American Dream.* New York: New American Library, 1988.
Cripps, Thomas. *Slow Fade to Black.* New York: Oxford University Press, 1977.
Cronon, Edmund D. *Black Moses.* Madison: University of Wisconsin Press, 1955.
Cruse, Harold. *The Crisis of the Negro Intellectual.* New York: Morrow, 1967.
Daniels, John. *In Freedom's Birthplace.* Boston: Houghton Mifflin, 1914.

Davidson, Edmonia W. "Education and Black Cities: Demographic Background." *Journal of Negro Education* XLII (Summer, 1973).

Davis, Allen Freeman. *Spearheads for Reform: The Social Settlements and the Progressive Movement, 1880-1920.* New York: Oxford University Press, 1967.

Delany, Sarah, and Delany, A. Elizabeth. *Having Our Say.* New York: Dell, 1993.

DuBois, W. E. B. *The Autobiography of W. E. B. DuBois.* New York: New York International Publishers, 1968.

————, ed. *The Negro American Family.* Cambridge: Negro Universities Press, 1909 (rev. ed. 1970).

————. *The Philadelphia Negro: A Social Study.* New York: Schocken Books, 1899 (rev. ed. 1967).

————. *Souls of Black Folk.* Chicago: A. C. McClurg and Co., 1903.

Duster, Alfreda M., ed. *Crusade for Justice.* Chicago: University of Chicago Press, 1970.

Ehrlich, Richard. *Immigrants in Industrial America.* Charlottesville: University Press of Virginia, 1977.

Farley, Reynolds. "The Urbanization of Negroes in the United States." *Journal of Social History* 1 (Spring, 1968).

Feldman, Egal. "Prostitution, the Alien Women and the Progressive Imagination, 1910-1915." *American Quarterly* XIX (September, 1967).

Field, Phyllis F. *The Politics of Race in New York: The Struggle for Black Suffrage in the Civil War Era.* Ithaca: Cornell University Press, 1982.

Fillmore, Millard. *Millard Fillmore Papers.* Vol. 1. Buffalo: Buffalo Historical Society, 1879.

Foner, Philip, and Lewis, Ronald, eds. *Black Workers: A Documentary History from Colonial Times to the Present.* Philadelphia: Temple University Press, 1989.

Fordham, Monroe. "BCES, Inc., 1928-1961: A Black Self-Help Organization." *Niagara Frontier* (Summer, 1976).

————. *A History of Bethel AME Church, Buffalo, New York, 1881-1977.* Buffalo: Bethel AME Church, 1978.

Fox, Stephen R. *The Guardian of Boston.* New York: Atheneum, 1970.

Franklin, John Hope. *Race and History.* Baton Rouge: Louisiana State University Press, 1989.

Franklin, John Hope, and Moss, Alfred A., Jr. *From Slavery to Freedom.* New York: McGraw-Hill, 1994.

Franklin, V. P. *Black Self-Determintion.* Brooklyn: Lawrence Hill, 1992.

————. *Living Our Stories, Telling Our Truths.* New York: Scribner, 1995.

Franklin, Vincent, and Anderson, James, eds. *New Perspectives on Black Educational History.* Boston: G. K. Hall, 1978.

Frazier, E. Franklin. *The Negro Family in the United States.* Chicago: University of Chicago Press, 1939.

Frisch, Michael H. *Town into City, Springfield, Massachusetts and the Meaning of Community 1840-1880.* Cambridge: Harvard University Press, 1972.

Gardner, Bettye. "Blacks in Baltimore, 1830-1860." Ph.D. dissertation, George Washington University, 1974.

Gayraud, Wilmore. *Black Religion and Black Nationalism: An Examination of the Black Experience in Religion.* Garden City, N.Y.: Doubleday, 1972.

Gerber, David. *Ohio and the Color Line, 1860–1915.* Urbana: University of Illinois Press, 1976.

Glasco, Laurence. "Ethnicity and Occupations in the Mid-Nineteenth Century: Irish, Germans, and Native-Born Whites in Buffalo, New York," in *Immigrants in Industrial America, 1850–1920,* edited by Richard Ehrlich.

———. *Ethnicity and Social Structure: Irish, Germans, and Native-Born of Buffalo, New York, 1850–1860.* New York: Arno Press, 1980.

———. "The Life Cycles and Household Structure of American Ethnic Groups: Irish, Germans, and Native-Born Whites in Buffalo, New York, 1855." *Journal of Urban History* (May, 1975).

Goings, Kenneth W. *The NAACP Comes of Age: The Defeat of Judge John J. Parker.* Bloomington: Indiana Universtiy Press, 1990.

Goings, Kenneth W., and Mohl, Raymond A., eds. *The New African-American Urban History.* Thousand Oaks, Ca.: Sage Publications, 1996.

Gordon, Michael. *The American Family in Social-Historical Perspective.* Second edition. New York: St. Martin's, 1978.

Gottlieb, Peter. *Making Their Own Way: Southern Blacks' Migration to Pittsburgh 1916–30.* Urbana and Chicago: University of Illinois Press, 1987.

Gray, Brenda Clegg. *Black Female Domestics during the Depression in New York City, 1930–1940.* New York: Garland, 1993.

Greenberg, Cheryl L. *"Or does it explode?": Black Harlem in the Great Depression.* New York: Oxford University Press, 1991.

Greene, Gwendolyn. "A Study of Social Group Work as a Function of the Buffalo Urban League, Inc." Master's thesis, University of Pittsburgh, 1952.

Groneman, Carol. "Working-Class Immigrant Women in Mid-Nineteenth Century New York. The Irish Women's Experience." *Journal of Urban History* 4 (May, 1978), 255–274.

Grossman, James R. *Land of Hope: Chicago, Black Southerners, and the Great Migration.* Chicago: University of Chicago Press, 1989.

Grover, Kathryn. *Make a Way Somehow: African-American Life in a Northern Community, 1790–1965.* Syracuse: Syracuse University Press, 1994.

Guthrie, Patricia. "Catching Sense." Ph.D. dissertation, University of Rochester, 1977.

———. *Catching Sense: African American Communities on a South Carolina Sea Island* (Westport, Conn.: Bergin and Garvey, 1996).

Gutman, Herbert. *The Black Family in Slavery and Freedom.* New York: Pantheon, 1976.

———. "The Negro and the United Mine Workers of America: The Career and Letters of Richard L. Davis and Something of Their Meaning: 1890–1900." *The Negro and the American Labor Movement.* Edited by Julius Jacobson. New York: 1968.

———. "Persistent Myths About the Afro-American Family." *Journal of Interdisciplinary History* IV (Autumn, 1975), 181–210.

Gutman, Herbert, and Glasco, Laurence. "The Negro Family, Household Structure and Occupational Structure, 1855–1925." Paper prepared for the Yale Conference on Nineteenth-Century Cities, November, 1968. (Mimeographed.)

Hacker, Andrew. *Two Nations: Black and White, Separate, Hostile, Unequal.* New York: Scribner's, 1992.

Hamilton, Kenneth Marvin. *Black Towns and Profit: Promotion and Development in the Trans-Appalachian West, 1877-1905*. Urbana: University of Illinois Press, 1991.

Handlin, Oscar. *Fire Bell in the Night*. Boston: Little, Brown and Company, 1964.

———. *The Newcomers*. Cambridge: Harvard University Press, 1959.

Hannerz, Ulf. *Soulside: Inquiries into Ghetto Culture and Community*. New York: Columbia University Press, 1967.

Hapgood, Hutchins. *The Spirit of the Ghetto: Studies of the Jewish Quarter of New York*. New York: Schocken Books, 1967 (orig. 1902).

Hareven, Tamara. *Family and Kin in Urban Communities, 1700-1930*. New York: New Viewpoints, 1977.

Harlan, Louis. *Booker T. Washington*. New York: Oxford University Press, 1972.

———. *Separate and Unequal: Public School Campaigns and Racism in the Southern Seaboard States, 1901-1915*. Chapel Hill: University of North Carolina Press, 1958.

Hausauer, Kenneth C. *The Second Fifty Years*. Buffalo, N.Y.: Y.M.C.A., 1970.

Haynes, George E. *Negro Migration in 1916*. Washington, D.C.: U. S. Department of Labor, 1919.

Higginbotham, Evelyn Brooks. *Righteous Discontent: The Women's Movement in the Black Baptist Church, 1880-1920*. Cambridge: Harvard University Press, 1993.

Hill, Joseph A. *Women in Gainful Occupations 1870-1920*. Washington, D.C.: U.S. Government Printing Office, 1929.

Hill, Robert. *The Strengths of Black Families*. New York: Emerson Hall Publishers, 1972.

Hill, Robert A., ed. *The Marcus Garvey and UNIA Papers*. Los Angeles: University of California Press, 1983-1987.

Hine, Darlene Clark. *Black Women in White: Racial Conflict and Cooperation in the Nursing Profession, 1890-1950*. Bloomington: Indiana University Press, 1989.

———. *Hine Sight: Black Women and the Re-construction of American History*. Bloomington: Indiana University Press, 1997.

Hine, Darlene Clark, and Thompson, Kathleen. *A Shining Thread of Hope: The History of Black Women in America*. New York: Broadway Books, 1998.

Hine, Darlene Clark, et al. *Black Women in America: An Historical Encyclopedia*. Bloomington: Indiana University Press, 1994.

Hofstader, Richard. *The Age of Reform: From Bryan to F. D. R.* New York: Knopf, 1955.

Horton, James O. *Black Bostonians: Family Life and Community Struggle in the Antebellum North*. New York: Holmes and Meier, 1979.

———. *Free People of Color: Inside the African American Community*. Washington, D.C.: Smithsonian Institution Press, 1993.

Howard, William Travis, Jr., M.D. *Public Health Administration and the Natural History of Disease in Baltimore, Maryland 1797-1920*. Washington, D.C.: Carnegie Institution of Washington, 1924.

Hunt, David. *Parents and Children in History*. New York: Basic Books, 1970.

Jackson, Kenneth. *The Ku Klux Klan in the City, 1915-1930*. New York: Oxford, 1967.

Jacques-Garvey, Amy. *Philosophy and Opinions of Marcus Garvey*. New York: Atheneum, 1970.

Jahn, Janheinz. *Muntu.* New York: Grove Press, 1961.

James, Joy. *Transcending the Talented Tenth.* New York: Routledge, 1997.

Johnson, Charles. "The Negro in Buffalo." Buffalo, N.Y.: State University of New York at Buffalo Archives, 1923. (Mimeograpahed.)

———. *Shadow of the Plantation.* Chicago: University of Chicago Press, 1935.

Johnson, James Weldon. *Black Manhattan.* New York: Atheneum, 1968 (orig. 1930).

Katz, Michael B. "Occupation Classification in History." *Journal of Interdisciplinary History* III (Summer, 1972), 63–88.

———. "The People of a Canadian City: 1851–1852." *Canadian Historical Review* 53 (1972), 402–426.

———. *The People of Hamilton, Canada West.* Cambridge: Harvard University Press, 1975.

Katzman, David. *Before the Ghetto: Black Detroit in the Nineteenth Century.* Urbana: University of Illinois Press, 1973.

———. *Seven Days a Week.* New York: Oxford University Press, 1978.

Kelley, Robin. *Hammer and Hoe.* Chapel Hill: University of North Carolina Press, 1990.

———. "'We Are Not What We Seem': Rethinking Black Working-Class Opposition in the Jim Crow South." *Journal of American History* 80 (June, 1993).

Kellogg, Charles F. *NAACP.* 2 vols. Baltimore: Johns Hopkins University Press, 1967.

Kincheloe, Samuel Clarence. *The American City and Its Churches.* New York: 1938.

King, Wilma. *Stolen Childhood.* Bloomington: Indiana University Press, 1995.

Kiser, Clyde Vernon. *Sea Island to City.* New York: Atheneum (orig. 1932).

Knights, Peter. *The Plain People of Boston, 1830–1860: A Study in the City Growth.* New York: Oxford University Press, 1971.

Komarovsky, Mirra. *Blue-Collar Marriage.* New York: Random House, 1962.

Krause, Corinne. "Urbanization Without Breakdown: Italian, Jewish, and Slavic Immigrant Women in Pittsburgh, 1900–1945." *Journal of Urban History* 4 (May, 1978), 291–306.

Kusmer, Kenneth. *A Ghetto Takes Shape: Black Cleveland 1870–1930.* Urbana: University of Illinois Press, 1976.

Lammermeier, Paul J. "The Urban Black Family of the Nineteenth Century: A Study of Black Family Structure in the Ohio Valley, 1850–1880." *Journal of Marriage and the Family* 35 (August, 1975).

Lamphere, Louise, and Rosaldo, Michelle Zimbalist, eds. *Woman, Culture, and Society.* Stanford: Stanford University Press, 1974.

Lee, Everett. "A Theory of Migration." *Demography* 3 (1966), 47–57.

Lehmann, Nicholas. *The Promised Land.* New York: Knopf, 1991.

Lewis, Earl. *In Their Own Interests.* Berkeley: University of California Press, 1991.

Lewis, Elizabeth Clark. *Living In, Living Out.* Washington, D.C.: Smithsonian Institution Press, 1995.

Lieberson, Stanley. *Ethnic Patterns in American Cities.* Glencoe, Ill.: Free Press of Glencoe, 1963.

Liebow, Elliott. *Tally's Corner.* Boston: Little, Brown and Company, 1967.

Litwack, Leon. *North of Slavery: The Negro in the Free States, 1790–1860.* Chicago: University of Chicago Press, 1961.

Logan, Rayford. *The Negro in American Life and Thought: The Nadir, 1877–1901.* New York: Collier, 1954.

Lubove, Roy. *The Professional Altruist: The Emergence of Social Work as a Career 1900–1920.* Cambridge: Harvard University Press, 1963.

————. *The Urban Community: Housing and Planning in the Progressive Era.* Englewood Cliffs, N.J.: Prentice-Hall, 1967.

Mandel, Bernard. "Samuel Gompers and Negro Workers." *Journal of Negro History* 40 (January, 1955).

Marx, Gary T. *Protest and Prejudice: A Study of Belief in the Black Community.* Revised edition. New York: Harper and Row, 1969.

Massey, Douglas S., and Denton, Nancy A. *American Apartheid: Segregation and the Making of the Underclass.* Cambridge: Harvard University Press, 1993.

Mayer, Joseph. *The Regulation of Commercialized Vice: An Analysis of the Transition from Segregation to Repression in the United States.* New York: 1922.

Mays, Benjamin E. *The Negro's God.* New York: Antheneum, 1968.

McCarthy, Kathleen. *Lady Bountiful Revisited: Women, Philanthropy, and Power.* New Brunswick: Rutgers University Press, 1990.

McDonald, Patricia. "Baltimore Women, 1870–1900." Ph.D. dissertation, University of Maryland, 1976.

McKay, Claude. *Harlem: Negro Metropolis.* New York: E. P. Dutton and Company, 1940.

McPherson, James. "White Liberals and Black Power in Negro Education, 1865–1915." *American Historical Review* 75 (June, 1970).

Meier, August. *Negro Thought in America, 1880–1915.* Ann Arbor: University of Michigan Press, 1963.

Meier, August, and Rudwick, Elliott. *Black Protest Thought in the Twentieth Century.* Indianapolis: Bobbs-Merrill, 1971.

————. *The Making of Black America.* Vol 2. New York: Atheneum, 1969.

Melder, Keith. "Ladies Bountiful: Organized Women's Benevolence in Early Nineteenth Century America." *New York History* XLVIII (July, 1967), 231–254.

Modell, John. *Into One's Own: From Youth to Adulthood in the United States, 1920–1975.* Berkeley: University of California Press, 1989.

Modell, John, and Hareven, Tamara. "Urbanization and the Malleable Household: An Examination of Boarding and Lodging in American Families. *The Journal of Marriage and the Family* 35 (August, 1973).

Morrison, Toni. *Sula.* New York: Knopf, 1973.

Moynihan, Daniel Patrick. *Employment, Income, and the Ordeal of the Negro Family.* Washington, D.C.: Department of Labor, 1965.

Muller, Edward K., and Groves, Paul A. "The Evolution of Black Residential Areas in Late Nineteenth Century Cities." *Journal of Historical Geography* I (1965), 169–191.

Murray, Pauli. *Pauli Murray: The Autobiography of a Black Activist, Feminist, Lawyer, Priest, and Poet.* Knoxville: University of Tennessee Press, 1987.

Nelli, Humberto. *The Italians in Chicago 1880–1930: A Study in Ethnic Mobility.* New York: Oxford University Press, 1970.

Neufeldt, Harvey, and McGee, Leo, ed. *Education of the African American Adult: An Historical Overview.* Westport, Conn.: Greenwood Press, 1990.

New York State Manuscript Census Schedules for Buffalo, 1905, 1915, and 1925.

Nie, Norman H. *Statistical Package for the Social Sciences.* 2nd Ed. New York: McGraw-Hill, 1975.

Norusis, Marija. *SPSS—Introductory Statistics Guide.* Chicago: SPSS, 1988.

O'Neill, William L. *Divorce in the Progressive Era.* New Haven, Conn.: Yale University Press, 1967.

Osofsky, Gilbert. *Harlem: The Making of a Ghetto.* New York: Harper and Row, 1963.

Ottley, Roi. *New World A-Coming.* New York: Houghton Mifflin, 1969 (orig. 1943).

Ovington, Mary White. *Half a Man: The Status of the Negro in New York.* New York: Hill and Wang, 1911.

Pleck, Elizabeth. "Two Parent Household: Black Family Structure in Late Nineteenth Century Boston." *Journal of Social History* 6 (Fall, 1972), 3131.

Porter, Connie. *All-Bright Court.* Boston: Houghton Mifflin, 1991.

Record, Wilson. *The Negro and the Communist Party.* New York: Atheneum, 1971.

Rhines, Charlotte. "A City and Its Social Problems: Poverty, Health, and Crime in Baltimore, 1865-1875." Ph.D. dissertation, University of Maryland, 1975.

Riegel, Robert E. "The Changing American Attitudes Toward Prostitution 1800-1920." *Journal of the History of Ideas* XXIX (July-September, 1968), 437-452.

Rose, Harold M. "The All-Negro Town: Its Evolution and Function." *The Geographical Review* 4 (July, 1965).

Ross, B. Joyce. *J. E. Spingarn and the Rise of the NAACP.* New York: Atheneum, 1972.

―――. "Mary McLeod Bethune and the National Youth Administration: A Case Study of Power Relationships in the Black Cabinet of Franklin D. Roosevelt. *Journal of Negro History* 60 (January, 1975).

Rowan, Richard L. *The Negro in the Steel Industry.* Philadelphia: University of Pennsylvania Press, 1968.

Rudwick, Elliott. *Race Riot at East St. Louis.* Carbondale, Ill.: Southern Illinois University Press, 1964.

Ryan, Mary P. *Womanhood in America from Colonial Times to the Present.* New York: New Viewpoints, 1975.

Salmon, Lucy Mayard. *Domestic Service.* 2d ed. Newport, R.I.: McMillan, 1902.

Schlesinger, Arthur M. *The Rise of the City 1878-1898.* New York: McMillan, 1933.

Scott, Emmett J. *Negro Migration During the War.* New York: Arno, 1920.

Scott, Patricia Bell, et al. *Double Stitch: Black Women Write about Mothers and Daughters.* Boston: Beacon Press, 1991.

Seller, Maxine. "The Education of the Immigrant Woman: 1900 to 1935." *Journal of Urban History* 4 (May, 1978), 307-330.

Sennett, Richard. *Families Against the City: Middle Class Homes of Industrial Chicago 1872-1890.* New York: 1970.

Sharpless, John B., and Shortridge, Ray M. "Biased Underenumeration in Census Manuscripts: Methodological Implications." *Journal of Urban History* 1 (August, 1975), 409-439.

Shaw, Stephanie. *What a Woman Ought to Be and to Do.* Chicago: University of Chicago Press, 1996.

Shimkin, Dimitri. *Extended Families and Black Society.* World Anthropology Series. Chicago: Aldine Press, 1978.

Silberman, Charles. *Crisis in Black and White.* New York: Random House, 1964.

Sims, Mary S. *The Natural History of a Social Institution: The Young Women's Christian Association.* New York: Woman Press, 1935.

Smith, Daniel Scott. "Parental Power and Marriage Patterns: An Analysis of Historical Trends in Massachusetts." *Journal of Marriage and the Family* 35 (August, 1973).

Smith, Jessie Carney, ed. *Notable Black American Women.* Detroit: Gale Research, Inc., 1992.

Smuts, Robert W. *Women and Work in America.* New York: Schocken Books, 1971.

Spear, Allan. *Black Chicago.* Chicago: University of Chicago Press, 1967.

Spero, Sterling, and Harris, Abram. *The Black Worker.* New York: Atheneum, 1969 (orig. 1931).

Stack, Carol. *All Our Kin.* New York: Harper and Row, 1974.

Stein, Robert L. "The Economic Status of Families Headed by Women." *Monthly Labor Review* 93 (December, 1970), 3-10.

Stephenson, Charles. "Tracing Those Who Left." *Journal of Urban History* 1 (November, 1974), 73-84.

Sternsher, Bernard, ed. *The Negro in Depression and War.* Chicago: Quadrangle, 1969.

Strickland, Arvarh. *History of the Chicago Urban League.* Urbana: University of Illinois Press, 1966.

Sutch, Raymond. *One Kind of Freedom.* New Rochelle, N.Y.: Cambridge University Press, 1977.

Tauber, Karl and Alma. *Negroes in Cities, Residential Segregation and Neighborhood Change.* New York: Atheneum, 1972 (orig. 1957).

Taylor, Henry Louis, Jr. *African Americans and the Rise of Buffalo's Post-Industrial City, 1940 to the Present.* Buffalo: Buffalo Urban League, 1990.

Terkel, Studs. *Race: How Blacks and Whites Think and Feel About the American Obsession.* New York: New Press, 1992.

Thernstrom, Stephan. *The Other Bostonians: Poverty and Progress in the American Metropolis, 1880-1970.* Cambridge: Harvard University Press, 1973.

———. *Poverty and Progress: Social Mobility in a Nineteenth Century City.* New York: Basic Books, 1969.

Thernstrom, Stephan, and Sennett, Richard, eds. *Nineteenth Century Cities.* New Haven, Conn.: Yale University Press, 1969.

Thornbrough, Emma Lou. "Segregation in Indiana During the Klan Era of the 1920s." *Mississippi Valley Historical Review* 47 (March, 1961).

Thomas, Bettye. "Black Community in Baltimore, 1870-1910." Ph.D. dissertation, George Washington University, 1974.

Thomas, Richard W. *Life for Us Is What We Make It: Building Black Community in Detroit 1915-1945.* Bloomington: Indiana University Press, 1992.

Tilly, Louise A.; Scott, Joan W.; and Cohen, Miriam. "Women's Work and European Fertility Patterns." *Journal of Interdisciplinary History* IV (Winter, 1976), 447-476.

Trotter, Joe. *Black Milwaukee: The Making of an Industrial Proletariat.* Urbana: University of Illinois Press, 1985.

———. *Coal, Class, and Color: Blacks in Southern West Virginia, 1915-32.* Urbana: University of Illinois Press, 1990.

Trotter, Joe William, ed. *The Great Migration in Historical Perspective.* Bloomington: Indiana University Press, 1991.

Tunnard, Christopher. *The Modern American City.* Princeton: Van Nostrand, 1968.

Tuttle, William. "Labor Conflict and Racial Violence: The Black Worker in Chicago, 1894-1919." *Labor History* 10 (Summer, 1967).

————. *Race Riot.* New York: Atheneum, 1970.

Uya, Okon. *The African Diaspora and the Black Experience in New World Slavery.* New Rochelle: Okpaku Communications, 1992.

Warner, Sam B., and Burke, Colin B. "Cultural Change and the Ghetto." *Journal of Contemporary History* 4 (October, 1969), 173-187.

Washington, Booker T. *Up From Slavery.* New York: Doubleday, 1901.

Waskow, Arthur. *From Race Riot to Sit-In.* Garden City, N.Y.: Doubleday, 1966.

Watkins, Ralph Richard. "Black Buffalo 1920-1927." Ph.D. dissertation, State University of New York at Buffalo, 1978.

Watts, Jim, and Davis, Allen. *Generations.* New York: Random House, 1974.

Weare, Walter. *Black Business in the New South: A Social History of the North Carolina Mutual Life Insurance Company.* Urbana: University of Illinois, 1973.

Weaver, Robert. *The Negro Ghetto.* New York: Harcourt Brace, 1948.

————. *Negro Laborer.* New York: Kennikat, 1946.

Webster, Janice. "Domestication and Americanization: Scandinavian Women in Seattle, 1888 to 1900." *Journal of Urban History* 4 (May, 1978), 275-290.

Weiss, Nancy. *The National Urban League, 1910-1940.* New York: Oxford University Press, 1974.

Wells-Barnett, Ida. *On Lynchings.* New York: Arno, 1969 (orig. *Southern Horrors*, 1897; *Mob Rule in New Orleans*, 1900).

West, Cornell. *Race Matters.* Boston: Beacon Press, 1993.

White, Deborah Gray. *Ar'n't I a Woman.* New York: Norton, 1985.

Willet, Mabel Hurd. *The Employment of Women in the Clothing Trade.* Columbia University Studies in History, Economics and Public Laws, XVI, No. 2, 1902.

Williams, Lillian S. *The Bridge to the Future: The History of Diversity in Girl Scouting.* New York: Girl Scouts of the USA, 1996.

Williams, Lillian Serece, ed. *The Records of the National Association of Colored Women's Clubs*, Parts I and II. Bethesda, Md.: University Publications of America, 1993, 1994.

Wilson, William Julius. *The Declining Significance of Race.* Chicago: University of Chicago Press, 1978.

————, ed. *Sociology and Public Agenda.* Newbury Park, Ca.: Sage, 1993.

Winchester, Ian. "The Linkage of Historical Records by Man and Computer." *Journal of Interdisciplinary History* I (1971), 107-125.

Woodward, C. Vann. *The Strange Career of Jim Crow.* 3d ed. New York: Oxford University Press, 1966.

Woofter, Thomas J. *Negro Migration.* New York: Negro Universities Press, 1920.

Worthman, Paul. "Black Workers and Labor Unions in Birmingham, Alabama, 1897-1904." *Labor History* 10 (Summer, 1969).

Wye, Christopher. "The New Deal and the Negro Community: Toward a Broader Conceptualization." *Journal of American History* 59 (December, 1972).

Yans-McLaughlan, Virginia. *Family and Community*. Ithaca: Cornell University Press, 1978.

———. "The Fingers of the Hand: A Study of Italians in Buffalo." Ph.D. dissertation. State University of New York at Buffalo, 1970.

Zaretsky, Eli. "Capitalism, the Family, and Personal Life." Part I and Part II, *Socialist Revolution*, 14 and 15 (1973).

PERIODICALS AND NEWSPAPERS

Buffalo American
Buffalo Courier
Buffalo Courier Express
Buffalo Criterion
Buffalo Evening News
Buffalo Forum
Buffalo Illustrated News
Buffalo Morning Express
Buffalo Star
Buffalo Times
Crisis
Men of Buffalo
National Association Notes
National Notes
Opportunity

MANUSCRIPT COLLECTIONS

Albany, New York

New York State Library, Archives

Buffalo, New York

Buffalo and Erie County Public Library
Buffalo and Erie County Historical Society
Durham Memorial AME Zion Church Archives (papers of St. Luke's AME Zion)
National Urban League Archives
St. Philip's Episcopal Church Archives
University at Buffalo, SUNY Archives

New York, New York

Girl Scouts of the USA, Archives
The Schomburg Center for Research in Black History, New York Public Library

Northampton, Massachusetts

YWCA Papers, Sophia Smith Collection, Smith College

Oberlin, Ohio

Oberlin College, Alumni Records

Tuskegee, Alabama

Tuskegee University Archives, Hollis Burke Frissell Library

Washington, D.C., Library of Congress

Brotherhood of Sleeping Car Porters Papers, 1926–1950
Carter G. Woodson Papers, Migration Files
Mary Church Terrell Collection
NAACP Papers, 1909–1950

Nannie Helen Burroughs Papers
Urban League Papers, 1926-1950

Washington, D.C., Moorland Spingarn Research Center at Howard University

Mary Church Terrell Papers

Washington, D.C., National Archives

R.G. 257 Bureau of Labor Statistics
R.G. 228 Committee on Fair Employment Practice
R.G. 174 Department of Labor
R.G. 195 Federal Home Loan Bank System
R.G. 31 Federal Housing Administration
R.G. 4 Food Administration
R.G. 183 Lawrence Oxley File
R.G. 2 National War Labor Board
R.G. 119 National Youth Administration
R.G. 73 President's Organization on Unemployment Relief
R.G. 196 Public Housing Administration
R.G. 3 United States Housing Corporation

Washington, D.C., National Association of Colored Women's Clubs, Inc.

Hampton, Virginia

Peabody Collection, Hampton University, Hollis Collingwood Library

Index